The Stone Garden Guide

Armenia and Karabagh

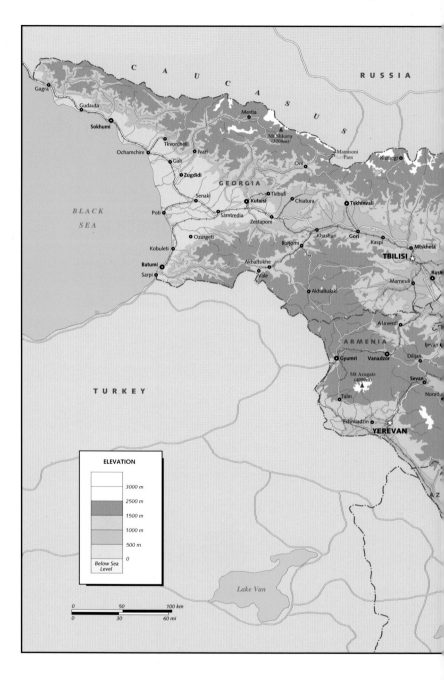

Requests for permission should be addressed to:
Stone Garden Productions; PO Box 7758; Northridge, California 91327
info@StoneGardenProductions.com / 1-888-266-7331

Library of Congress Control Number: 2004093620
ISBN 0-9672120-8-1 24.95

The publisher and authors are solely responsible for the content of this
book. They have made every effort to make the information in this travel
guide as accurate as possible. However, they accept no responsibility for
any loss, injury or inconvenience sustained by anyone using this book.

The Stone Garden Guide

Armenia and Karabagh

Matthew Karanian
Robert Kurkjian

Stone Garden Productions

Los Angeles / Yerevan

For Armenia,
Ancient Nation
And New Republic

CONTENTS

Photograph, Page 6: Church of the Holy Cross at Aghtamar Island, Western Armenia

FOREWORD

Armenia is a remarkable destination. Most travelers and tourists tend to explore culture and history, and Armenia offers a healthy diversity of those elements, as it sits along the old Silk Road, at the crossroads of migration and trade for many Middle Eastern, Mediterranean and European neighbors. Perhaps more significantly however, and less appreciated, is the fact that Armenia also hosts an astounding diversity of flora and fauna, making it a fascinating destination for the serious eco-tourist. Plant and bird lovers will be especially well rewarded, and very likely surprised, by the biological richness of this relatively small country.

Armenia lies at the convergence of three bio-geographic regions, the Caucasian, the Iranian and the Mediterranean and—blessed by this overlapping of biological systems—it hosts seven of the eight major biological communities in the world. This gives Armenia one of the world's highest vegetation densities, some of which are considered ancient crops—the ancestral wild relatives of plants now domesticated for food production.

The country also lies in the migratory path of birds from many regions of the world and it is estimated that there are approximately 350 species present in the country, a veritable treasure for avid bird watchers. The authors provide rich details of much of this information. They have personally experienced what they discuss, and they elaborate honestly about all the subjects they introduce. The have traveled, eaten, and slept at virtually every location they recommend, and their individual educational backgrounds allow them to make excellent and insightful commentary about the environmental issues within Armenia. Their experience, and the insights which flow from it, pervade every chapter.

It is seldom that a traveler is presented with a guide such as this, which is accurate because of actual on-the-ground investigation, and rich with history, research and anecdotes that broaden the user's viewpoints, particularly regarding Armenia's biodiversity.

This is a guide that the casual traveler should not do without. For the traveler who enjoys a more profound experience of the natural world, this guide is unparalleled. We would all be much better informed as visitors if all guidebooks provided this breadth of information, revealing not only what we need to know with regard to our own creature comforts to enjoy being there, but also what we should know about the many wonderful creatures that live in the place we are visiting.

Robert Glenn Ketchum
Los Angeles, 2004

Robert Glenn Ketchum is an environmental conservationist and nature photographer. He is the author of many books, including *Rivers of Life, The Legacy of Wildness*, and *Northwest Passage.*

Photographs, left: Azat River, east of Yerevan;
previous page: Moon rise over mountains near Garni village

PREFACE

Tourism has become an economic force in the world and it may even be the world's largest industry. Annual revenue from tourism worldwide is even said to rival revenue from sales of the ubiquitous automobile. Although in the short term this might be good for people who earn their livings from tourism, it is not necessarily good for the host country as a whole, or for the environment.

Over the past few decades, the global environmental movement has become vocal about the harm that often accompanies conventional tourism—harm such as the destruction of forests and wetlands and the loss of habitats. Ecotourism has been promoted as an alternative to conventional tourism. There are many different ideas of just what constitutes ecotourism but most experts agree that ecotourism is tourism that simultaneously benefits tourists, the environment, and the local society and economy.

Development of ecotourism in Armenia and Karabagh is probably many years away. Responsible tourism and environmental awareness, however, is developing. There has been a growing realization among tourism professionals in Armenia and Karabagh that tourism's impact on the environment can be enormous. Along with this realization, many people now agree that progressive strategies are needed for a sustainable approach to tourism.

The local, regional, and international effects of tourism need to be addressed, with cooperation among the various travel organizations and businesses. Education of both the tourists and the hosts is critical. This is especially important in the south Caucasus where there is vast biodiversity but where for decades, the environment has been treated merely as an exploitable resource. With this in mind, we hope that the information about conservation and ecology in this guidebook will encourage tourists to tread lightly and to be environmentally friendly.

Tourism in Armenia and Karabagh has increased steadily over the past few years, despite the combination of a global economic slowdown, modern-day conflicts, and health epidemics. Tourism is projected to continue to grow there, both among Diaspora Armenians and non-Armenians. For Diaspora Armenians, traveling to Armenia is like going home. For many of them, a single visit kindles a life-long connection to the country. For non-Armenians, Armenia is a fascinating country with an ancient culture, beautiful landscapes, and unequaled hospitality.

We hope this book encourages visitors to Armenia and Karabagh and that the people who visit, whether they are tourists, business people, or politicians, become aware of environmental issues. Decisions that each of us makes every day can contribute to environmental protection, whether it is through conserving water, promoting the use of renewable energy, or helping to preserve cultural artifacts.

We are excited to be a part of this growing movement, and we hope this book will encourage more responsible tourism. Enjoy Armenia and Karabagh's spectacular outdoors and help preserve the environment!

Matthew Karanian
Robert Kurkjian
Los Angeles / Yerevan, 2004

ACKNOWLEDGEMENTS

The authors express their profound thanks to Sarkis Acopian and Gerard L. Cafesjian. Mr. Acopian supported this publication through a grant, and by graciously allowing the use of the Birds of Armenia maps. Mr. Cafesjian also supported this book through a grant, which was provided by the Cafesjian Family Foundation. Without this support from both Mr. Acopian and Mr. Cafesjian, this guidebook could not have been realized.

The realization of this book has also been a collaborative effort in many other ways. We are grateful to Jeff Acopian for his unwavering support and for his confidence in us. He introduced us to leading conservation experts, and he always had time to take our phone calls and to be a friend.

For their valuable contributions to the text, we are thankful to the scientists and environmental scholars Dr. Dan Klem, Dr. Keith Bildstein, and Jason Kauffeld, and to the public health specialist Dr. Alina Dorian. We are thankful to members of the Birds of Armenia Project in Yerevan for their assistance with our conservation research, and to Dr. Artak Hambarian for helping us with the renewable energy text. We are grateful, as well, for the encouragement we received from the world-renown environmental photographer and conservationist Robert Glenn Ketchum (Internet: www.robertglennketchum.com).

The authors relied upon the assistance of many colleagues and friends throughout the research, writing, and production of this book. There are too many to list, but a few of them must be noted. For help with research and writing, we are thankful to the historians and scholars Dr. Vahakn Dadrian, Dr. Ronald Grigor Suny, and Dr. Richard Hovanissian.

Every author needs an editor, and Vicken Yeghparian proved himself, once again, to be a true friend by tirelessly editing the text and checking our statements for accuracy. Anna Grigoryan worked the phones in Yerevan to check facts, and logged a lot of internet time while verifying our listings. The Karabagh Representative in the US, Vardan Barseghian, reviewed the Karabagh chapter and provided valuable information.

We sincerely thank Dr. Charles Kurkjian for helping with the tiresome task of proofreading and assisting us to make sure that everything fit together at the end. Thanks, also, to three great brothers who accompanied us on a few of our research trips: Aren, Vahn, and Narek Kurkjian.

Finally, we thank the people of Armenia for their hospitality, their kindness, and for profoundly enriching our lives.

ABOUT THIS GUIDE

The authors have each lived, worked, and traveled in Armenia and Karabagh since 1995, and this book is the product of their countless miles of excursions to the most remote reaches of the region. Their travel research is original, and when the authors recommend a site, or suggest a travel route, it's because they've been there, and they know the best—and the worst—way to go. They've flown to Armenia through all the major European hubs—London, Amsterdam, Paris, Frankfurt, Vienna, and Istanbul—and they've traveled the countryside by bus, van and car. The authors haven't stayed in every hotel, but they've visited every one and verified each hotelier's claim. If they name a restaurant or café, you can be sure that they've eaten there and are offering first hand observations and recommendations. These are things that you cannot do in a couple of weeks.

Your Comments Are Invited

Every guidebook must be selective in deciding what to list. Omission is not necessarily a criticism (although it may be). If you have comments about what is printed, or if you have information to add or correct, we invite your correspondence. This will help us to make improvements in subsequent editions. You may write to us at: Stone Garden Productions; PO Box 7758; Northridge, California 91327. For periodic updates on the information in this guide, please check our website, www.stonegardenproductions.com.

Photographs

The images in this book are available for commercial licensing and also as original fine art prints from Stone Garden Productions (Tel. 1-888-266-7331; E-mail:info@stonegardenproductions.com; Internet: www.StoneGardenProductions.com.) You may also write to us at: Stone Garden Productions; PO Box 7758; Northridge, California 91327. For additional images, please visit www.armenianphotography.com.

Field of poppies, southern Armenia

ABOUT THE AUTHORS

Matthew Karanian is a professional photographer, writer, and attorney. He is a principal of Stone Garden Productions, a photography and publishing company, and he has worked as a journalist for several international magazines. Matthew is a Nikon Professional Shooter®.

Matthew graduated with a degree in international law from Georgetown University. He has worked in the Republic of Georgia as a Caucasus specialist for Georgetown University's Institute for the Study of International Migration, and he has practiced law in the US for several years, specializing in environmental issues.

Matthew has been working and traveling in Armenia since 1995, as a photographer and journalist, and as a Professor of Law at the American University of Armenia, where he currently teaches International Environmental Law and serves as Associate Dean of the Law Department. He and his law students founded Armenia's first English-language law journal, the Armenian Law Review, in 2003. He splits his time between the US and Armenia.

Robert Kurkjian is a professional photographer and an international environmental consultant. He is the principal of Kurkjian Images, which specializes in worldwide stock photography. He studied photography both in New York, at the School of Visual Arts, and in Los Angeles. Robert is a Board Member of the American Society of Media Photographers (ASMP), Los Angeles Chapter, and is a Nikon Professional Shooter®.

Robert has lived, worked, and traveled extensively in Armenia since 1995, as a photojournalist and Professor of Environmental Science at the American University of Armenia. Robert has done extensive environmental research throughout Armenia and the US, and he earned his Ph.D. in Geochemistry from the University of California. His work on air and water quality is widely published in scientific journals.

Robert has been traveling and photographing worldwide since the early 1980s. Photographs from his extensive travels throughout Armenia, Karabagh, South and Central America, Europe and Asia have been published in numerous books and periodicals. His environmental consulting and stock photography businesses are based in Los Angeles, but he frequently travels overseas.

The photography and writing of Robert Kurkjian and Matthew Karanian has been featured in the acclaimed photography book "Out of Stone, and in the photography-based guidebook "Edge of Time: Traveling in Armenia and Karabagh." Their images have also been shown on several PBS-TV documentaries.

Their work has also been featured in magazines and newspapers of wide distribution in the US, Europe, and Canada. A representative sampling includes: Arthur Frommer's Budget Travel (US); Geographical (UK); Global Adventure (UK); Impressions (the in-flight magazine of British Airways); Outpost (Canada); Photo District News (US); Photographer's Forum (US); Photo Life (Canada); and Photo World magazine (US).

Robert and Matthew are currently working on several projects documenting Armenia's historic lands and diaspora communities around the world.

Land and People

one

Map of Armenia © 2004 Stone Garden Productions

We drank some Armenian brandy, followed by Armenian coffee. We ate some pastries. We told some stories and we listened to plenty more. The only thing the villagers asked of us was that we return. They asked that we return and visit with them again, sleep in their homes, share in their lives.

—Edge of Time: Traveling in Armenia and Karabagh

INTRODUCTION

When Armenia re-established its independence in 1991, it was not particularly concerned about positioning itself as a tourist destination. The fledgling republic had other priorities. Except for a brief blip from 1918 to 1920, the Armenian nation had not been self-ruled for more than 600 years. The institutions of statehood had to be created. Armenia needed to develop a foreign policy and establish its place in the world. And it needed to start a market economy almost from scratch.

On the home front, Armenia was struggling to care for the victims of a 1988 earthquake who, three years later, were still homeless. Everywhere, even in the capital, there was almost no electricity and no fuel. There was little industry. There was little work. But somehow, contrary to the forecasts of the pundits, the Armenians made their tiny country work.

During its first decade of renewed independence, Armenia had made progress in its state-building efforts. It had developed into the most stable democracy in the Caucasus, and it had plotted a course of Western-style reform. But it hadn't developed as a tourist destination.

Only in the past few years have travelers discovered Armenia. Travelers have continued to go to Armenia for the humanitarian reasons that had brought so many foreigners here during the first few years of independence. With greater frequency, travelers are now visiting Armenia on holiday, to have fun! Foreign tourists have ceased to be a novelty in the capital. The number of tourists broke the 100,000 mark in 2001, and it has continued to grow each year, according to Armenia's National Statistical Service. Almost half of these visitors are from the United States and Europe.

Private investors have responded to this increased interest. They have added hundreds of new hotel rooms in Yerevan, the capital city, as well as many more in the countryside. Business people have opened dozens and dozens of restaurants offering Armenian and international cuisine. There are scores of new shops offering Western-manufactured goods. By 2004 it seemed that renting a car in Yerevan had become as easy as sending out for Thai food or getting a pizza delivered.

All this progress hasn't spoiled Armenia. This is a land of magnificent mountains and vistas, with a treasure trove of ancient cultural sites. This is a country where you can still get a cup of coffee for 20 cents, and where you can still get invited back for a homemade dinner each time you visit a different village. Despite the changes, the heart of Armenia is still there, and it's bigger than ever.

Photograph, previous page: Azat Reservoir and Mt. Ararat

Monument honoring General Andranik at the recently-built St. Gregory the Illuminator Cathedral, Yerevan

A BRIEF HISTORY OF ARMENIA

By Ronald Grigor Suny

For three thousand years historians and travelers have recorded the presence of a people called the Armenians in what is today eastern Turkey and the South Caucasus. The history of Armenia has been told as a tale of heroes and martyrs, of an ancient people who somehow survived the onslaughts of invasions, conquests, natural disasters, and near annihilation at the hands of imperial powers.

A central theme has been survival and endurance, a search for security and dignity. For many centuries these people maintained an identity—first pagan and later Christian—without a state of their own. Their national church provided the focus of unity, and its priests and monks perpetuated the literary and artistic traditions that marked the Armenians. In the early twentieth century, after more than five hundred years without a state, Armenians set up an independent republic in the South Caucasus. That state was soon Sovietized, and for seven decades was part of the Soviet Union. At the dawn of the twenty-first century, Armenians are once again divided between those who live in the newly independent Republic of Armenia and those who are scattered around the world in the Diaspora.

Armenia historically was a mountainous land of more than 100,000 sq mi with its ancient centers in the valley of the Arax River and the region around Lake Van in what is now the Republic of Turkey. Living on the Armenian plateau continuously from the seventh century BC until driven out of Turkish Armenia in 1915, most Armenians were peasant farmers who managed to cultivate the rugged land despite the bitterly cold winters and fiercely hot summers. Throughout their long history, threats from invaders and marauding nomads encouraged many Armenians to migrate to towns or to foreign countries and form new Armenian communities in the Middle East, Russia, Poland, Western Europe, India, and America. Today more Armenians live outside the borders of the modern Armenian Republic than within. That tiny country of 11,000 sq mi today faces hostile countries to the east and west, bears up under a crippled economy and an inconclusive struggle for the historically Armenian region of Karabagh, which had recently been part of the neighboring Soviet Republic of Azerbaijan. The capital of the Armenian Republic, Yerevan, is the country's largest city, a modern city of more than a million inhabitants.

The Earliest Times

Humans first settled on the Armenian plateau about six thousand years BC, and the first major state was the kingdom of Urartu, with its center around Lake Van. Excavated and restored monuments from the Urartian period can be found in Yerevan, which was founded by the Urartians as the citadel of Erebuni. Shortly after the fall of Urartu, the Indo-European-speaking proto-Armenians migrated, probably from the West, onto the Armenian plateau and mingled with the local peoples. The first mention of the Armenians dates from the mid-sixth century BC in an inscription at Behistun.

Culturally, Armenia stood between the world of ancient Persia and ancient Greece, its traditions a blend of Hellenism and Iranism. Ruled for many centuries by the Persians, Armenia became a buffer state between the Greeks and Romans to the West

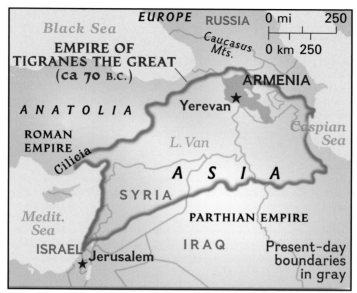

EUROPE

Black Sea

EMPIRE OF
TIGRANES THE GREAT
(ca 70 B.C.)

RUSSIA

Caucasus Mts.

0 mi   250

0 km 250

ARMENIA

A N A T O L I A

Yerevan

Caspian Sea

ROMAN
EMPIRE

Cilicia

L. Van

A S I A

SYRIA

PARTHIAN EMPIRE

Medit.
Sea

ISRAEL

Jerusalem

I R A Q

Present-day
boundaries
in gray

National Geographic Maps / NGS Image Collection, Reprinted with permission

and the Persians or Arabs of the Middle East. It reached its greatest size under King Tigran II, the Great, (95-55 BC), who fought but ultimately succumbed to the Romans. Tigran, whose crowned head can be seen on coins of his era, built his capital at Tigranakert in southeastern Anatolia. A major monument in the Republic of Armenia, the temple at Garni, bears witness to the classical heritage in Armenia.

Religion

A distinctly Armenian culture may be said to begin with the conversion to Christianity. Armenian tradition traces Armenian origins back to Haik, the lover of independence, who killed the evil Bel, but these tales come down to us in early sources of the Christian era. Grandparents tell their grandchildren about the earliest Armenians, descendents of Noah, whose ark landed on Mount Ararat, or of the Armenian language spoken by all humanity before the Tower of Babel confused the tongues. And Armenians repeatedly tell their acquaintances, Armenian or odar (non-Armenian), that they were the first Christian state. Even before the official conversion of the Armenians, there were Christians in Armenia. This is attested to in the Armenian tradition of the antiquity of the Armenian Church, which was founded by apostles of Christ.

At the end of the third century AD, Armenia came under the protection of Rome once again. Parts of the eastern Roman Empire, like Cappadocia, were already Christianized, and a priest from Caesarea named Gregory (Grigor) entered Armenia to proselytize the faith. The Armenian king, Trdat III, was a protégé of the Roman emperor Diocletian, who persecuted the Christians in the empire. Trdat loathed the Christians as well and had Gregory tortured and thrown into a pit (Khor Virap). In the story told by the fifth century historian Agathangelos, Gregory remained in the pit for fifteen years.

Meanwhile, the king cruelly murdered Christian nuns, Hripsime and Gayane, who were escaping from Diocletian, and for his actions Trdat was turned into a wild boar. Trdat's sister dreamt that Gregory could save the king. The holy man preached to the king for sixty-five days after which Trdat agreed to accept Christianity and build a cathedral at Vagharshapat (Echmiadzin). Nearby he erected chapels to commemorate the martyred nuns. Saint Gregory the Illuminator became the first Catholicos of the new church.

Both theologically and politically the Armenians stood apart from the Orthodoxy of the Byzantine Empire to the west and the Mazdeist, and later Muslim, world of Persia to the east. Armenia was a buffer zone to be sure, but this also meant that it would be buffeted by more powerful states in their wars against one another.

In the first years of the next century Saint Mesrop, known as Mashtots, invented an alphabet so that the Gospel could be revealed to the Armenians. In the fifth century, considered the "Golden Age" of Armenian literature, important religious and historical works appeared that provided a foundation for a distinguished literary tradition. The Armenian historian Yeghishe tells the story of the struggle of Armenians under Prince Vardan Mamikonian against the attempt of the Persians to impose their religion on Armenia. At the battle of Avarair in 451, the Armenians fought to the death against the Persians to preserve their faith. That day, Vardanants, when hundreds of Armenians died in service of Christianity, is still marked as a major national holiday by Armenians, and Vardan is venerated as a saint. Later generations of writers turned the Armenian martyrs of Yeghishe, who were largely concerned about salvation and eternity, into patriotic defenders of the nation who loved the soil of their motherland, Armenia.

In the late classical and medieval periods, Armenians made up a broad ethno-religious community, whose primary loyalty was to their church and their local prince. The most cherished ancient Armenian historian, Movses Khorenatsi, demonstrated the pride of Armenians in their glorious past already in the eighth century when he wrote, "Although we are a small country and very restricted in numbers, weak in power and often subject to another's rule, yet many manly deeds have been performed in our land worthy of being recorded in writing."

The Middle Ages

Small kingdoms and princedoms characterized medieval Armenia. Faced by powerful enemies in the East, like the Persians, and in the West, by Rome and later Byzantium, the Armenians seldom united under a single monarch. Very often the various noble houses of Armenia fought with one another and with their kings. Indeed, in 428 the nobles petitioned the Persian king to eliminate the monarchy in Armenia.

Some analysts argue, however, that it was precisely the diversity of the Armenian principalities that helped preserve Armenia. Instead of a single kingdom that could have been conquered by invaders seizing the capital and subduing the king, Armenia presented its enemies with many semi-independent polities that had to be overrun one by one.

This powerful system of autonomous princes, or nakharars, marked the social structure of Armenia from antiquity until the Mongol invasions of the thirteenth century. Seventy or eighty important families, like the Mamikonians, the

Bagratunis, and Artsrunis, commanded thousands of armed warriors, lived off landed estates, and governed their realms from fortified castles. The nakharars held their land in hereditary tenure, though occasionally a king might seize the land for some reason. In Armenia these aristocrats were as powerful, sometimes more powerful, than the person designated king.

Armenian medieval civilization was faced by two great threats in the seventh century. From the west, the expanding Byzantine Empire moved against the Persians and attempted to integrate Armenians back into the Orthodox religious world. From the south, the Arabs, newly converted to Islam, moved through the Middle East into Armenia and the South Caucasus. Armenians used the competing imperialisms to maneuver a degree of autonomy in the face of these dual dangers. The Armenian princes estimated that the Arabs were the lesser danger and did not resist the Arab invasions very vigorously at first. In the words of Sepeos the Bishop, the nakharars "made an accord with death and an alliance with Hell."

Armenians actually thrived after the initial Arab conquest of Greater Armenia, but later Arab rulers proved to be far more brutal than their predecessors. In the eighth century, Armenians revolted against the Arabs, and the Muslims crushed the rebellions and turned their rage against the Armenian princes. Yet one Armenian princely family, the Bagratunis, benefited from their alliance with the Arabs and soon emerged as the new kings of Armenia and Georgia. The repeated invasions of the Byzantines and Arabs brought chaos and destruction to Armenia. In 855 the Caliph sent an enormous army that killed 30,000 Armenians. Whole areas of the country were de-Armenized and settled by Muslims. Arab emirates co-existed with small Armenian principalities and the kingdoms of the Bagratunis. Where Armenians were able to keep control and maintain a degree of internal security, they continued building their churches, writing their histories, and illustrating their manuscripts. The eighth to the eleventh centuries were simultaneously a period of high culture amid great danger.

In the tenth century the Byzantine Empire annexed parts of historic Armenia, even as the Bagratuni kingdoms reached their zenith. King Gagik I "the Great" expanded his kingdom and crowned it by building the Cathedral at Ani (now lying across the border in Turkey). The mystical writer Grigor Narekatsi composed his eulogies to the cross and the Madonna in those years. But Gagik's relatively peaceful and prosperous reign corresponded to the reign of the energetic Byzantine emperor, Basil II, who continued the imperial expansion to the east. Almost all of western Armenia came under Byzantine control by the early eleventh century. Armenia was no longer a serious buffer for the Byzantines when suddenly from the east came the first Turkish invaders, the Seljuks. In the 1030s the Seljuks entered Armenia, and in 1064 they took the Bagratuni capital, Ani. The Armenian chronicler, Aristakes Lastivertsi, lamented: "The number of people massacred and the incalculable number of corpses turned the great river that flows near the city red with blood. The dead found their graves in the stomachs of savage beasts and domesticated animals, for no one was able to bury them or spread dirt on their bodies." In 1071 the Seljuks defeated the Byzantine army at Manzikert and captured the emperor, initiating the long, slow decline of the Byzantine Empire.

One by one, the independent Armenian kingdoms in Greater Armenia collapsed. Thousands of Armenians fled south to the Mediterranean coast where several princes established small states that eventually formed the princedom, later kingdom, of Cilician Armenia. The Armenian kingdom received the Crusaders from Western Europe and fought against the rising Muslim threat to Christendom until Mamluks overran it in 1375. Cilician Armenia's greatest moments came in the reign of Levon II "the Magnificent" (1187-1219). As ruler of one of the most important states in the Middle East, the king joined with Richard the Lionhearted in the conquest of Cyprus. The tiny kingdom imitated the feudal political forms of the Western Europeans and engaged in vigorous trade with Genoa and Venice. The Armenian Church drew close to the Roman Catholic Church for a time, as European influence flooded over the Armenian kingdom. The last kings of Armenia were, in fact, more French than Armenian. Overwhelmed by superior forces, the last king of Armenia, Levon VI, was taken captive by the Mamluks to Egypt. Later ransomed by the king of Castile, Levon died in Paris and was buried with the kings of France in the church at St. Denis outside of Paris.

After several centuries of devastation and despair at the hands of Turks and Mongols, Greater Armenia was once again divided between the Ottoman Turks and the Persians. Population in Armenia fell; towns shrank in size; and much of Armenia reverted to agriculture. From the fifteenth century until the early twentieth century, most Armenians lived in the Ottoman Empire, while a smaller number in eastern Armenia were ruled by the Persians. A few surviving Armenian nobles maintained some political power in the small melikdoms of Karabagh, Sisian, Kapan, and Lori.

The Modern Era

The nineteenth century has been called the "Age of Nationalism." The idea that humanity is naturally divided into nations and that these nations should have the right to govern themselves became a powerful source of political mobilization in the decades after the French Revolution of 1789-1799. Already in the eighteenth and early nineteenth centuries, Armenian scholars wrote patriotic histories, poems, and plays extolling the notion that an ancient Christian people was unjustly suffering under the Muslim yoke.

In the late nineteenth century, as the Ottoman Empire declined, Armenians in Turkey complained of arbitrary taxation, seizures of property, and the periodic attacks of armed Kurds. Russia and Britain took an interest in their plight, and after the Russo-Turkish War of 1877-1878, the victorious Russians forced the Turkish sultan to agree to reforms in the Armenian provinces of eastern Anatolia. But at the Congress of Berlin in 1878, the Great Powers of Europe forced the Russians to back down and left the Armenians with few gains. Although much talk revolved around the so-called "Armenian Question," no real reforms were carried out to protect the Armenians from their Muslim rulers. Frustrated and angry, young Armenians turned from working within the Ottoman system to organizing small revolutionary parties. The Turkish authorities responded brutally to what they perceived to be an Armenian threat to the stability of the empire. The "Bloody Sultan" Abdul Hamid II armed Kurdish irregulars and sanctioned the massacre of hundreds of thousands of Armenians in 1894-1896.

Genocide and Wrongful Denial

When World War I broke out and Turkey went to war with Russia, Armenians found themselves on both sides of the front. In a fierce campaign in the winter of 1914-1915, the Russian army, aided by Armenian volunteers from Russia, dealt a severe blow to the Ottoman forces. The Young Turk leaders, fueled by the accumulated hatreds and suspicions of the Armenians, decided to deport Armenians from their historic homeland into the deserts of Mesopotamia. Orders went out to demobilize the Armenian soldiers serving in the Ottoman Army, and they soon were murdered. Then the authorities turned on civilians, women and children, forcing them out of their homes and marching them through mountains and valleys toward Syria. In the process, hundreds of thousands of Armenians, perhaps as many as a million and a half, died or were massacred in what most historians call the first genocide of the twentieth century. International opinion at the time condemned the "holocaust" launched by the Turks against their Armenian subjects, but in time the events of 1915 were slowly forgotten – though not by Armenians.

Decades later, the Turkish government organized and financed an official campaign to deny that the Ottoman state was responsible for the killings of the Armenians or that the massacres constituted genocide. Rather the deaths and deportations, they claimed, were the unfortunate result of a civil war in which Muslims as well were killed. Official Turkish historians and their supporters worked tirelessly to turn an undeniable tragedy into a controversy, while Armenian and other scholars established a documentary record of archival materials, memoirs, and historical accounts to preserve the historical memory of official mass murder. For twentieth-century Armenians, particularly in the Diaspora, the Genocide of 1915 became the most potent source of their national identity, an ineradicable pain that remains unrecognized by much of the rest of the world.

The Ottoman Empire collapsed in the wake of World War I, as did the Russian Empire. Many Armenian survivors fled north to Russian Armenia, where on May 28, 1918, an independent republic was established, with Yerevan as its capital. This independent Armenia lasted only until the end of 1920. The first Armenian republic was a land of refugees, disease, and hunger. Some aid came from the United States, but famine was rampant in Yerevan. Isolated and insecure, independent Armenia had to fight all its neighbors to establish its borders. The Dashnak Party managed to organize elections, however, and a relatively representative government ran the country. The expectation that military aid would come from Europe or America never materialized, and ultimately Armenia was abandoned by the Allies. The United States Senate rejected a request by President Woodrow Wilson that the Americans establish a protective mandate over Armenia. Threatened by the nationalistic Kemalist movement in Turkey, the Dashnak government agreed on December 2, 1920 to turn the new state over to Communists as the lesser danger to Armenian existence.

With Western Armenia in the hands of the triumphant Kemalists, only Eastern Armenia, that small portion of historic Armenia that had been under Persian rule until 1828 and then part of the Russian Empire until 1917, remained under the control of Armenians. The country was at the nadir of its modern history. By 1920 only 720,000 lived in Eastern Armenia, a decline of thirty percent. In the seven years of war, genocide, revolution, and civil war (1914-1921), Armenian society had in many ways been "demodernized," thrown back to its pre-capitalist agrarian economy and more traditional peasant-based society.

Soviet Era

After an initial period of harsh rule, the Soviet Armenian government introduced the more moderate economic program known as NEP (the New Economic Policy), which denationalized much of the economy and gave the peasants the right to control their own grain surpluses. The leader of the Russian Communists, Vladimir Lenin, called this new policy a tactical retreat to "state capitalism."

I the view of supporters of Soviet Armenia the new republic provided a degree of physical security that Armenians had seldom known in their long past. Armenia was part of the largest country in the world, a Great Power that could easily prevent incursions from Turkey or Iran. But, in the view of the opponents of Soviet Armenia, the state was a fraudulent homeland that did not represent the national aspirations of Armenians. The Soviet government would not push the "Armenian Agenda" and attempt to retrieve lost lands in Turkey. Indeed, the Soviets had granted to the neighboring republic of Soviet Azerbaijan the Armenian-populated region of Nagorno Karabagh. Soviet Armenia was recognized by only a minority of the Armenians living outside the Soviet Union, and for decades many Diaspora Armenians spoke as if no Armenian state existed. The Diaspora and the Armenians within the Soviet Union grew distant from each other, with very little direct knowledge of how the other half was developing.

Stalin, who ruled with little opposition from roughly 1928 until 1953, established the rigid authoritarian political system and state-run economy that lasted until the fall of the Soviet Union. Anything that was suspected of nationalism was attacked and could condemn its author to prison. The Armenian Church was ruthlessly disciplined and made subordinate to the Soviet authorities. This led to disaffection among Diaspora Church members, and a schism eventually divided the international Armenian Church. Some churches recognized the direct and exclusive authority of the Holy See of Echmiadzin, which lay in Soviet Armenia, while others rejected any but formal association with the Catholicos at Echmiadzin and gave their loyalty to a rival see at Antelias in Lebanon. The Cold War and the Iron Curtain led to a deep division between Armenians, both within the Diaspora and between the Diaspora and the Armenians of the Soviet Union.

During World War II, the Soviet state and the Armenian Church made an uneasy peace. In its desperate struggle for survival, the Soviet government quickly made a number of concessions to the Armenian Church, which became the major link between Soviet Armenia and the Diaspora. In late 1942 some of the closed churches in Armenia were reopened, and exiled clergy returned from Siberia. The interests of the Church, the Armenian Diaspora, and the Soviet government most closely coincided in the brief interlude between the end of World War II and the onslaught of the Cold War. Stalin made claims to historic Armenian lands across the border in Turkey. Shortly after the Yalta Conference, the Soviet government initiated a campaign to encourage Armenian settlement in the Armenian republic and to recover Armenian lands in eastern Turkey. But the advent of the Cold War and Turkey's integration into the United States-led Western alliance made any border change impossible.

The Church supported the Soviet claims and encouraged the efforts to "repatriate" Diaspora Armenians to the Soviet republic. Tens of thousands migrated to

Armenia, only to find an impoverished country with no political freedom. Some of them were exiled from their new homeland to prison camps in Siberia. A bitter anecdote of the time told of a repatriate who told his relatives and friends before migrating to Soviet Armenia that he would send them a photo of himself on arrival. If he was standing, things were good and they should also come to Armenia; if he was sitting, things were bad and they should stay where they were. When the photo arrived, the man was lying on the ground!

With the death of Stalin in 1953, life became easier in the USSR. The worst aspects of political terror ended, and though the monopoly of Communist party power remained, there was a significantly greater degree of social and cultural freedom in the years that Nikita Khrushchev ruled the Soviet Union (1953-1964). This period of reform, known as "the Thaw," improved the material and social life of the Armenians. Visitors from abroad became more common in Yerevan, and many Soviet Armenians moved from communal to private apartments. While the standards of living lagged far behind the most developed countries in the West, Armenians were able to meet their needs and many of their desires through the semi-legal "second economy." Almost everyone knew someone who could get something outside of the official governmental stores, which were often marked by empty shelves. Consumer taste improved, and people began to discriminate in their preferences, seeking out foreign-made goods whenever possible.

The long stolid years of Leonid Brezhnev's rule (1964-1982) provided a stable, secure life for Armenians, but the arteries of the system were hardening. Corruption and cynicism increased, and few Armenians believed in the goals of the Communists. Along with new interest in the ordinary material amenities of normal life, Armenians comforted themselves with a renewed interest in their own history and culture, and nationalism became a unifying sentiment among both intellectuals and ordinary folk. While a quiet official commemoration of the fiftieth anniversary of the Armenian Genocide (April 24, 1965) took place in the Opera House, thousands of Armenians demonstrated without permission in the streets of Yerevan. They called on Moscow to return Armenian lands to Armenia. Even the revered Catholicos of All Armenians, Vazgen I, had difficulty trying to calm the crowds. The Kremlin reacted by removing the head of the Armenian Communist Party, but eventually it agreed to have an official monument to the Genocide built on the high hill of Tsitsernakaberd.

Armenian nationalism had its roots in the long textual tradition that Armenian clerics and scholars had elaborated ever since the invention of the Armenian alphabet in the fifth century. While the Soviet regime was ostensibly anti-nationalist, in fact Soviet nationality policies contributed to a powerful feeling of territorial nationalism. Soviet Armenians were better educated, and knew their history, language and culture more thoroughly than most of their predecessors. Once the heavy hand of Stalin's terror was replaced by the greater tolerance of the late 1950s and 1960s, the pent-up demand for greater national and personal expression exploded in the form of a new nationalism. The achievements of Soviet Armenian culture were respected both within the USSR and throughout the world. Most famous was the composer Aram Khachaturian, author of The Gayane Ballet from which the popular composition, "The Sabre Dance," originated. The painter Martiros Sarian painted the landscapes and portraits of Armenia, and the filmmaker Sergei Parajanov turned the static images of Armenian miniatures into a unique form of cinematic art.

Mikhail Gorbachev became General Secretary of the Communist Party of the Soviet Union in March 1985 and soon initiated his own revolutionary changes that eventually led to the demise of the USSR. Armenians reacted to the new liberal atmosphere by organizing a broad-based national movement by 1988. At first it focused on ecological issues. The transformation of Armenia into an industrial-urban country had brought in its wake severe ecological problems, most importantly the threat from a nuclear plant at Metsamor. But soon many Armenians expressed anger at the pervasive corruption and arrogance of the local Communist regime. Finally and most importantly, Armenians were concerned about the fate of Karabagh, the Armenian-populated enclave that lay in the Azerbaijani republic. Demonstrations both in Karabagh and Armenia in February 1988 led to a violent response from Azerbaijanis in the industrial town of Sumgait. More than two dozen Armenians were killed and a cycle of violence began that escalated over the next few years into a full-scale shooting war between the two republics.

After more than two years of the Karabagh conflict, Armenians moved from being one of the most loyal Soviet nations to one that had a complete loss of confidence in Moscow. On December 7, 1988, more than 25,000 Armenians perished in a devastating earthquake that hit the towns of Spitak, Leninakan (now Gyumri), and Kirovakan (now Vanadzor). When Gorbachev came to Armenia to express his sympathy, crowds turned on him, insisting that Karabagh be joined to Armenia. What had begun as a peaceful constitutional movement for Armenian rights in Karabagh degenerated by the spring of 1990 into vicious pogroms in Azerbaijan, the evacuation of the Armenian community of Baku, and a guerilla war between two nations in the southern Soviet Union. With the Communist Party in rapid decline and the popular nationalist forces far from united, a vacuum of power could be felt in Armenia. Both the incomplete political reform, in part democratic, in part preserving the old structures, and the national revolts had negative effects on the economy. In January 1990, pressured by the Pan-Armenian National Movement (Hayots Hamazgayin Sharzhum or HHSh), the Armenian Supreme Soviet revised the republic's constitution and gave itself the power to validate USSR laws. Central state authority withered, and the writ of the Kremlin could only be enforced by police and soldiers.

Independence

In the elections of the spring and summer of 1990, non-Communists won a parliamentary majority. After several rounds of voting, the newly elected Armenian parliament chose Levon Ter Petrosian instead of the Communist chief as its chairman. With HHSh in power and the Communists in opposition, Armenia began a rapid transition from Soviet-style government to an independent democratic state. The following year, on September 23, 1991, Armenia declared itself independent of the Soviet Union.

The first years of the second independent republic were a time of nationalistic enthusiasm and extravagant hope for a prosperous, secure future. A parliamentary democracy with an elected president was established. By the spring of 1992 Armenian paramilitary forces had taken control of Karabagh, and despite some setbacks the Armenians essentially won the war with Azerbaijan by 1994, when a cease-fire was declared. At this time there were signs that the government was becoming more authoritarian. Some newspapers were suppressed, and the major opposition party, the Dashnaktsutiun, was banned. In July 1995 a new constitution providing for an extremely strong presidency was adopted.

Ter Petrosian was reelected to the presidency the following year, but the outcome was disputed and he became far weaker and less popular than he had been. Nevertheless, he decided to try to break the impasse on peace in Karabagh. He proposed a bold compromise solution that would leave Karabagh formally within Azerbaijan while retaining the fullest possible autonomy and self-government for the local Armenians. Even his closest political allies turned against him, forcing his resignation in February 1998. New elections confirmed Robert Kocharian, formerly the leader of Karabagh, as Armenia's second president. Within a short time, two other politicians emerged as the most influential in Armenia – Vazgen Sargsian, the minister of defense and later prime minister; and Karen Demirjian, the former Communist party boss, who was, by the late 1990s, the most popular leader in Armenia. Sargsian and Demirjian allied in the elections of 1999 and won handily. But before they were able to carry out their policies, they were assassinated in the parliament building in October 1999. In the uncertain political environment at the end of the millennium, Kocharian once again emerged as the most powerful leader in Armenia.

In 2001 Armenia observed the 1,700th anniversary of its adoption of Christianity as a state religion, and the Pope made his first visit to the country as part of this celebration. Robert Kocharian was re-elected to a second five-year term as president in 2003, and the country has been the most stable democracy in the Caucasus. The president's opponents say the election was invalidated by ballot stuffing and other alleged frauds, however. The accusation that the election had been rigged was an accusation that continued to haunt Kocharian into 2004, when opposition parties clamored for his ouster. The country's impoverishment—the World Bank reported in 2004 that roughly 50 percent of the population lives in poverty—gave the political opposition a fertile ground to cultivate. An ostentatious class of the wealthy grew larger during the first few years of the millennium, but a middle class did not develop. This great disparity between the rich and the poor has contributed to dissatisfaction among many Armenian citizens. By 2004, it is estimated that more than one million of them had left the country in search of better lives.

Armenia's future appears at the moment, as in many times in its past, quite uncertain. The small republic is once again isolated and economically strapped. But one is reminded of other moments of Armenia's long history – of the early Christian era when it was between Byzantium and Persia; of the long centuries after the fall of the last Armenian kingdoms; of the years of genocide and dispersion in the early twentieth century. At each of these moments, Armenians revived and reconstructed their society, restored their cultural traditions, and reconceived their future.

The themes of Armenian history remain regeneration and survival, hope and faith in the darkness of the present. Knowing and appreciating the heroic efforts that this small people have made through time allows optimism about the years to come.

The authors thank Armenian history scholar Ronald Grigor Suny, Ph.D. for writing this article for *The Stone Garden Guides*.

Courtesy of the Birds of Armenia Project, American University of Armenia, Oakland, CA, 1999

GEOGRAPHY

The Republic of Armenia is located in southwestern Asia, east of Turkey (40.0°N, 45.0°E). Its total area is 29,793 sq km (11,490 sq mi), which is roughly the size of Belgium, or the US state of Maryland. It is the smallest republic in the Former Soviet Union. The country is landlocked, and there are no navigable waterways. There are several fast-flowing rivers, however, which are a significant source of electricity.

The country is mountainous, and has an average elevation of 1,800 m above sea level. Only about 10 percent of the country lies below 1,000 m. Forty percent lies at least 2,000 m above sea level. The tallest mountain of historic Armenia is Mt. Ararat, which the Armenians also call Masis. The taller peak, Mets (Big) Masis, reaches 5,165 m (16,946 ft). The smaller, and conical, peak Pokr (Little) Masis, or just Sis, is 3,990 m (13,100 ft). The two peaks are separated by 11.3 km (seven mi). The town of Meghri, on Armenia's southern frontier, has the lowest altitude at only 400 m above sea level.

Ararat dominates the skyline of Yerevan, as well as much of the region around the Armenian capital. But this mountain is actually located in modern Turkey, just across the border. Inside modern Armenia, the tallest peaks are those of Mt. Aragats, which rises to 4,095 m (13,435 ft).

Geologists consider the twin peaks of Ararat and the four peaks of Mt. Aragats to be dormant volcanoes. There is no historical record of any of them having been active, but evidence of their eruptions is plentiful. Soil of volcanic origin is present in the surrounding Ararat Valley, and there is an abundance of obsidian and tuff throughout the region. Obsidian is a volcanic glass, which is considered to be a semi-precious stone. It is also known as "Satan's nail" in Armenian. Tuff is a lightweight volcanic rock from which many homes and offices are built.

Forested lands are not common and can be found mostly in the northern region surrounding Dilijan. Only approximately 8 percent of the country is either forest or woodland and there are no natural woodlands in the Yerevan area. Approximately 10 percent of the land is arable, and less than four percent is devoted to agriculture.

Lake Sevan, one of the largest alpine lakes in the world, is Armenia's largest surface water resource. Four percent of the surface area of Armenia is covered by this lake, and roughly 16 percent of the country lies within the vast Sevan watershed. The lake lies at an altitude of 1,890 m (6,240 ft) and it stretches to a length of 117 km (73 mi) with a width of 62.4 km (39 mi). It covers an area of 1,250 sq km (554 sq mi).

Other significant natural resources include deposits of copper, zinc and aluminum. There are small gold deposits as well, and rocks and minerals are a valuable commercial resource.

Seismic activity is common throughout the country, and the susceptibility of the region to earthquakes has influenced the ancient architectural design of the churches, many of which have withstood repeated quakes. A significant earthquake struck the northern regions on December 7, 1988. Armenia's second largest city, Gyumri, was devastated by the quake and Spitak, the town nearest the epicenter was leveled. More than 25,000 people were killed. Significant progress on reconstruction wasn't made for more than a decade, during which time the survivors lived in shipping containers that had been fashioned into trailer homes, which they call "domiks."

A young girl in her village in northern Armenia

CLIMATE

Armenia has a highland continental climate, marked by dry, hot summers and cold winters. The mountainous terrain contributes to the formation of several microclimates. As a result, it is not unusual for the weather to be hot and sunny in the capital city of Yerevan, while it is cold and rainy 60 km away at Lake Sevan. The best weather for travelers occurs during September and October. April and May can sometimes be rainy, but are otherwise fine times to travel. The intense sun and soaring temperatures of August, however, can be unpleasant.

Average temperatures in Yerevan and the Ararat Valley are -5°C to +5°C (25°F to 40°F) in winter. The absolute low is about -30°C (-22°F). Summer temperatures average 25°C to 27°C (75°F to 80°F) and top out at no more than 42°C (106°F). In the Lake Sevan region, winter temperatures range from -12°C to +8°C (10°F to 28°F), and summer temperatures are a more moderate 18°C to 20°C (65°F to 70°F).

Annual precipitation ranges from 1,000 mm in the mountains to less than 250 mm in the Ararat Valley. Most of the precipitation occurs in April and May and the driest months are July through September. Current weather conditions for several locations throughout Armenia are available at the Weather Channel's website www.weather.com and at Weather Underground's site www.wunderground.com.

POPULATION

Armenia's population is slightly more than 3 million according to the republic's most recent official census, which was conducted in 2001. This is Armenia's first census as an independent state. A tally conducted in 1989 during Soviet rule had revealed a population of 3.7 million. The decline is attributed to emigration, which has been caused by poor economic conditions. More Armenians live outside Armenia, than within its borders. Armenians comprise 0.06 percent (six one-hundredths of one percent) of the world's population.

Official government statistics from the Nagorno Karabagh Republic in 2002 reveal a population of 144,000, of whom more than one-third lived in the capital city of Stepanakert. Both Karabagh and Armenia have ethnically homogenous populations. Ninety-six percent of Armenia's population is Armenian, and 90 percent of them are members, at least nominally, of the Armenian Apostolic Church. Kurds account for about two percent, and the balance is comprised of Russians, Greeks, Jews and expatriates from the West.

LANGUAGE

These are people who jangle the keys of their language even when they are not using them to unlock any treasures.
–Osip Mandelstam, poet

Armenian is the official language of Armenia and Nagorno Karabagh, and it is spoken and written by nearly everyone. Russian is widely spoken, especially among the older generation.

Two major dialects of Armenian are spoken in the world today. Eastern Armenian is spoken in the Republic of Armenia and among the Armenians of Iran. Western

Armenian was prevalent among Armenians in western Armenia until 1915, and is today still spoken by many Armenians in the Diaspora. There are other regional dialects spoken throughout Armenia and Karabagh. The Armenian Apostolic Church uses an ancient form of the language for its liturgy known as Classical Armenian.

Armenian is an Indo-European language, but it's on a branch by itself, unaffiliated with any other language. Armenian uses a unique alphabet with two cases, which was devised by Mesrop Mashtots in the fifth century AD. Although it started with 36 letters, two more have been added over the centuries, in order to allow the sounds of some foreign words to be written.

ECONOMY

Armenia had virtually no industry in 1914 but by the end of the Soviet era it had an economy that was estimated to be based 70 percent on industrial production, according to some sources. By the close of World War II, Armenia was noted as a center for the manufacture of precision instruments, for synthetics and plastics, and electrical products. Armenia entered a period of economic decline beginning in 1988, when a massive and devastating earthquake struck its northwestern region, including Gyumri, the country's second-largest city. The economy was stabilized and inflation was brought under control by 1995, but the country is still today struggling to develop a free-market system. These efforts have been discouraged by Armenia's neighbors, Turkey and Azerbaijan, which have both closed their borders to Armenia for the past decade. As a result, supply routes are circuitous, and trade is hampered.

There is an abundant supply of electricity, however, thanks to a combination of thermal, hydroelectric, and nuclear power. Indeed, there is a surplus at times, which is sold to electricity-starved Georgia. The waters of Lake Sevan have been exploited for hydroelectric generation, but its exploitation has imperiled the ecosystem and as a result the lake cannot be counted upon to meet the nation's increasing energy use. Armenia's nuclear plant, which went online in 1976, is nearing the end of its useful life. The president, Robert Kocharian, pledged to close the plant by 2004, but only if alternative energy sources are located. Alternatives are unlikely as long as its neighbors blockade the country, however, and the plant remains open. And so, with international assistance, the Armenian government has instead spent millions of dollars on upgrades and safety precautions at the nuclear power plant. Despite these expenditures some critics say that the plant, which does not have a Chernobyl-style design, is still not safe. Gasoline is readily available, but at more than two dollars per gallon, is very expensive when considering local wages.

Ample supplies of electricity have not resulted in significant economic growth. The per capita Gross Domestic Product (GDP) is roughly $490, and the total GDP is about $1.9 billion, according to recent figures released by the World Bank. Major natural resources are copper, zinc, aluminum. There are also small deposits of gold. The primary agricultural products are fruits and vegetables, wines, and some livestock.

Jewelry and precious stones account for 34 percent of Armenia's exports. Minerals and metals account for an additional 24 percent. Roughly one third of the country's imports are foodstuffs. Rough diamonds are imported from Belgium so that they can be cut and polished. The finished gems are then exported back to Belgium, where they are resold.

Fifty-five percent of the labor force is employed in agriculture. Twenty-five percent works in the services sector and 20 percent of the workforce is employed in manufacturing, mining and construction. Forty-five percent of the population lives below the poverty line.

For additional information and statistics about the economy, try www.state.gov, which is the site operated by the US Dept. of State, and www.odci.gov/cia/publications/factbook/geos/am.html, which is operated by the Central Intelligence Agency. The National Statistical Service website www.armstat.am/ has a database of official figures for anything that the government counts. The World Bank and the United States Agency for International Development (USAID) are also good sources of information.

POLITICS

Framework

Armenia is a democratic republic. The government is hybrid in form, and consists of both an elected president and a prime minister who is selected by the president. The President is chief of state. The Prime Minister is the head of government. The cabinet is selected by a council of ministers that is appointed by the prime minister.

The legislature consists of a unicameral parliament, which is known as the National Assembly. Its 131 members represent several political parties, ranging from Republicans to Communists. The nation's judicial branch consists of both a Supreme Court and a special Constitutional Court that is empowered to hear only cases of constitutional significance.

Armenia's constitution was adopted by referendum in 1995, and it is a document of great aspiration. Extraordinary constitutional guarantees include housing, medical care, and education, but the government lacks the money to implement them. Other guarantees, such as the right to travel, are reminders of past repression while under Soviet rule. There is universal suffrage for all citizens who have reached the age of 18 years. In addition to being a document of high aspirations, it is also a document of strong presidential power.

Several changes and amendments to the constitution were proposed in 2001 in an effort to limit the president's authority, and to increase citizen access to the courts. The proposals failed after a nationwide referendum on the constitution in 2003. Voters were presented with an entirely new constitution, which they were asked to either adopt in its entirety with a "yes" vote, or to reject by voting "no." There was little publicity about the referendum, and many voters simply didn't know how to vote. The referendum ended up becoming little more than a sideshow to the Parliamentary elections that were held at the same time. In order for the new constitution to be adopted, at least one third of Armenia's eligible voters must participate in a referendum on it, and of those voters, a majority must vote to approve its adoption. Armenia has assured the Council of Europe—the organization that had encouraged the constitutional reforms—that there would be another referendum before 2005.

The legal system is based upon civil law, which is dramatically different from the common law system in the US and the UK. There are no juries, but it is common for a case to be heard by three judges, each of whom takes such an active role in the proceedings that the private lawyers sometimes appear to be superfluous. Cases are decided not by legal precedent, but instead by reference to the code of laws. This legal system is common in continental Europe.

Leadership

President Robert Kocharian assumed the office of president on February 3, 1998, upon the resignation of the country's first elected president, Levon Ter Petrosian. Kocharian was elected in a special election the following month, and re-elected in March, 2003 in a run-off election that was perceived as having been marred by fraud. International observers reported that there had been irregularities at many polling stations. In some precincts, there were more ballots cast than registered voters. Kocharian's ballot tally was 67.5 percent of the vote. Opponent Stepan Demirchyan's tally was 32.5 percent.

The role of Prime Minister is filled by Andranik Margarian, who has been in office since May 12, 2000. Vartan Oskanyan is Foreign Minister.

There are nearly 100 political parties, 84 of which are marginal and considered to be largely dormant. The leading political parties are the Republican Party of Armenia, Armenian Peoples Party, Agro-Technical Peoples Union (formerly Stability Faction), Constitutional Rights Union, Armenian National Movement, National Democratic Union, Republic Party, Self Determination Union, Liberal Democratic Party, Ramkavar-Christian Democratic Party, Communist Party of Armenia, National Accord Party, Armenian Revolutionary Federation-Dashnaktsutyun, and the Country of Laws (Orinats Yerkir) Party.

Role in International Community

Armenia participates in many international organizations and is a party to many multilateral treaties. It is of course a member of the United Nations, and it has occupied a leadership role through its membership (from 2002 to 2004) on the UN Commission on Human Rights and also (since 2003) on the Economic and Social Council. Membership on those important UN organizations is determined by the UN General Assembly.

Armenia is also a member of the Council of Europe and of the Organization for Security and Cooperation in Europe (OSCE). Armenia is not a member of the European Union, but membership is something that many Armenian leaders hope to someday achieve. For now it is unlikely. One would expect, at minimum, that Armenia would not be considered for EU membership until it shares a border with an EU state, which it presently does not. There would of course be many other pre-requisites to membership, as well.

Major environmental and cultural conventions of which Armenia is a party include the Convention on Wetlands of International Importance Especially as Waterfowl Habitat (Ramsar); the UN Educational Scientific and Cultural Organization (UNESCO); and the UN Framework Convention on Climate Change.

Armenia is a member of Interpol and is a signatory of the International Criminal Court. It is also a member of Partnership for Peace, which is an organization supported by NATO.

TWO THOUSAND YEARS OF CHRISTIANITY

The Armenians count themselves among the world's first Christians and they attribute their survival as a distinct people to their faith. Christianity united the nation during its long periods of foreign domination, and it enabled the Armenians to preserve their culture and national identity. As Christians in a part of the world that would become, and which still is, predominantly Muslim, the Armenians were able to avoid assimilation and maintain a cohesive society even without political independence.

The earliest Christians in Armenia had been converted in the first century AD by Christ's apostles Thaddeus and Bartholomew. The missionary work of these Apostles eventually resulted in Armenia's official repudiation of paganism. In an acknowledgement of its ancient origins, the church of Armenia is called the Armenian Apostolic Church.

The nation officially adopted Christianity in AD 301 when a man named Gregory persuaded King Trdat that the king's realm should be Christian, and not pagan. The king, ironically, had imprisoned this man thirteen years earlier for the crime of preaching Christianity. Gregory had been sent to prison, actually a dungeon pit, for his supposed lunacy, and he survived only because other Christians had secretly brought him food and water.

The king didn't fare as well and had gone mad in the meantime. According to the legend, Gregory prayed for the king and cured him. And so the king expressed his gratitude by proclaiming Christianity as the official faith for the nation. Gregory was sainted, and he is now known as St. Gregory the Illuminator. The pit where he was imprisoned still exists, and a monastery was built above it as a demonstration of Christianity's triumph. Visitors can climb down into the pit, at the monastery of Khor Virap, in the town of Artashat.

Of course, Christianity in Armenia predates AD 301. And since the church traces its lineage directly to Christ, the Armenians might just as properly be celebrating their nation's 2,000-year-old Christian heritage. But the practice of Christianity wasn't freely permitted until the king's decree, so Armenians logically settled upon 2001 as the year for commemorating the 1,700th anniversary of their faith. Special activities were held all year long to mark the date. The two biggest events were a visit by the Pope and the consecration of the new St. Gregory the Illuminator Cathedral in Yerevan.

Katoghikeh, a thirteenth century chapel in central Yerevan

Visitors who missed the opportunity to travel to Armenia for the 1,700th anniversary celebrations can still take advantage of many holy site pilgrimages that are arranged by church authorities each year. Mail or telephone inquiries may be directed to the Diocese of the Armenian Church, 630 Second Avenue, New York, NY 10016 (Tel. 212-686-9893; Fax 212-686-0245) or the Prelacy of the Armenian Church, 138 East 39th Street, New York, NY 10016 (Tel. 212-689-7810; Fax 212-689-7168).

ARCHITECTURE

The history of Armenian architecture is more than 4,000 years old, dating back to the late Neolithic period. The ruins of many megaliths and mortar-less fortresses from this era can still be found. Many more, however, have vanished under layers of earth or have been destroyed. Armenia's ecclesiastic architecture has fared better.

Churches and monasteries are among the oldest surviving examples of Armenian architecture, and their survival is not happenstance. Much of the Armenian heartland is prone to earthquakes, and many of the nation's most important public buildings have been designed with this in mind. The designs that made these churches resistant to earthquakes have also helped to make them resistant to the ravages of time and war. As a result, it is possible for us today to view stone churches throughout the countryside that are often more than 1,000 years old.

Dating back to the fifth century, the major elements of church architecture have been repeated throughout Armenia, partly out of need, and partly as a result of what is known as cultural memory. This cultural memory has resulted in the repetition of some design elements long after their intended purpose was forgotten. As a result, it is possible for art historians to identify Armenian churches as having a distinct style, which makes them all part of a recognizable group.

Two of the most recognizable elements of the Armenian churches are their domes and their floor plans. The domes, of course, are also the most visible. The dome is typically a double construction with a conical exterior and a hemispheric, or rounded, interior. This design may have permitted the conical exterior to protect the load-bearing drum and walls. But it might also have been strictly cosmetic. The shape mimics both the volcanic cone of Mt. Ararat, and the head-cover worn by Armenian clergy. Whether the mimicry is intentional or fortuitous is not clear.

The basic floor plan is drawn in the shape of a cross, and is repeated in many church buildings. The dome is located above the center of the cross, and this dome sits atop a drum. This floor plan makes it possible for the weight of the dome to be distributed first to the drum, and then to the side niches and to the pillars of the central prayer hall. Vertical external niches were often used as an additional means of load distribution. Floor plans became more elaborate in the twelfth through fourteenth centuries and the buildings became more grandiose. But the distinctly Armenian style nevertheless persisted.

There are deviations from this style, and these variants sometimes offer clues to various periods of Armenia's foreign domination. The tiny seventh-century church of Karmravor, in the town of Ashtarak, is one example. The tile-capped circular roof is suggestive of an Arabian influence on Armenian architecture, which was the result of a period of Arab dominion over the region.

One of the construction techniques that has contributed to the survival of these ancient buildings appears within the walls of some buildings. The stone walls of these churches are built in three layers. The core is mortared, and this core is lined with stone blocks on the inside and outside of the building, resulting in a three-layered design that is strong and flexible enough to withstand much seismic activity. This triple layer design also made it possible for the walls to be built higher and thinner without sacrificing strength and stability.

Earthquakes were not the only enemy of Armenia's buildings. Churches and monasteries also had to be designed to withstand foreign invasion, and this concern is part of the reason for the sparing use of windows. The few windows that exist are often high above the ground, and too small for a person to squeeze through. Another reason for the tiny windows, however, is the mysticism of the Armenian Church itself. An altar drenched in sunlight would have been inconsistent with this mysticism.

This mysticism may have also played a role in the survival of the church buildings. Invaders who destroyed the Armenian towns and villages may have intentionally overlooked the churches, for fear of some mystical and divine retribution. Still, the Armenians didn't take unnecessary chances: they built their churches in mountains, on hilltops, and in other inaccessible locations.

Armenian churches in historic Armenian lands outside the Republic of Armenia are today at great risk, and not merely from neglect. In Turkey, thousand-year-old Armenian churches have been dismantled for their building materials or even dynamited to clear the land for other uses. The cut stones of the church have found their way into the foundations of municipal buildings, and there's no one to object to the practice. Others have been modified to serve as granaries, barns and warehouses. Foreign armies have even used them as munitions depots.

During the past decade within Armenia's current political borders, however, church buildings have been targeted for repair and renovation. Visitors can see the fruits of these labors at Noravank in Yeghegnadzor, at Saghmosavank in Ashtarak, at Tatev near the town of Goris, and at many more throughout the countryside. Religious services are regularly conducted at many of these churches, and visitors are always welcome.

Protecting Cultural and Historic Monuments

In 1972, the United Nations Educational, Scientific and Cultural Organization (UNESCO) adopted a treaty known as the World Heritage Convention. The goal of the organization is to recruit the world community in identifying cultural and natural properties of "outstanding universal value." Since then, 172 of the world's 192 nations, including Armenia, have signed the treaty. The World Heritage List now includes 754 sites, including 149 natural, 582 cultural, and 23 mixed sites.

Armenia has three sites included on the World Heritage List: (1) the Cathedral and Churches of Echmiadzin and the Archaeological Site of Zvartnots; (2) the Monastery of Geghard and the Upper Azat Valley; and (3) the Monasteries of Haghpat and Sanahin [see Chapter 5, Central Armenia, and Chapter 7, Northeast Armenia, for more information about each of these sites]. Additional information may be found on the internet at www.whc.unesco.org/nwhc/pages/home/pages/homepage.htm.

Essentials

two

PLANNING YOUR TRIP

Visitors from the United States and Canada usually travel to Armenia by way of Europe. Karabagh is accessible only overland from Armenia, however. Because of this, it is usually just a side trip for many visitors, although it deserves to be treated as a destination in its own right. If you are visiting for just one week, you will want to concentrate your travels in Yerevan and the surrounding area. In one week you should be able to plan half-day trips to Echmiadzin, Garni temple, Geghard monastery, Amberd fortress, Khor Virap, and Lake Sevan.

If you have two weeks in country, you will easily be able to add to your itinerary the historic sites around Yeghegnadzor, which is south of Yerevan, and also the Dilijan resort area, the monasteries of Sanahin and Odzun, and the city of Gyumri, all in the north. Ambitious travelers will find that two weeks is plenty of time to add visits to Goris and Karabagh, as well. Many of these trips can be done with public transportation, but you will save a lot of time (without spending a lot of money) using a private driver.

WHEN TO GO

Autumn weather in Armenia and Karabagh is typically dry and warm, with cool evenings, making this the best season for travel. September is also one of the busiest months for tourism. The landscape is golden brown in most parts of the country at this time of year. **Spring** arrives in mid-March in many parts of Armenia, and by mid-April you can count on mild weather in all but the highest elevations. This is the rainiest time of year, however, and in Karabagh you should plan on plenty of fog and drizzle until May. Late April to mid-May is the best time to visit in Spring. The landscape is colorful at this time of year, with fields of flowers in bloom all over the countryside. This is also a time of year when the sky is usually clear enough in Yerevan to permit awesome views of Mt. Ararat.

Summer is intensely sunny and dry in Yerevan and in much of Armenia. The days can get hot, dusty and parched, especially in Yerevan and the Ararat Valley, so if this is when you plan to travel, you will need to take precautions against dehydration and excessive exposure to the sun. Haze during the summer will obstruct the view of Mt. Ararat on most Summer days. You will want to avoid traveling during **Winter**, which runs from December through February. The weather can get cold and snowy and roads outside Yerevan may not always be passable.

The high season for tourism is June through September, and this is when you will pay the highest airfares and find the fewest hotel vacancies in Yerevan, at Lake Sevan, and in Karabagh.

WHAT TO WEAR

Summers in most parts of Armenia are hot and dry during the day, and cool in the evening. Lightweight clothes, made from natural fabrics, are best. Hats and sunscreen are also advisable to protect against the intense sun. Bring sunscreen with a high SPF rating. Yerevan's semi-arid climate can make it dusty in the summer, so

Photographs, left: Field of wild flowers, southwest Armenia;
previous page: Khor Virap Monastery and Mt. Ararat

bring clothing that can be easily cleaned, or which will not show dirt. Average annual precipitation is 550 mm (21.6 inches). Ararat Valley is the driest part of the country, and annual rainfall is just 200-250 mm (7.9 to 10 inches).

Armenians take pride in the way they dress, and their attire is generally conservative. Short pants and tank tops are rarely worn in Armenia, except by young children, even on the hottest days. Men wear long pants. Women usually wear dresses or skirts. Dark colors are common year-round. When going out for the evening, to the theater or to dinner, Armenians in Yerevan, especially women, generally dress stylishly and avoid the casual clothing that is more common in the West.

If you are traveling in winter, be aware that most apartments and offices do not have central heating. Long underwear and woolen garments are advisable for use indoors as well as outside. Dressing in layers is the best way to trap your body's heat, and thereby stay warm. Most body heat is lost through the top of the head, so be sure to wear a hat. Men will have to bring hats from home. We have found that stores frequently do not sell hats and gloves in men's sizes.

Bring a flashlight and treat it as a part of your daily attire, too. Use a small key-chain flashlight that will be easy for you to carry all the time. In Yerevan, many streets and public areas don't have lights and are therefore dark at night.

MAJOR HOLIDAYS

Most businesses and offices are closed on these dates. Holidays are recognized by both Armenia and Karabagh, unless noted otherwise in parentheses.

New Year's, December 31 through January 2
This is perhaps the most joyous of the Armenian holidays and is marked by feasts, gatherings of family and friends, and the exchange of gifts. Neighbors and even strangers are welcomed into the home. Most businesses and offices are closed all three days.

Christmas Day, January 6
Armenians celebrate the birth of Christ according to the Old Julian calendar, on January 6. This holiday is religious, and has not been commercialized.

Independence Day (Karabagh), January 6
Commemorates Karabagh's declaration of independence in 1992. Karabagh's referendum on independence was held December 10, 1991.

Women's Day, March 8
This holiday is a hold-over from the Soviet Union.

Day of Maternity and Beauty, April 7
This is a new holiday in Armenia, which celebrates not only mothers, but all women.

Easter, (varies)

Armenian Genocide Memorial Day, April 24
This is the most somber of national holidays. Tens of thousands make pilgrimages to the Genocide memorial, Tsitsernakaberd (Fortress of the Swallows) where they lay flowers at the eternal flame. Armenians here and around the world mourn the 1915-1923 slaughter of 1.5 million of their countrymen, and the destruction of their 3,000 year-old homeland. Shops and offices are closed, and many Armenians attend solemn church services.

Shushi Liberation Day (Karabagh), May 8
Recognizes the day in 1992 that the Karabagh army recovered Shushi, thereby ending a several-months-long siege of Stepanakert by enemy forces.

Victory and Peace Day, May 9
This hold-over holiday from the Soviet Union commemorates the conclusion of World War II.

St. Vardan's Day, May 26
Commemorates Vardan Mamikonian's battle against Persia in AD 451, which preserved Armenia's Christian status. Also known as Vardanants, which is a term used to describe the wars between Armenia and Persian in which Armenia fought for freedom of religion.

First Republic Day (Armenia), May 28
Also known as Independence Day, recognizing the first Armenian republic's independence in 1918.

Constitution Day (Armenia), July 5
Commemorates Armenia's adoption, by plebiscite in 1995, of the national constitution. Most businesses and stores remain open.

Independence Day (Armenia), September 21
Also known as Re-establishment Day, recognizing the Republic of Armenia's independence in 1991.

Earthquake Victims Commemoration Day (Armenia), December 7
Recognizes the victims of the 1988 earthquake. Most businesses and stores remain open.

WATER FESTIVAL

By tradition, Armenian children dump buckets of water on passersby during the summer holiday known as **Vardavar**. The origins of this tradition are murky. Many believe that the holiday originated during Armenia's pagan era, when Armenians worshipped Vishaps— stone monuments of water dragons— for bringing life-giving water to the land. Vardavar may have been celebrated as early as the Bronze Age (5000-3500 BC).

Today the holiday is celebrated on a Saturday fourteen weeks after Easter, which usually occurs in July. The primary rule is clear: children may splash buckets of water on people with near-impunity. There's no indignity in being doused with water, but plenty of shame if you complain about it. Pleading to be spared is not unheard of, but we've even seen soldiers who prefer to simply accept the soaking rather than make a fuss. The dry weather, unrelenting sun, and temperatures that approach 40°C (106°F) may be the reason for the tolerance.

GETTING THERE

Getting to Armenia and Karabagh is relatively simple, although tiring. There are several commercial flights to Armenia each week, and there is reliable ground transportation to Karabagh from Armenia. Because of the time difference, many flights to Armenia from the US arrive two mornings after departure. The lost time is made up on the return flight, when the morning flight out of Yerevan arrives in the US later that same day. The most convenient connections are offered on British Airways [see "Getting There By Air," below].

Two passing women get splashed during the annual Vardavar water festival

BEFORE YOU GO

A passport is required for all travelers, even infants. Passports must be valid for at least six months beyond the date of entry into the country. First-time applicants must apply for their passports in person at a US post office or passport agency, but renewals may be made by mail. When applying for your first US passport you will need to provide proof of citizenship, such as an original birth certificate. For a renewal, your old passport is acceptable. The fee for a first-issue passport is $85. Renewals are $55. Applications typically take about six weeks to fulfill, but expedited service is available for an additional fee of $60. You can get an application form and more information from your local post office or from www.travel.state.gov/passport_services.html.

A visa is required for citizens of most western countries. Children are required to obtain visas, too, but the fee is waived for children under the age of 16. A **three-week tourist visa** can be obtained from the Armenian Embassy in Washington, DC either by regular mail, in person, or on the internet. Visas are also available at the airport upon arrival in Yerevan.

To apply by mail in the US, write to the Consular Section of the Armenian Embassy, 2225 R Street, NW, Washington, DC 20008 (Tel. 202-319-2983), or the Consulate General of Armenia in California at 50 N. La Cienega Boulevard, Suite 210, Beverly Hills, California 90211 (Tel. 310-657-6102). There's a short application form that is available by mail or online at www.armeniaemb.org. The fee is $60 and the processing time is seven business days. Faster processing is available for an additional fee. Personal checks are not accepted.

To apply online and get an electronic visa from the website of the Armenian Embassy, go to www.armeniaforeignministry.am. The **E-visa** allows travelers to get their visas entirely online, instead of by mail or in-person at an Armenian Consulate office. This is the simplest way to get a visa for Armenia. The fee is $60, which you can pay by credit card. Print a copy of your completed application before logging off, and bring the copy with you as proof that you applied online. This visa is valid for entry only at Yerevan's Zvartnots Airport, and not at land crossings.

An E-visa has the same effect as a regular visa, but there is no stamp or label in your passport. In most cases, the Armenian Embassy says it will be able to approve your application and issue an E-visa within one or two business days. You can also check the status of your E-visa using their website. This could become a worldwide trend, but at the moment Armenia is the only country that allows you to apply for a visa on the internet and to pay by credit card.

To apply upon arrival, go to the visa window at Zvartnots Airport as soon as you get off the plane, before passing through customs or immigration. Visas are issued routinely, with no added red tape. We've never heard of anyone being denied a visa upon arrival. You will have to pay in cash, but the fee is only $30, making this the least expensive tourist visa that Armenia offers.

Travelers who wish to stay more than three weeks must obtain a letter of invitation from a resident of Armenia. For a **90-day business visa**, the letter of invitation must be sent directly to the Consular Department of the Ministry of Foreign Affairs in Yerevan. For a 90-day tourist visa, the letter of invitation must be sent directly to the Passport and Visa Department of the Ministry of Internal Affairs in Yerevan. The consular section of the Armenian Embassy will provide particulars on how to file these letters and it will process the paperwork and issue the visa. The cost is $35 for a single-entry visa and $65 for a multiple-entry visa. Full details on other types of visas are available on the Armenian Embassy's website or directly from the embassy in Washington, DC.

Business travelers who intend to reside in Armenia for more than three months are required to obtain a residency permit from the Ministry of Internal Affairs after their arrival in Armenia. Travelers from the US must obtain a separate national visa for each of the Newly Independent States that they intend to visit. For travelers who are just passing through, **three-day transit visas** are usually offered, and a three-day visa to Armenia is available for $18.

Keep in mind that standard tourist visas permit only one entry into Armenia. If you intend to cross the border into Armenia more than once, you will need either a multiple entry visa, or you will have to get a new visa either online, from the Consular section of an Armenian Embassy, or at the airport upon your return to Armenia. If you're returning to Armenia from Karabagh, this restriction is not enforced.

If you need to overstay your visa, you can get an extension—with great aggravation and difficulty—from OVIR, which is the Armenian Ministry of Internal Affairs' Passport and Visa Department, located at 13a Mesrop Mashtots Avenue (Tel. 52-14-16). If you attempt to leave Armenia with an expired visa, you will merely be assessed a fine of $3 for each day that you overstay. If you expect that you will need to overstay your visa by only a week or two, you are better advised to simply pay the three dollar per day fine at the airport when you leave, instead of trying to deal with the people at the OVIR office. OVIR is also the office where you can apply for a residency permit.

ARMENIAN EMBASSIES WORLDWIDE

Austria: Neubaugasse 12-14, 1070 Vienna (Tel. 43-1-522-7479; Fax 43-1-522-7481) (E-mail: armenia@ycom.or.at) or (armenia@armembassy.at)

Canada: 7 Delaware Avenue, Ottawa, Ontario K2P 0Z2 (Tel. 613-234-3710; Fax: 613-234-3444) (E-mail: embottawa@rogers.com; erac@ican.net) (Internet: www.armembassycanada.ca)

France: 9 Rue Viete, 75017 Paris (Tel. 331-4-212-9800; Fax 331-4-2129803) (E-mail: ambarmen@wanadoo.fr)

Georgia: 4 Tetelashvilis Street; Tbilisi (Tel. 995-32-95-17-23; Fax 995-32-99-01-26) (E-mail: aspet@access.sanet.ge) or (armemb@caucasus.net)

Iran: 1 Ostad Shahriar; Tehran (Tel. 982-1-670-4833; Fax 982-1-670-0657) (E-mail: emarteh@yahoo.com)

Lebanon: Jasmine Street, Beirut (Tel. 961-4-402-952; Fax 961-4-418-860) (E-mail: armenia@dm.net.lb)

Russia: Armianski Pereulok 2; Moscow (Tel. 095-924-1269; Fax 095-924-5030) (E-mail: info@armem.ru; armembru@df.ru) (Internet: www.armenianembassy.ru)

United Kingdom: 25A Cheniston Gardens, London, England W8 6TG (Tel. 011-44-20-7938-5435; Fax 44-20-7938-2595) (E-mail: armembuk@onetel.net.uk)

United States: 2225 R Street, NW; Washington, DC 20008 (Tel. 202-319-1976). Additional office, consulate only, at 50 N. La Cienega Boulevard, Suite 210, Beverly Hills, California 90211 (Tel. 310-657-6102; Fax 202-319-2982) (E-mail: amembusadm@msn.com) (Internet: www.armeniaemb.org)

Armenia also maintains embassies or consulates in Argentina, Belarus, Belgium, Bulgaria, China, Egypt, Germany, Greece, India, Iraq, Italy, Kazakhstan, Poland, Romania, Switzerland, Syria, Turkmenistan, Ukraine, and the United Arab Emirates.

TRAVEL INFORMATION

Travel Safety Advisories

The US Dept. of State provides Travel Warnings and Consular Information Sheets on all countries, including Armenia (Tel. 202-647-5225; Fax 202-647-3000) (Internet: www.state.gov). For emergency information about an American traveling overseas, call the Office of Overseas Citizens Services (Tel. 202-647-5225). The Dept. of State characterizes the relationship between Armenia and the US as excellent, and points out that the US Embassy was the first embassy to open in Yerevan in February 1992. It is not likely that civil disturbances, if they occur, would be directed against US businesses or the US community. Most travelers also report that Americans and other Westerners are generally well liked and warmly received.

There are also travel advisories that are intended specifically for citizens of Canada (Tel. 800-267-6788; 613-944-6788) (Internet: www.voyage.gc.ca). The Canadian Dept. of Foreign Affairs reports that foreigners in Armenia have not been targeted for attack. The British Foreign Office (Tel. 20-7008-0232) (Internet: www.fco.gov.uk) reports that most visits to Armenia are "trouble free" for British citizens. It sees no specific threats to British nationals and considers the public order situation in Armenia to be "calm."

Travel Insurance

Travel insurance is available from many providers in the US. There are many types of policies, covering different risks. Some policies will insure against theft or loss while traveling. There are other policies available that will reimburse you for the cost of airfare and lodging in the event that you become ill and physically unable to take your vacation. Be sure to read the policy carefully, and pay attention to the risks that are excluded. Some insurers, for example, will not provide coverage if you cancel your vacation voluntarily, even if your decision is in response to a government travel advisory. Check with your local travel agent or call a company such as Travel Guard Travel Insurance (Tel. 800-826-7488), which writes policies that cover trip cancellation, or World Travel Center (Tel. 800-234-1862) (Internet: www.worldtravelcenter.com), or Clements International Insurance (Tel. 202-872-0060; Fax 202-466-9064) (Internet: www.clements.com).

Some insurance policies will cover the cost of transportation to a hospital in Europe or the US in a medical emergency. Insurers call this "med-evac" insurance. [for more information on medical insurance for travelers, see the section on Health later in this chapter].

Tourist Information

The Armenian Tourism Development Agency in Yerevan has a library of more than 100 books on Armenia's historic sites which visitors are invited to use for free. This is a good source for books about Armenian culture and travel. You can also pick up free tourist maps and brochures about many sites of interest to visitors. Open daily 10 am to 7 pm. Located at 3 Nalbandian Street near Republic Square (Tel. 54-23-03) (E-mail: help@armeniainfo.am) (Internet: www.armeniainfo.am).

Travelers with a passion for learning about Armenia's archaeological treasures should consult www.cilicia.com. This non-commercial website is operated as a hobby by an Armenian American and it features detailed descriptions of just about every historic monument in Armenia.

CALLING ARMENIA

Placing Calls to Yerevan from Abroad: To reach Yerevan from outside Armenia, connect to an international operator (In the US, enter 011), and then Armenia's country code (374) plus the Yerevan city code (1). If you are calling a cell phone, enter (09) immediately before you enter the local phone number.

Placing Calls to Other Cities in Armenia from Abroad: To reach cities other than Yerevan from outside Armenia, enter (011) and then Armenia's country code (374) plus the code for the city you are calling [for a list of city codes, and for instructions for placing phone calls when you are in Armenia, see Chapter 4, Yerevan].

MAPS

Good maps of Armenia were scarce until just a few years ago. Now, visitors have their choice of several. Many of the Armenia country maps in this book were created by Mr. Sarkis Acopian and the American University of Armenia for the Birds of Armenia project (Internet: www.aua.am/boa). Their wall-sized version of the maps is one of the best that exists, and it is sold for about $12. Information about how to order the map is available in the Appendix.

In Yerevan, many stores sell booklets of maps of the country in a pocket-sized format for about $5. They're not as good as the Birds of Armenia maps, but they are convenient to use while driving around the country. You can get a large street map of Yerevan for free from most hotels in Yerevan. Street maps for most other cities and towns are difficult to find, and the ones in this book are the best in print. A great street map of Gyumri is available from the Shirak Development Center (www.shirakinfo.am) and is also included in this book with their permission.

CUSTOMS REGULATIONS

There have been significant reforms of customs procedures in Armenia during the past few years, resulting in a painless procedure for most travelers. It's no longer necessary to write down every item you carry in, such as your wedding band or your wristwatch. But it has been routine during the past few years for customs officers to x-ray all baggage. There is no limit on the amount of Armenian or foreign currency that can be brought in or out of the country. Transfers of $10,000 or more are subject to reporting requirements according to Armenian law, however, and the transfer must be made electronically. US law obligates travelers who enter or depart the US while carrying $10,000 or more in US currency to file a declaration with the US Customs office.

Travelers who carry rare or expensive items into the country, and who intend to carry them back out, should declare these items upon their arrival. You will be given a form that you must present to customs upon your departure, so that you may avoid an export tax. Commercial goods (items fresh from the factory that look like you might sell them) that exceed $500 in value are taxable. Personal items are excluded from this calculation.

There are no restrictions on the type of food that may be imported, but quantity limits are imposed on many items, unless you have an import license. There's a 20-pack import and export limit on cigarettes, a 2-liter limit on alcohol, and a 1-kilogram limit on coffee. There is an absolute prohibition on the import or export of pornography, drugs and explosives. Prescription medicine should be left in its original drug store container, with a note from your doctor if you are carrying a large quantity.

Customs officers in Armenia are trained to look for carpets, paintings and antiquities when travelers are departing the country. Exporting antiquities with cultural or historic value is restricted. If you intend to export any item that is, or might be mistaken for, an antique, then you should apply for a special license at the Ministry of Culture. Without this license, you should expect that your carpet will be seized. Either obtain the license from the merchant, or apply in person at the Ministry of Culture, Government House #3, Republic Square (Tel. 52-93-49; 52-12-76). You will need to show the item to an officer, and provide two photographs for documentation. If you attempt to leave the country with antiquities—no matter how seemingly insignificant—that you have pilfered from a cultural site, it's almost a certainty that you'll be apprehended at the airport. Pilfering is treated as a serious criminal offense.

When you return to the US you will not be permitted to bring many food products through Customs, in order to protect American agriculture from pests and diseases. When returning to the US, you must declare any meats, fruits, vegetables, plants, animals, and plant or animal products that you are carrying in your checked or carry-on baggage. Bakery goods, candies, roasted nuts, and canned fruits and

Potato farmer near Sisian

vegetables are usually allowed. Details about what food items you can bring back to the US are available from the USDA Animal and Plant Health Inspection Service, at www.aphis.usda.gov/travel/usdatips.html.

As a result of the new, higher limits that took effect in 2002, you can now bring back as much as $800 worth of goods for personal use without paying a customs duty when entering the US. More information on US customs procedures is available from the website of the US Customs and Border Protection website, www.cbp.gov.

GETTING THERE BY AIR

Most Western travelers arrive in Armenia by air at Yerevan's **Zvartnots Airport**. Round trip airfares from the US are typically about $1,300 but they can range from $900 to as much as $1,700 during the high season. The airport is about 17 km from Yerevan, and the 20-minute cab ride should not cost more than $5 to $8 unless you're traveling with a group or have excess luggage. **City Cab** (Tel. 24-79-99) has a dispatch office at the airport. There's a bus that makes the journey, too, but departure times are not reliable.

The other commercial airport in Yerevan, **Erebuni Airport**, was at one time used for domestic flights, but there are no domestic flights in Armenia now and that airport is now used by the military, instead.

Shirak International Airport operates in Gyumri, which is Armenia's second-largest city. At time of research, the only available flights at this airport were on Aeroflot to and from Moscow each Saturday; to and from Krasnodar, Russia, each Thursday; and to and from Rostov-on-Don each Friday. Still, the people of Gyumri speak with pride about their international airport.

Commercial Airlines

Aeroflot Russian International Airlines (www.aeroflot.com) (Tel. 888-340-6400) provides service through Moscow, but travelers have reported poor service and difficulties making transfers at the Moscow airport. They have several ticket offices in Yerevan, including one at 12 Amirian Street (Tel. 52-24-35; 53-21-31) (E-mail: evnsu@arminco.com; evnsu@cornet.am).

Armavia, a private carrier, has taken over many of the routes of the defunct, state-operated, Armenian Airlines, including the flights to Yerevan from Amsterdam and Frankfurt. The airline has added an Istanbul flight, too. Armavia has a reputation for poor service and late flights, however, and this has encouraged many travelers to choose other airlines. Armavia is a subsidiary of Siberian Airlines. It has a ticketing office in Yerevan at 3 Amirian Street (Tel. 56-48-05; 56-48-06) (E-mail: armavia@infocom.am) (Internet: www.armavia.am).

Armenian International Airways, another private carrier, has also taken over several routes of the former Armenian Airlines, including the popular route to Yerevan from Paris, and from Beirut. This airline does not have a US office. Their offices in Yerevan are located at Zvartnots Airport and at 15 Mesrop Mashtots Avenue (Tel. 28-77-54; Fax 28-76-37) (Internet: www.armenianairways.am) (E-mail: aa@armenianairways.com) (Internet: www.armenianairways.com).

Austrian Airlines (www.aua.com) (Tel. 800-843-0002) has three weekly flights to Yerevan (four weekly flights during the Summer), with connections through its hub in Vienna. Flights are direct and non-stop, but many travelers tell us that they avoid this flight because of long layovers in Vienna. At time of research, scheduled flights departed Vienna on Tuesdays, Thursdays and Sundays. Return flights from Yerevan departed on Mondays, Wednesdays and Fridays. The AA office in Yerevan is located in the AUA Business Center at 9 Alek Manukyan Street (Tel. 51-22-01; Fax 51-22-06) (Internet: www.austrianairlines.am) (E-mail: armenia@aua.com).

British Airways (www.britishairways.com) (Tel. 800-247-9297) is the leading carrier offering service to Armenia. The airline offers direct non-stop flights from London to Yerevan, with very short layovers and, hence, convenient arrival times in Yerevan. BA's partner, British Mediterranean, actually operates the flight, using BA planes and personnel, and the airline offers the flight three times weekly during the high season, usually on a modern Airbus A320. At time of research, scheduled flights departed London on Mondays, Wednesdays and Fridays. Return flights from Yerevan departed on Saturdays, Tuesdays and Thursdays. The flight is popular with travelers who find that London is a good break point between Yerevan and the US. The BA office in Yerevan is located at 10 Sayat Nova Avenue (Tel. 52-13-83; 52-82-20) (E-mail: britair@arminco.com).

Czech Airlines (www.csa.cz) began operating flights between Prague and Yerevan in 2003. The airline has a good reputation for service, and has been operating a new Airbus on this route. Round trip airfares may be a bit higher than the competition. The Czech Airlines office in Yerevan is located at 2 Marshal Baghramian Avenue (Tel. 56-40-99; Fax 52-21-62) (E-mail: info@visaconcoRoadam) (Internet: www.visaconcoRoadam).

At time of research there were also flights available (1) between Yerevan and Istanbul on **Fly Air**, 25 Sarian Street (Tel. 52-03-03) (E-mail: bagratour@netsys.am); (2) between Yerevan and Aleppo on **Syrian Air**, 3 Khorenatsi Street (Tel. 53-85-89) (E-mail: astrontravel@netsys.am); and (3) between Yerevan and Tbilisi on both **Caucasus Airlines**, 10 Sayat Nova Boulevard (Tel. 52-52-10) and **Caspian Airlines**, 19 Nalbandian Street (Tel. 52-44-01).

Booking Agents

Sidon Travel specializes in arranging flights from the US to Armenia, and can often book a seat for a fare that is lower than the airlines. They can be reached at 428 South Central Avenue, Glendale, California (Tel. 818-553-0777; Toll-free 800-826-7960; Fax 818-553-0779) (Internet: www.sidontravel.com). In Yerevan: 50 Nalbandian Street (Tel. 52-29-67; Fax 15-16-84) (www.sidontravel.com/html/armenia.html).

Levon Travel is also an Armenia travel specialist. Located at 1132 North Brand Boulevard, Glendale, California (Tel. 818-552-7700). In Yerevan: 10 Sayat Nova Boulevard (Tel. 52-52-10; Fax 56-14-83) (E-mail: sales@levontravel.com). In Stepanakert: 16a Vazgen Sargsian (Yerevanian) Street. In Tbilisi: 20 Chavchadze Avenue (Tel. 995-32 + 25-00-10) (E-mail: levont@access.sanet.ge).

With the exception of the conveniently-scheduled flights from London on British Airways, flights to Yerevan from European hubs are almost always red-eyes. Departure times are generally in the evening, and the flights generally do not arrive in Yerevan until the following morning. Connecting flights into Europe from the US are usually red-eyes, too. This means that by the time you finally arrive in Armenia, you may have spent two full nights in the air, and a full day of layover at an airport in Europe. After such a marathon of travel, you probably won't want to schedule too many activities for your first day in Armenia. To make the journey more pleasant, you should include a toothbrush and some other toiletries in your carry-on luggage so that you can freshen up between flights.

GETTING THERE OVERLAND

The only overland route to Armenia that an American can conveniently take is through the Republic of Georgia, which is located to the north. Armenia's borders with Turkey and Azerbaijan are closed and militarized. Armenia's border with Iran is open, but crossing from Iran may not be comfortable for someone traveling on a US passport.

Buses make a daily run between Tbilisi, Georgia, and Yerevan, but the cheap 3,000-dram (about $6) fare is made less enticing by the painful six-to-eight-hour ride on an old run-down heap. A small van, generally one that is in good condition, operates on the same route twice daily. The fare is 6,500 dram (about $13), and travel time is only about four or five hours. Departures for both buses and vans are from Tbilisi's Ortajella Bus Station at 8 am and 10 am. All arrivals are in Yerevan at the Kilikia Central Bus Station on Admiral Isakov Avenue, but the driver will often discharge passengers in the center of the city, as well, in exchange for a gratuity.

There is also an overnight **train** from Tbilisi that departs at 4 pm. The train makes stops in Alaverdi, Vanadzor, and Gyumri before arriving at Yerevan's central train station at 6:30 am the next day. This is about twice as long as the journey would take by bus, so it's not recommended. Fare is 2,150 drams (less than $4). This train has compartments, each with four beds, but none has a door for privacy.

For the truly adventurous, buses also operate four times each week between Tehran, Iran, and Yerevan. The fare is $55, and travel time is roughly 32 to 36 hours. Departures from both Tehran and Yerevan are on Tuesday, Wednesday, Friday and Sunday. At time of research, the Yerevan departures were from Hotel Erebuni, in the city center.

When making the crossing in a private car, you can expect to be scrutinized by border guards on both the Georgian and Armenian sides. It may sometimes be necessary to offer a modest "grease" payment of $10 in order to expedite the process. This is usually enough to put everything in order and to get you on your way.

ORGANIZED TOURS AND TRAVEL AGENCIES

If you are already in Armenia and you want to join (or form) an organized tour with a guide, there are several reputable tour guides to choose from. Leading local tourist agencies are Sati Tours and Menua Tours [see "Getting Around" later in this chapter for more details].

In the US, Levon Travel and Sidon Travel have been operating for several years and have good reputations [see "Getting There by Air" earlier in this chapter].

ARRIVING AND LEAVING

The US Embassy encourages US citizens to register their presence. You don't have to do this, but if you do it will make it easier for the embassy staff to locate you in an emergency. To register, stop by the consular office of the embassy in Yerevan. The entrance is located on the left side of the embassy building at 18 Baghramian Avenue (it will be located there until late 2005 when a new embassy compound at the edge of the city replaces it). Whether you register or not, you should make a couple of photocopies of your passport and keep them in a safe place. Having a photocopy will make it easier to get a replacement passport if the original is lost.

At the airport upon your departure from Armenia and before you can check your bags you must pay an airport tax, in Armenian currency, at a special window. The 10,000-dram tax is equivalent to about $20.

FOREIGN EMBASSIES AND CONSULATES IN YEREVAN

Belarus: 12 Dumani Street (Tel. 59-73-09; Fax 56-70-18) (E-mail: 27-56-11; Fax 26-03-84) (E-mail: armenia@belembassy.org)

Bulgaria: 11 Nor Aresh Street (Tel. 45-82-33; Fax 45-46-02) (E-mail: bularm@arminco.com)

Canada: 25/22 Demirjian Street. Consulate only (Tel. 56-79-03)

China: 12 Marshal Baghramian Avenue (Tel. 56-00-67; Fax 54-57-61) (E-mail: chiemb@mbox.arminco.com)

Egypt: 6a Sepuh Street (Tel. 22-67-55; Fax 22-64-25) (E-mail: egyemb@arminco.com)

Estonia: 43 Gulbenkyan Street (Tel. 26-39-73; Fax 25-15-26) (E-mail: aries@arminco.com)

France: 8 Grigor Lusavorich Street, behind Republic Square (Tel. 58-35-11; Fax 56-98-31) (E-mail: admin@ambafran.am) (Internet: www.ambafran.am)

Georgia: 42 Aram Street, near Abovian Street (56-41-83; 56-43-57; Fax 56-41-83) (E-mail: geomb@netsys.am)

Germany: 29 Charents Street (Tel. 52-32-79; Fax 52-47-81) (Internet: www.deutschebotschaft-eriwan.am/de/home) (E-mail: germemb@arminco.com)

Greece: 6 Demerjian Street (Tel. 53-00-51; Fax 53-00-49) (E-mail: grembarm@arminco.com)

India: 50/2 Dzorapi Street (Tel. 53-91-74) (E-mail: inemyr@arminco.com)

Iran: 1 Budaghian Street, near Komitas Avenue (Tel. 28-04-57; 23-29-20; 52-98-30; Fax 23-00-52) (E-mail: info@iranembassy.am) (Internet: www.iranembassy.am)

Iraq: 24 Sevastopol Street (Tel. 26-12-23; Fax 26-13-22)

Italy: 5 Italy Street (Tel. 54-23-35; Fax 54-23-01) (E-mail: ambitaly@arminco.com) (Internet: www.ambitarm.am)

Lebanon: 7 Vardanants Street (Tel. 52-65-40; Fax: 52-69-90) (E-mail: libarm@arminco.com)

Norway (consulate only): 50 Khanjian Street (Tel. 55-15-82; Fax 57-46-39) (E-mail: admin@nrc.am)

Poland: 44a Hanrapetutian Street (Tel. 54-24-93: Fax 54-24-98) (E-mail: polemb@arminco.com)

Romania: 3 Sepuh Street (Tel. 27-47-01; Fax 54-41-44)

Russia: 13a Grigor Lusavorich Street (Tel. 56-74-27; Fax 56-71-97) (E-mail: russia@arminco.com) (Internet: www.armenia.mid.ru)

Syria: 14 Marshal Baghramian Avenue (Tel. 52-40-28; Fax 52-40-58) (E-mail: syrem_ar@intertel.am)

Thailand (consulate only): 8 Amirian Street (Tel. 56-04-10; Fax 54-44-25) (E-mail: info@thaiconsulate.am)

Turkmenistan: 72 Dzorap Street, Hotel Hrazdan (Tel. 53-83-56) (E-mail: serdar@arminco.com)

Ukraine: 58 Yerznkian Street (Tel. 58-68-56; 56-70-18; Fax 22-74-02) (E-mail: ukremb@internet.am) (Internet: www.erevan.am/ukrembassy)

United Kingdom: 34 Marshal Baghramian Avenue (Tel. 26-43-01; Fax 26-43-18) (E-mail: britemb@xter.net) (Internet: www.britemb.am)

United States: 18 Marshal Baghramian Avenue (Tel. 52-46-61; 52-16-11). The US Embassy will be at this location until late 2005, when its new 23-acre compound opens on Admiral Isakov Highway, next to Lake Yerevan (Internet: www.usa.am)

Uruguay: 26/9 Ghazar Parpetsu Street (Tel. 53-49-10; Fax 53-49-30) (E-mail: Uruguay@freenet.am)

Essentials

ONCE THERE

Safety

World events have not affected one's ability to travel safely throughout Armenia. Armenian officials have not reported any new restrictions on travel and Western visitors—particularly Americans and Canadians—are well-liked and warmly received. The US Embassy is replacing its centrally-located facility with a secure compound at the edge of the city, but this is being done as part of an upgrade of US-government sites worldwide, and not in response to any unique concerns about security in Armenia. By most accounts Armenia is a safe destination.

Violent street crime is almost unheard of in Armenia, but travelers are nevertheless advised to take the same precautions that they would take in any major city. Don't walk alone late at night; be aware of your surroundings, especially when in a crowded area, and wear a money belt or neck pouch if you are carrying a lot of money.

Armenia and its neighbor Azerbaijan are at war, but a cease fire has been in force since 1994. Nevertheless, hostile relations with Azerbaijan and Turkey make it necessary for travelers to avoid straying close to the frontiers with these countries. The borders are militarized and are well marked, so you need not worry about accidentally entering a dangerous area. Motorists on the remote roadway between the northeastern towns of Ijevan and Noyemberian are occasionally subjected to hostile fire from Azerbaijan, but there have been no problems reported elsewhere in the country.

The greatest safety risk that is likely to be faced by most tourists is the risk of accident involving a motor vehicle. Pedestrians are rarely granted the right of way by automobile drivers in Yerevan, making it potentially dangerous to walk down the street. Automobiles and taxis do not generally have seat belts, air bags, or other safety features that are taken for granted in the West. Public transportation, and particularly the passenger vans that flood the streets of Yerevan, are frequently overcrowded and lack basic safety equipment. Tourists are urged to use added caution when walking in Yerevan and when using public transportation anywhere in Armenia.

Pedestrians who are out at night will discover that many streets, and common areas inside apartment buildings, are dark. Bring a small flashlight with you, to help you avoid stepping in potholes or into open manholes, or tripping on stairs. A small key-chain flashlight is adequate, and it's small enough to ensure that you will always carry it. You will also want to have a flashlight when visiting ancient churches that have no electricity.

If you drive a car, one of the greatest daily nuisances in Armenia is from the traffic police. It is customary for police to stop drivers without reason, in order to check their documents. These are purported to be safety stops, but what the police are really looking for is money, usually only about 1,000 drams ($2), in exchange for which the driver is allowed to continue on his way. Foreigners generally don't have to pay anything, unless they have actually committed an infraction, but the stops can nevertheless be annoying.

Note About Telephone Listings

Unless stated otherwise, we list local Armenia phone numbers according to how they would be dialed from Yerevan. Thus, Yerevan phone numbers are listed without the Yerevan area code, which isn't needed for calls placed from within the city.

Phone numbers in other cities and villages are listed with their local area code, because that area code must be dialed when calling from Yerevan.

Armenia's land phone system (as opposed to its wireless system) is not always reliable, and the technology to rollover calls from one line to another doesn't exist. We have therefore listed more than one telephone number for each listing whenever possible.

MONEY

Armenia has a cash economy. Credit cards are not widely accepted outside of the major hotels. Visitors should therefore plan to bring enough cash for their entire stay, or rely upon ATM machines for cash withdrawals. HSBC, the international banking institution, has several ATM machines in Yerevan, but their ATMs are not available outside the capital [for ATM locations see Chapter 4 Yerevan].

The local currency is the dram, which trades at approximately 560 dram to the dollar. Coins circulate in denominations of 10, 20, 50, 100, 200 and 500 drams. Paper notes are used for denominations of 500, 1,000, 5,000, and 10,000 dram.

As part of a phase-out of small bills, the 500-dram note will be withdrawn from circulation in 2005. Bank notes with smaller denominations were withdrawn from circulation in April 2004. There are also notes in denominations of 20,000 dram (about $35) and 50,000 dram (about $85), but they can rarely be negotiated, except at a bank or hotel.

Exchanging Money

The US dollar is widely accepted for larger transactions, but new bills, without marks or tears, are preferred. For most retail purchases, however, you will need to have Armenian dram. You can lawfully exchange dollars, without a commission, from merchants located in post offices, hotels, and even on the street. Dollars are preferred, but you may also be able to exchange euros and rubles. British currency, however, is more difficult to exchange. Bills should always be new and clean. The worst exchange rates are offered at Yerevan's airport and at the major hotels. For the best rates, try any of the shops located along Tigran Mets Avenue in Yerevan, just off Republic Square.

Exchange Rates

Armenia's currency, the dram, has remained fairly stable for the past several years. The exchange rates at the time of research are presented below. These rates can be used as a guide to what costs will be when you travel. For up-to-the-minute rates for the dram and for every other currency in circulation worldwide, consult www.xe.com. The US dollar is the most popular foreign currency.

Exchange Rates	
United States	1 dollar: 560 dram
Europe	1 euro: 495 dram
Russia	1 ruble: 18 dram
Great Britain	1 pound: 806 dram
Canada	1 dollar: 357 dram

TIME

Local time in Armenia and Karabagh is 12 hours ahead of California, nine hours ahead of New York, and four hours ahead of Greenwich Mean Time. When it's 9 am Sunday in Los Angeles, it's already 9 pm Sunday in Yerevan. Time changes for daylight savings have not always been made in unison with the rest of the world, however, and so it is possible that the time differences may for brief periods be reduced by one hour.

MAIL

Mail within Armenia is frequently lost or misdirected, and the post office should not be relied upon for delivering anything important in Armenia. You might have better success with the Armenian post office for mail that is to be delivered outside the country. To send a letter or package from Armenia, to a destination outside of Armenia, it is best to mail it from a post office in Yerevan. Private couriers such as FedEx and DHL also operate in Yerevan. [For more information about shipping see Chapter 4, Yerevan].

WEIGHTS AND MEASURES

Armenia uses the metric system for weights and measures. If you are not familiar with the metric system you can make some quick and approximate conversions into measures that you are more familiar with by using the methods below.

To quickly convert degrees Celsius into Fahrenheit, multiply the Celsius temperature by two and then add 32. To convert degrees Fahrenheit to Celsius, subtract 32 and then divide in half. The result is not exact, but it's close.

To convert distances from meters to feet, divide by three for a rough approximation. To convert feet to meters, multiply by three. To convert kilometers to miles, multiply by 0.6.

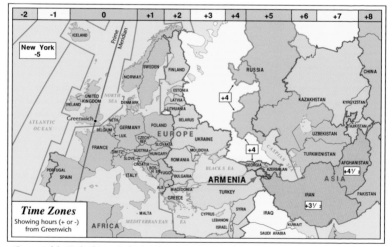

Courtesy of the Birds of Armenia Project, American University of Armenia, Oakland, CA, 1999

Measurement Conversions	
1 centimeter: 0.4 inches	1 gram: 0.04 ounce
1 meter: 3.3 feet	1 kilogram: 2.2 pounds
1 meter: 1.1 yards	1 liter: 1.1 quart
1 kilometer: 0.6 miles	1 liter: 0.26 gal

To convert the value of kilograms to pounds, just multiply by two and then add 10 percent. One liter is equivalent to roughly one quart. One gallon is approximately four liters.

ELECTRICITY

Standard voltage in Armenia and Karabagh is 220V. Appliances from the US are designed for 110V, however, so you will need a voltage converter if you plan to use US appliances here. The voltage sometimes deviates from the standard, so you should also bring a surge protector for computers and other valuable equipment. It may be difficult to find stores in Armenia that sell transformers or surge protectors, so bring these from home. For the past few years, power outages have been uncommon in Armenia. Therefore, back-up power sources are less important than they once were.

Electric outlets use European-style plugs with two round pins. You will therefore need to use plug adaptors for US appliances, in addition to the voltage converter. These are sold in the US, and they are also readily available in Yerevan at electronics stores such as Zig Zag and at the many new electronics stores that have opened on Mesrop Mashtots Avenue.

GETTING AROUND

A tour of Armenia can easily be arranged independently by hiring a private driver. This means finding someone, anyone, with a car and agreeing on a fare. Because of the high unemployment rate, finding a driver is not difficult. Most hotels and tour operators will help you locate someone suitable. The going rate is about 100 dram (twenty cents) for each kilometer traveled.

A **private driver** to Lake Sevan will usually charge about $30 for a stay of several hours. Other typical fares are: $20 to Garni and Geghard; $20 to Khor Virap monastery; $15-$20 to Echmiadzin, but fares will vary depending upon the type of vehicle used and the length of time one stays at a destination. Most cars will accept three or four passengers. A van will usually accept up to 11 passengers. There are several taxi services that will provide a driver at a reasonable rate.

Road conditions are highly variable. Most roadways outside Yerevan are not lighted, and safety features such as guardrails are used sparingly. As a result, driving on secondary roads at night is difficult and many drivers will prefer to get you back to your hotel before sunset. Armenia's days are long in the summer, so this often means you'll be able to return to your hotel as late as 10 pm. Most of the primary roads have been repaired and repaved during the past few years, however, making intercity travel a little safer and more convenient.

Keep in mind that in most parts of rural Armenia, you'll be sharing the road with farm animals. There have been times while driving around the country that we have felt as if we were playing a video game: first we swerve to avoid a gaggle of geese that crosses the highway in front of us; then we dodge a wayward chicken, a mixed herd of cows and sheep block the road and we slam on the brakes.

Hitchhiking is generally safe, and it's common among all groups, including even the elderly. We've even seen soldiers and police hitching rides. In the villages and towns, it is customary for drivers to offer rides to just about anyone, and pedestrians seem to expect that cars will stop for them. The greatest danger from hitchhiking is from the cars themselves, which usually lack seatbelts and other safety features.

Many **tour operators** offer traditional guided group tours. Some of the local agents that we have received good reports about are: **Armintour** (Tel. 58-22-82); **Delta-Armenia**, 30-12 Kievyan Street (Tel. 56-59-99) (E-mail: delta@netsys.am) (Internet: www.delta-armenia.am); **First Travel and Service Agency**, 12/2 Parpetsi Street (Tel. 53-40-24; 53-99-01) (E-mail: first@arminco.com); **Menua**, Sayat Nova Ave, in the lobby of the Ani Plaza Hotel (Tel. 52-73-72; Fax 58-39-01) (E-mail: info@menuatours.com) (Internet: www.menuatours.com); **Prana Tour**, 18 Kievian Street (Tel. 22-54-88; 27-15-42; Fax 27-31-41) (E-mail: prana@arminco.com); **Sati Tours**, 21 Mashtots Avenue (Tel. 53-99-00) (E-mail: armenia@satiglobal.com) (Internet: www.satiglobal.com); **Shirak Hotel Tours**, 13 Movses Khorenatsi Street (Tel. 52-33-15; Fax 58-35-93) (E-mail: shirak_hotel@infocom.am) (Internet: www.shirak-hotel.am); **Tatev Tour Agency**, 45 Komitas Avenue (Tel. 23-18-48; 23-18-58; Fax 15-14-39) (E-mail: info@tatev.com) (Internet: www.arminco.com/tatev); **Tourism Management, Ltd.**, 29 Komitas Avenue, 2nd floor (Tel. 22-41-11; Fax 27-73-44) (E-mail: mtourism@arminco.com).

Armenian Church organizations often sponsor tours, which they advertise as pilgrimages, to Armenia and to historical Armenian areas outside the republic. These are comprehensive tours that must be arranged well in advance. For details contact the Diocese of the Armenian Church, 630 Second Avenue, New York, NY 10016 (Tel. 212-686-9893; Fax 212-686-0245); or the Prelacy of the Armenian Apostolic Church, 138 East 39th Street, New York, NY 10016 (Tel. 212-689-7810).

It is finally possible to find **rental cars** in Armenia which do not come with drivers. There are three car rental companies doing business in Yerevan from which you can rent a new sedan complete with air conditioning, seat belts, and everything you would expect in a rental car [for details see Chapter 4, Yerevan].

If you plan to live in Armenia and want to buy a car, you'll need a valid license from your home state and an international driver's license, which you can get from the American Automobile Association in the US. If you do not have a driver's license from the US, you will need an Armenian license. To get the license you will have to sit for a written examination that is currently offered only in Armenian.

Bicycles are not common sights in Armenia, and there aren't any bike rental companies that we know of. If you bring a bicycle to Armenia, the most practical type is a mountain bike, so that you can cover the country's mountainous terrain. Bring spare parts, too. Riding a bicycle in Yerevan can be dangerous because automobile drivers aren't accustomed to seeing and accommodating bicyclists, so use extreme caution.

PUBLIC TRANSPORTATION

Yerevan

In Yerevan, a **subway** cuts a single swath through the center of the city, and reliably arrives at each station within five minutes of the previous train. Fare is 50 dram (less than ten cents). This is a convenient way to go across town now that Yerevan has developed, in the past year or two, a morning and evening rush hour.

There's a local shuttle service on small **passenger vans**, which everyone calls by the Russian name marshrutni. These marshrutni vans operate throughout the city for a fare of 100 dram (about twenty cents). Seating is cramped, and it's not always easy to determine where a particular van will go. Still, at this price, if you end up in the wrong place, at least you will not have wasted much money getting there. Trams once operated in Yerevan, but were discontinued in 2003.

Cabs are plentiful, and often times you can find one that's parked on the curb. Gasoline is too expensive, and customers too few, for cabbies to drive around looking for fares. A foreigner should expect to pay about 1,000 dram (less than $2) regardless of the destination within the center city. Drivers usually expect a little more for late-night trips. Fares should be metered or negotiated in advance.

Intercity

For trips between cities, **buses** are available and cheap, but they should be avoided unless you have lots of spare time. The inter-city vans are a more expensive, but faster choice. For a current schedule of both, it's best to check with the bus station one or two days before you intend to travel.

Mother Armenia statue from Mesrop Mashtots Ave.

Go, in person, to the **Kilikia Central Bus Station**, located on Admiral Isakov Street, or call (Tel. 56-53-70), for timetables and tickets. Admiral Isakov Street is also known as the Echmiadzin road, because it leads, predictably, to Echmiadzin. The bus station is located just past the Ararat Brandy factory, on the same side of the road.

In addition to service from the bus station, there are several vans that depart from central Yerevan for Lake Sevan every Saturday and Sunday morning during the summer. Fare is 900 dram (less than $2). The vans depart from the **Komitas Park** located near the corner of Sayat Nova Avenue and Mesrop Mashtots Avenue. Departure times are when all the seats in a particular van are filled, and generally start around 10 am and conclude by noon. Year round bus service to Lake Sevan is available daily from the bus stop at 28 Isahakian Street, in front of the Drama Theater [for more information see Chapter 6, Lake Sevan].

Essentials

Other intercity vans depart from points throughout Yerevan, with destinations throughout Armenia. Departure times are flexible because the vans depart only when all the seats are filled. Even allowing for this inconvenience, these vans still offer the safest and swiftest public transportation in the country. Some of the more popular tourist destinations are: , 250 dram (about 50 cents) departure from corner of Mashtots and Amirian; Sevan, 1,000 dram (about $2) departure from Moskovian Street near the Conservatory; Gyumri, 1,000 dram (about $2); and Vanadzor, 1,000 dram (about $2), both of which depart from St. Gregory the Illuminator Cathedral.

There are also **intercity trains** operating within Armenia, but they are slow and old, and we recommend that you avoid them. There is train service between Yerevan and Gyumri each day with departures from Yerevan's **Sasuntsi Davit train station** at 8 am. The return trip departs Gyumri at 5:15 pm. Fare is 500 dram (less than $1) which is quite a bargain for a journey of 120 km. Travel time is typically five and one-half hours, however, which is quite a long time to be seated on a wooden bench, and also unreasonable, considering that one can drive the distance in a private car in about 90 minutes. Still, if you want to try, you can get to Yerevan's central train station by taking the metro to the Sasuntsi Davit station, which is located right next door. One of our readers, a tourist from the Czech Republic who traveled on this train, advises "it was terrible. It was a 40-year old train with wooden benches crowded with people and their goods from local markets on the way. More of an adventure than travel."

International (To Neighboring Countries)

Nagorno Karabagh Republic: Daily vans from Yerevan to the Karabagh capital of Stepanakert depart from the Kilikia Central Bus Station (Tel. 56-53-70). Departures begin at 7:30 am and continue each 30 minutes until 10 am. Travel time is roughly eight hours and the fare is 5,000 dram (less than $10). Arrive about an hour before departure so you can select a good seat. A window seat on the right side of the van will provide unobstructed views of Mt. Ararat. To guarantee a seat, buy your ticket the night before [for more information about traveling to Stepanakert and the surrounding countryside, see Chapter 10, Karabagh]. There are no regularly scheduled commercial flights to Karabagh.

Republic of Georgia: Buses and vans from Yerevan operate daily to Georgia, but the buses are dreadfully slow and should be avoided. Vans are cleaner, faster, and still reasonably priced. They all depart from Yerevan's Kilikia Central Bus Station. Departures by van to Tbilisi are daily at 7 am, 8 am, and 9 am. Travel time is only about four or five hours, and the fare is 6,500 dram (about $13). Arrive early to claim a good seat. The actual departure time will be when all the seats are sold. All vehicles arrive in Tbilisi at the Ortajella Bus Station. From there, a five-minute cab ride of 8 Georgian lari (about $4) will take you to the center of town. Within Tbilisi, foreign tourists should expect to pay 4 lari (about $2) for just about every fare.

A modern van makes the daily trek from Yerevan to **Akhalkalak**, the Armenian-populated region of Georgia, which is located north of Gyumri, at 8 am. Travel time is at least 8 hours, most of which occurs on the miserable, rocky roads in Georgia. The fare is 2,000 dram (about $4).

There are regularly scheduled commercial flights between Yerevan and Tbilisi on two Georgian airlines. See "Getting There By Air" earlier in this chapter for details.

Iran: A slow bus to Tehran departs from Hotel Erebuni in Yerevan, for a fare of about $50. Departures from both Tehran and Yerevan are on Tuesday, Wednesday, Friday and Sunday, and travel time is roughly 36 hours. Check with the Iranian Embassy in Yerevan for visa applications, and to learn about restrictions on travelers who are US citizens. Located at 1 Budaghian Street (Tel. 52-98-30; 28-04-57) (Fax 15-13-85). Commercial flights from Yerevan to Tehran are available on Caspian Air. Tickets are available from the airline's agent, Tatev Travel, 45 Komitas Street (Tel. 23-56-67; 23-18-48).

Turkey: There is also a bus to Istanbul, Turkey that departs from Yerevan's Kilikia Central Bus Station every Saturday at 10 pm. The bus cannot cross directly to Turkey from Armenia because the border is closed, so it takes a detour through Georgia. Travel time is approximately 36 hours, with six rest stops. The $50 fare ends up being $90 after adding the cost of the border visa in Georgia. The return bus from Istanbul to Yerevan departs every Saturday at 7 pm. The bus is operated by Emniyet Kesebirler Tours, a Turkish company with an office in Yerevan (Tel. 54-07-56) (E-mail: eminet@netsys.am).

US citizens can purchase a Turkish visa at the border. The visa fee for Americans is currently a hefty $100. If you are in Istanbul and wish to travel to Yerevan, call the bus company at their office in Turkey to make arrangements (Tel. 0-212-658-38-34). Armenia does not have an embassy in Turkey, so get your Armenia visa before going to Turkey or at the border. There's also another bus line that can take you as far as Istanbul. For tickets and schedule information, check with AST Turizm Ltd. at their Yerevan office on 50 Nalbandian Street (Tel. 56-44-54).

There is also a once-weekly flight between Yerevan and Istanbul operated by the Yerevan-based Armavia Airlines, which is a subsidiary of Siberia Airlines. This flight is an exception to Turkey's policy of keeping its frontier with Armenia closed. The airline is notorious for making late changes to its schedule on this route. Check with a travel agent to confirm flight times, even after your ticket has been issued.

A privately-owned Turkish airline called Fly Air began operating a twice-weekly flight between Istanbul and Yerevan in 2003, and thereby became the first Turkish company to operate direct flights to Armenia. At time of research it was unclear whether the airline would be financially able to keep this route open. Check with a travel agent to confirm that the flights are still operating.

Azerbaijan: It is not possible to travel directly to Azerbaijan. If your passport contains a Karabagh visa you will certainly be denied entry to Azerbaijan. You might also be arrested, and your safety could be in jeopardy. Do not attempt to travel to Azerbaijan if you have a Karabagh visa in your passport. If your passport contains an Armenian visa, or if you have an Armenian surname, the official line is that you will not be denied entry to Azerbaijan. But when we spoke to an official of the Azerbaijan Embassy in Washington, DC, he acknowledged that travelers with Armenian names or Armenian visas would certainly face "difficulties."

Essentials

SPECIAL CONCERNS

Disabled Travelers and the Elderly

Armenia is not hospitable to travelers with disabilities. Many hotels and buildings do not have elevators, and even when they do, the elevator car is typically too narrow to accommodate a wheelchair. Doorways are often too narrow for wheelchairs and stairs seem to create obstacles everywhere—even on the sidewalks outdoors. Public transportation offers no accommodation to physically challenged travelers, either. If you use a wheelchair or if you walk with crutches or a cane, you will need to make special arrangements with your hotel or tour operator to make certain that your needs will be filled. Wheelchair users should expect that they will need assistance whenever moving about on the streets of Yerevan.

Senior citizens are respected, but the law does not generally afford them special considerations when boarding public transportation, or when paying for goods and services. Elderly and disabled travelers will want to avoid using the mini vans that are ubiquitous in Yerevan. These vans are apt to make sudden, unannounced stops, pickup and discharge passengers from the traffic lane, and be overcrowded. Most vans also lack basic safety features such as seatbelts and many are in poor mechanical condition.

Women and Children

Although Armenia is an ancient Christian nation, it is also a secular democratic republic. Women's rights are respected in Armenia and women dress and conduct themselves in public just as they would in any modern Western country. Some segments of society are fairly conservative, however, and it is not unusual for local women, especially those in small towns and villages, to be expected to cook and be homemakers and to fill the so-called traditional women's roles.

Families with children can safely travel to Yerevan. Armenia is extremely child-friendly, and there is no safety or security reason to discourage families from bringing their kids. The greatest safety concerns for parents are probably the lack of seatbelts in most cars and the hazards that children, and all pedestrians, face when crossing the busy streets of Yerevan. Armenians love children and it is unthinkable that an adult here would victimize a child. As a result, there is no social taboo against strangers talking to children.

If you are detained by police, you have the right to contact your country's representative in Yerevan. For US citizens, this means you have the right to speak to the Consul of the US Embassy (Tel. 52-16-11; Fax 15-15-50) (Internet: www.usa.am). If the Consulate is closed, you can still get help in an emergency at any time of day or night by calling the Embassy switchboard (15-15-51).

Airport Security

Airport security x-rays can damage your film in some circumstances. Many airports use scanners for checked baggage that are so powerful they can penetrate lead bags. Therefore, absolutely never pack any film in the luggage that you check. Don't mail the film home, either, for the same reason. Instead, all of your film should be in your carry-on luggage when you travel by air. Remove all of the packaging and

place the rolls of film in a clear plastic bag. By doing this, you will be able to request for a hand inspection of your film.

If you cannot get a hand inspection, your best alternative is to place your film in a lead-lined film bag. These bags are designed for traveling with film, and you can purchase one at a camera shop. This lead won't stop the x-rays that are used for checked luggage, but it will protect most film from the low-dose x-rays at the passenger gate.

If your luggage has been selected for physical inspection and you have placed locks on the bags, security personnel in the US may break the locks in order to take a look at the contents. The Transportation Safety Administration (TSA) offers packing tips to avoid security problems (Tel. 866-289-9673) (Internet: www.TSATravelTips.us). There are now special TSA-approved locks available for purchase, which the TSA can open with a passkey.

HEALTH

Traveling to developing countries such as Armenia and Karabagh presents travelers with the burden of anticipating medical needs that might arise during their visit. Medical supplies are often limited, and if serious needs arise, the patient's familiar network of medical providers won't be able to help.

For the latest information about the precautions you should take before traveling, contact the Centers for Disease Control (CDC), National Center for Infectious Diseases, and ask for their Travelers' Health Bulletin (Tel. 888-232-3299) (Internet: www.cdc.gov/travel). Health advisories for worldwide destinations, including Armenia, are available from the CDC hotline (Tel. 404-332-4559). This is the best source for health advisories on all worldwide destinations. The World Health Organization (WHO) also offers up-to-date information on health concerns worldwide (Internet: www.who.int/en). Canada's Travel Medicine Program is also a good source for the latest international public health advice (Internet: www.travelhealth.gc.ca).

Immunizations

Armenia and Karabagh do not require proof of any immunizations or vaccinations to gain entry. If you have special health needs, speak to your physician before traveling. Medical providers advise that travelers to Armenia should have current immunizations for Diphtheria, Tetanus, Typhoid, and Hepatitis A. Travelers who may come into contact with blood should ideally be vaccinated for Hepatitis B. The risk of contracting tuberculosis is low, but there is a renewed concern about Malaria [see below].

Many communities in the US offer special clinics for overseas travelers where you can get travel immunizations. Check with your local Department of Health. A private professional organization that can help you locate a travel clinic is the International Society of Travel Medicine, PO Box 871089, Stone Mountain, Georgia 30087 USA (Tel. 770-736-7060) (E-mail: istm@mediaone.net) (Internet: www.istm.org). One privately operated medical clinic that offers immunizations and which has locations throughout the US is Passport Health, Inc. (Tel. 888-499-7277) (Internet: www.passporthealthusa.com).

To learn about clinics in Canada, check with the International Association for Medical Assistance to Travelers (IAMAT) (Tel. 416-652-0137) (Internet: www.iamat.org). In the UK, check with the Berkeley Travel Clinic in London (Tel. 0-20-7-629-6233) or call the Medical Advisory Service for Travelers Abroad (MASTA) for the location of a clinic near you (Tel. 0-12-7-668-5040).

Malaria

After a period of absence, Malaria is once again a risk in the Ararat Valley region of Armenia, just south of Yerevan. Wetlands in this area were drained in the 1950s, and the mosquitoes and malaria both disappeared. From 1963 through 1995, there were no reported cases of malaria. Environmental degradation of the Ararat Valley, and the lack of irrigation and drainage systems, has provided ideal breeding grounds for mosquitoes, however. In 1996, 143 cases of malaria were reported in the Ararat Valley and in the adjacent region of Armavir, and malaria has been reported here every year since then. There have been no reports of malaria-related deaths. Anti-malaria tablets are not always effective, but tourists can take other precautions: if you plan to be in the Ararat Valley after sunset between the months of June and October, wear long pants and long sleeves, and use insect repellant with the ingredient DEET. Most tourists are not outdoors in this region after dark, however, and so their risk is much lower than for those who live here.

Medicine

Bring any special medications that you reasonably believe you will need, especially prescription drugs. Use a carry-on toiletry kit when traveling so that you don't risk losing your medical essentials. Leave your prescriptions in their original, marked containers, and bring enough to last for your entire stay. If you are planning a long stay, and are therefore bringing a large supply, bring a letter of explanation from your doctor. This will help you avoid problems with customs officers who might otherwise be understandably suspicious.

Medicine can be purchased at the many pharmacies throughout Yerevan, but their selections are often limited and are unlikely to include exactly what you want. Outside Yerevan, and in Karabagh, you are apt to find even less. Travelers should therefore bring: fever reducers such as ibuprofen, Tylenol® or aspirin, over-the-counter cold remedies, antidiarrheal medications such as Imodium®, and some antibiotics, as well. Use the antibiotics only under direction of a physician.

In the summer, bring sun block, sunglasses, and a hat for protection from Armenia's intense and relentless sun. Armenia's high altitude—Yerevan is situated at approximately 1,000 m above sea level—makes exposure to the sun something you need to protect yourself from. Exposure to insects may also be a problem in the countryside. Bring insect repellant with the ingredient DEET if you plan to travel outside Yerevan in the evening [see comment about Malaria, above]. Sun block and insect repellant are rarely available in Armenia.

Throughout Armenia and Karabagh, find a pharmacy by looking for a sign with the Russian word "Apteka." Most of the pharmaceuticals are Russian-manufactured, so if you have a preferred brand of over-the-counter medicine, bring it from home.

Sexually Transmitted Disease

Sexually transmitted diseases are present here, as they are in every community. Travelers should take appropriate precautions. Condoms are increasingly becoming available at locations other than under the glass counters at pharmacies, but the available brands may be of poor quality. Travelers should bring whatever they need from home. Although there is a low incidence of HIV in Armenia, medical authorities say that there has been an increase in the past few years.

Safe Food and Water

Food and waterborne diseases are the leading cause of illness in travelers. Travelers' diarrhea can be caused by viruses, bacteria, or parasites, all of which are found everywhere and can contaminate food or water. Infections may cause diarrhea and vomiting, fever, or hepatitis. To help ensure that your food is safe, consume only pasteurized dairy products.

In Armenia and Karabagh, drink only bottled water, or water that has been brought to a full boil. In villages and whenever the water quality is in doubt, you should brush your teeth with bottled or boiled water, too. Although the water supply may be good, the water delivery system may be old and may introduce contaminants that are not present at the source.

Boil water for ten minutes to destroy most pathogens. If you are unable to boil water, the addition of iodine is a good alternative. Iodine treatment kits are available at many sporting goods stores, and wherever camping supplies are sold. Iodine treatment will destroy bacteria and will help prevent Giardia. Chlorine treatment is an alternative, as well, and chlorine tablets may also improve the safety of water. Still, this technique may not destroy the microbe that causes Giardia, and does not purify water as effectively as boiling or iodine treatment. Simple filtration is the least effective water purification technique, and will not remove all pathogens.

Bottled waters such as Noy brand (without gas) and Jermuk (sparkling) are available throughout Yerevan, and offer the safest, cheapest, and most convenient option for most travelers.

When at a café or restaurant, remember to avoid ice cubes. Drinking coffee or tea while dining out should not be risky, provided the drinks were made with boiled

---

Basic Medicine and Toiletry Kit Check-list

pain reliever	Band-Aids®
cold medicine	insect repellant (with DEET®)
cough drops	contact lens solution
anti-diarrheal	anti-bacterial towelettes
antacid tablets	feminine hygiene products
analgesics such as Ben-Gay®	children's medicines
sun-block	multi-vitamin supplements
anti-septic such as Neosporin®	

water. Avoid buffets at restaurants—the food may have been sitting out all day, without refrigeration, by the time you get to it. Use caution when purchasing food from street vendors. Fruit and vegetables that can be peeled are safe, but others should be washed with either bottled or boiled water.

Treating Stomach Illness

If you develop diarrhea or a stomach illness, it should typically disappear within two or three days. Dehydration is a risk; so you can speed-up your recovery by drinking lots of clear liquids, especially water. Remember to make certain that it is sterile, and use only bottled or boiled water. If you treat your illness with Imodium®, be certain that you do not exceed the recommended dosage. Constipation can also be painful, and can be an unintended result. When you are ready to begin eating again, avoid spicy and fatty foods. Plain boiled potatoes, and rice, are a couple of safe foods to start with.

Medical Emergencies

Emergency facilities are limited. We suggest using **European Medical Center**. 3 Vazgen Sargsian Street (Tel. 54-00-03; 54-05-40). This modern clinic offers Western-style medical care, with English-speaking doctors and nurses, and 24-hour ambulance service. They will also provide you with a detailed receipt that most insurance companies require for claims, and they can arrange for medical evacuation from the country.

The American Embassy can offer a list of doctors in general practice and also in various specialties (Tel. 52-16-11; Fax 15-15-50). If the Consulate is closed, you can still get help in an emergency at any time of day or night by calling the Embassy switchboard (15-15-51).

Armenia's equivalencies of the "911" emergency number that most Americans are familiar with are 1-01 (Fire); 1-02 (Police); and 1-03 (Ambulance). Operators may not speak English, however, and we suggest these numbers to foreign visitors only as a last resort. If you need hospitalization, the Ministry of Health Hospital #4, located at 21 Paronian Street, usually has an English-speaking doctor or nurse on staff.

Emergency dental care is available at Deluxe System Dental Clinic, 31 Moskovian Street (Tel. 53-95-38).

Medical Evacuation Insurance

Travel insurance that covers medical emergencies while away from home is available from many providers in the US. Some policies will cover the cost of transportation to a hospital in Europe or the US in a medical emergency. Insurers call this "med-evac" insurance, and the benefits can be great. Some policies will cover the expenses, for example, if you become ill and need to be evacuated to a Western hospital on a special flight, accompanied by a nurse.

To learn more, check with an insurance agent in your community or contact one of these insurers: TravMed® 8501 (Tel. 800-732-5309) (Internet: www.medexassist.com); Wallach Insurance (Tel. 800-237-6615) (E-mail: info@wallach.com) (Internet: www.wallach.com); or Passport Health, Inc. (Tel. 888-499-7277) (Internet: www.passporthealthusa.com). The largest (but not necessarily the best) provider of medical evacuation insurance in the newly independent states is the Geneva-based company SOS International (Tel. 800-523-8930). Clements International Insurance also provides med-evac insurance (Tel. 202-872-0060; Fax 202-466-9064) (Internet: www.clements.com).

Personal Hygiene

Many Western-quality toiletries are readily available in Yerevan, at prices that are comparable to those in the West. For the best selection of Western-brand shampoos, deodorants and beauty items, try one of the many cosmetics stores on Abovian Street near Republic Square in Yerevan, such as Mary Parfums Salon, 1 Abovian Street (Tel. 56-17-84). You can also choose from many Western-style grocery stores [for stores and locations, see Chapter 5, Yerevan]. The products at pharmacies are often limited to Russian imports. For short visits, bring all the toiletries you anticipate needing.

If you wear contact lenses, bring a spare set or better yet, disposable lenses. You will also need to bring enough lens cleaning solution to last for your entire visit, since cleaning and disinfecting products are rarely available at stores. If you wear eyeglasses, bring a spare pair. Women should bring sanitary napkins and any other special items they may need, rather than hope to find their preferred products.

BUSINESS MATTERS

Special Residency Status

Armenian law permits foreigners to obtain special residency status if they are conducting business in Armenia or if they are of ethnic Armenian ancestry. The **"Special Residency Passport"** is valid for ten years and allows one to pass through immigration without a visa. Applications can be obtained from the Armenian Embassy in Washington, DC (Tel. 202-319-1976) or from the Consulate in Los Angeles, California (Tel. 310-657-6102). The application fee is $350 if you apply in the US, and $300 if you apply in Armenia. This residency passport is valid only for entry to Armenia, and cannot be used when arriving at any other country, including the country of your citizenship.

An alternative to the 10-year passport is a one-year or three-year **temporary residency permit,** which is available to non-citizens who live and work full time in Armenia. Business travelers who intend to reside in Armenia for more than three months are required to obtain this residency permit from the Ministry of Internal Affairs after they arrive in Armenia. The permit is available from the Armenian Ministry of Internal Affairs, Passport and Visa Department, located at 13a Mesrop Mashtots Avenue (Tel. 53-43-91).

Registering with the US Embassy

The US does not require US citizens in Armenia to register their presence, regardless of their residency status, but registering is advisable because it will make it easier for you to be reached in an emergency. To register, go to the consular office of the US Embassy in Yerevan.

Registering with the Armenian Authorities

A law enacted in 2004 makes it obligatory to obtain an Armenian Social Security card if you wish to do any of the following: (1) open a bank account in Armenia; or (2) receive income that is paid in Armenia (regardless of where it is earned); or (3) receive reimbursement payments in Armenia (regardless of where the debt was incurred). More information is available from the Armenian Ministry of Labor and Social Issues.

If you are working in Armenia as a professional journalist or photographer you must register with the Foreign Ministry. A letter of introduction from the journalist's employer is required. More information is available from the Ministry of Foreign Affairs on Republic Square. Registration is also required in Karabagh. For details contact Karabagh's Representative to the US in Washington, DC (Tel. 202-347-5166).

Business Directories

Spyur Company publishes an English-language business directory that is comparable to the Yellow Pages in the US. Purchase for roughly $12 from the publisher at 1/3 Pavstos Buzandi Street, Yerevan (Tel. 59-00-00), or look at the online versions (Internet: www.spyur.am) (www.yellowpages.am). For an online directory of just about any company in Armenia, complete with phone numbers and addresses, try www.arminco.com/hayknet/500pred/500_e.htm

Commercial Guides

The **US Embassy** in Yerevan produces an annual guide that provides helpful information for business people. This document, The Country Commercial Guide: Armenia, is available online at www.state.gov and at www.export.gov. Another helpful source is KPMG's "Investment in Armenia" guide. KPMG provides business counseling. Located at 8 Hanrapetutian Street, in the Hy Business building (Tel. 56-67-62) (Internet: www.kpmg.am).

The **Armenian Development Agency** (ADA) publication Armenia Country Investment Profile includes recent data, but might be difficult to find in the US. To obtain a copy in Armenia, contact the ADA office in Yerevan (Tel. 57-01-70; Fax 54-22-72).

Local Networking

The American Chamber of Commerce in Armenia (AMCHAM) sponsors seminars and breakfast meetings that are great for networking. Contact Elen Ghazaryan (Tel. 59-91-87; Fax 59-92-56) (E-mail: amcham@arminco.com) (Internet: www.amcham.am).

Legal Counsel

If you need legal counsel the Consular section of the US Embassy can provide you with a list of attorneys who speak English (Tel. 52-46-61; Fax 15-15-50). Information about lawyers from local sources is available from Union of Advocates of the Republic of Armenia, 3 Zakyan Street (Tel. 58-34-42); International Union of Armenian Advocates, 2 Buzant Street (Tel. 54-34-35); International Bar Union,

2 Mashtots Avenue (Tel. 58-76-84); and from the Bar Association of Armenia, c/o Yerevan State University Law Department (Tel. 55-06-30).

Notary Services

If you need to have a document notarized, go to the Consular Section of the US Embassy. For a fee of $30 per signature, the Consulate provides notary services to US citizens and to foreign nationals who are doing business with US citizens. The service is available weekdays from 2 pm to 5 pm. 18 Marshal Baghramian Avenue (Tel. 52-16-11; Fax 15-15-50) (Internet: www.usa.am).

British nationals can get documents notarized from the British Embassy. Located at 34 Marshall Baghramian Avenue (Tel. 26-43-01; Fax 26-43-18) (www.britemb.am). Canada does not have an embassy in Armenia, but the Canadian Consulate may be able to provide assistance (Tel. 56-79-03; Fax: 56-79-03) (E-mail: aemin@freenet.am).

Insurance

Liability, homeowners, and automobile insurance are available in Armenia from both local and foreign companies. **Clements International Insurance** is a US-based company that is used by many US foreign-service personnel. Contact Clements at 1660 L Street NW; Ninth Floor; Washington, DC 20036 (Tel. 202-872-0060; Toll-Free 1-800-872-0067; Fax 202-466-9064) (E-mail: info@clements.com) (Internet: www.clements.com). If you choose to use a local company, there are more than 20 to choose from in Yerevan. One of the leading companies is Prime Insurance (Tel. 55-94-74) (E-mail: prime@netsys.am).

Registering a Company

Registering a business in Armenia is a multi-step process which usually requires driving around from one government office to another. For detailed information, go to the **State Register of Legal Persons** at the Ministry of Justice, 15 Grigor Lusavorich Street (Tel. 52-45-16; 52-46-00; Fax 52-10-21) or contact one of the organizations listed early in this section.

Conference Facilities

Conference facilities and temporary offices are available in Yerevan at the American University of Armenia (AUA) **Business Center** (9 Alek Manukyan Street). Amenities include a 300-seat auditorium and a state-of-the-art communications technology. Further details are available from AUA headquarters, 300 Lakeside Drive, 4th Floor, Oakland, California 94612 (Tel. 510-987-9452; Fax 510-208-3576) or directly from the facility in Yerevan (Tel. 15-10-48) (E-mail: mmkrtchi@aua.am).

Corruption

The fear of corruption, as well as corruption itself, is a deterrent to foreign investment in Armenia and this is a concern for many Westerners who are thinking about doing business in Armenia. In late 1996, the Armenian government acknowledged that corruption is a significant problem, and it is accepting US technical assistance.

Note About Privatization

Armenia has already privatized most of its agricultural land, approximately 85 percent of its larger state organizations and most of its housing, according to World Bank figures. Some privatization is continuing. In this process, foreign and domestic investors are entitled to be treated equally. Armenia's Law on Privatization states that foreign companies have the same rights to participate in the privatization processes as Armenian companies. The privatization of so much of Armenian industry has resulted in a lessening of government control over the economy, according to an analysis by the US government. Still, factories that the government considers strategic will probably not be privatized. More information about the sell-off of government property is available from www.privatization.am.

Essentials

In 2003 the National Assembly adopted its first Criminal Code as an independent state. The country had previously relied upon the Soviet Criminal Code. In the new code, abuse of power is punishable by up to six years imprisonment. Taking or giving bribes is a criminal offense and is punishable by up to 12 years imprisonment.

These severe penalties have not yet had an apparent effect on corruption. Bribery is widespread and is believed to be common in government procurement and in transactions such as company registration and licensing.

A new Civil Service law that has been in force since 2002 operates to restrict the participation of civil servants in commercial activities. Tax fraud and unregistered businesses are the most prevalent illegal activities in the private sector.

Closing Information about Doing Business in Armenia

Concerns about political stability should not deter one from investing in Armenia. The country has a European orientation as well as many cultural, political and economic ties to the West. Its relations with the US are "excellent," according to the US government's 2004 Commercial Guide to Armenia, and it is "unlikely" that civil disturbances, should they occur, would be directed against US businesses or the US community. Another report, this one issued in 2004 by the US Agency for International Development (USAID), reports that Armenia is "a relatively stable country with low conflict vulnerability." The US funded $90 million in assistance programs for Armenia in 2002.

Further good news is found in Armenia's investment and trade policies, which are considered to be among the most liberal of the Newly Independent States (NIS). The Heritage Foundation ranks Armenia's economy as the most open of the NIS. Because its economy depends on foreign trade, the Armenian government is motivated to attract foreign investment. Foreign companies are encouraged to invest and are entitled so-called "national treatment," which guarantees them the same treatment that the locals receive. This is one of the provisions of the Bilateral Investment Treaty (BIT), which governs many of the private deals between US and Armenian business people.

Ecology

three

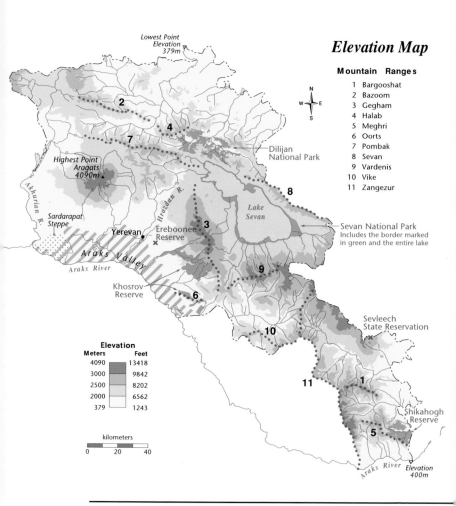

Elevation Map

Mountain Ranges

1 Bargooshat
2 Bazoom
3 Gegham
4 Halab
5 Meghri
6 Oorts
7 Pombak
8 Sevan
9 Vardenis
10 Vike
11 Zangezur

Lowest Point
Elevation
379m

Dilijan
National Park

Sevan National Park
Includes the border marked
in green and the entire lake

Highest Point
Aragats
4090m ▲

Lake
Sevan

Akhurian R.

Sardarapat
Steppe

Yerevan

Ereboonee
Reserve

Hrazdan R.

Araks Valley

Araks River

Khosrov
Reserve

Sevleech
State Reservation

Shikahogh
Reserve

Araks River Elevation
400m

Elevation

Meters		Feet
4090		13418
3000		9842
2500		8202
2000		6562
379		1243

kilometers
0   20   40

Courtesy of the Birds of Armenia Project, American University of Armenia, Oakland, CA, 1999

INTRODUCTION

In the early days of Armenia's independence movement, the environment was a high-priority political issue. By the late 1980s, 70 years of Soviet-era central planning had left a visible stain on the environment and had provoked national outrage. The haze of industrial air pollution had become so thick that it was difficult to see the majestic Mt. Ararat—located just 60 km from Yerevan—on many days, and the erasure of this national monument became a poignant symbol of the deterioration of Armenia's natural environment.

A greens movement became active during the 1980s and it developed a broad base of support. This support was evidenced by the shutdown in 1989 of Armenia's potentially-hazardous nuclear power plant, and by the closure of several other pollution-emitting industries. The governing structure was revamped, as well. The State Committee on Environmental Protection was scrapped, and in its place a full-fledged Ministry of Nature Protection was established and charged with protecting the environment and establishing a framework of environmental laws and regulations.

The economic consequences of independence and of conflict with hostile neighbors prompted the Armenian public to reconsider its priorities during the past dozen years. The economic crisis has led to an over-exploitation of natural resources and, following just four years of independence, a report about the condition of Armenia's environment concluded that there was no public constituency for conservation in Armenia. Armenia's National Environmental Action Plan reached the same conclusion five years later, in 1999, and noted that environmental issues, except for those associated with Lake Sevan, don't get much attention from the public. This was demonstrated by the "minor role" played by environmental organizations in public and private life.

Today it is still difficult to identify a significant public constituency. Most Armenians are simply not aware of the environmental issues and have given priority, instead, to economics. Environmental destruction has resumed during the past several years without much public outcry. This lack of public awareness and participation has contributed to a decline in environmental conditions in both urban and rural areas. Natural habitats have become imperiled. Wildlife populations are at risk. Economic losses and health risks to people are likely to increase.

One major challenge to the environment arises from the conflict between human development and the need to preserve our natural resources. Improper land use practices can lead to deforestation, desertification, lost habitats, reduced biodiversity, and increased pollution. Development of environmental legislation, implementation of environmental policy, and the enforcement of environmental regulations can assist with natural resource protection and ensure sustainable development.

The legacy of environmental problems throughout the former Soviet Union has been well documented and environmental contamination is serious and widespread. In Armenia, relatively little has been done to accurately assess these concerns. The problem from the lack of accurate assessments is further complicated by the unreliability of historical data and the limited availability of recent data concerning environmental contamination. Regulations designed to protect Armenia's environment exist but have been largely ignored both before and after Armenian independence.

Photograph, previous page: Stand of trees at Lake Sevan

Industrial production has decreased significantly from its level in the 1980s and consequently the release of pollutants to the environment has decreased. As Armenia's economy continues to improve, pollutant emissions will increase from industrial activities, more lands will be cleared for development or for their lumber, and air, water, and soil quality will deteriorate. It is therefore important to understand the environmental issues facing Armenia and to take a responsible approach to development.

HABITATS

Armenia's location at the junction of three bio-geographic regions permits it to have a great diversity of flora and fauna. The convergence in Armenia of these areas—the Caucasian, Iranian and Mediterranean floral regions—permits this small country to have great biological diversity. Armenia is host to seven of the eight major biological communities of the world. Within these biological communities, several prominent natural habitats exist. Exploitation of natural resources has put many of these habitats at risk. Of great concern are the depletion of water resources, soil erosion, and the degradation of sensitive ecosystems. Pollution to air, land and water, and the resulting health hazards are also of primary concern.

Desert habitat is found in a small area in the Ararat Valley that is situated at an altitude of less than 900 m. Semi-desert predominates in southern Armenia and is characterized by a cover of sage plants and rock. This area is typically below 1,000 m. Mountain steppe is also dry land at altitudes between 1,200 to 2,000 m and is host to grasses, with rocky outcrops and shrubs of varying heights. Sub-alpine and alpine meadows are typically found at 2,000 m above sea level. This habitat features grasses, shrubs, bare soil, rocks, and snow. Forests occur in various sized patches at elevations between 550 to 2,600 m and are composed mainly of deciduous beech, oak, and hornbeam trees. Forest cover is now less than eight percent of the land area of the country [see box, "The Forests of Armenia," below]. The primary azonal habitat is wetlands. Although water is moderately represented in the overall area within the republic, many Armenian wetlands have been drained or debilitated to support human development.

FLORA

There are approximately 8,800 plant species in Armenia. Vascular plants represent approximately 3,200 of the total. Fungi, algae, lichens, and mosses make up the rest, according to the First National Report of Armenia's Ministry of Nature Protection. By comparison, there are 6,000 vascular plant species throughout the entire Caucasus region. There are about 106 species of endemic plants, which are plants that are limited to a specific region. There are also estimated to be up to 200 relict species, which are species that have not changed genetically over thousands of years.

The Lake Sevan watershed contains more than 1,700 species of flower and seed producing plants, and more than 250 species of spore producing plants such as mosses and lichens. More than 150 of these plant species are considered to be threatened or endangered.

Biological Diversity

Armenia has one of the world's highest vegetation densities in the world, with more than 100 species per square kilometer. This biodiversity plays an important role in Armenia's economic development. Approximately 2,000 plant species in Armenia, for example, have nutritional properties or are used to produce drugs, paints, ether, and rubber. Economic uses of the country's biologically diverse resources have not been well planned, however. The Armenian Ministry of Nature Protection reported in 2003 that degradation and even the extinction of certain plant species have occurred, resulting in an overall impoverishment of biodiversity.

Armenia has taken steps to preserve its flora and fauna diversity through the designation of 28 Specially Protected Areas (SPAs). These areas include two national parks, 23 reservations, and three reserves [more information on SPAs appears later in this chapter].

Endangered Species

Throughout Armenia, approximately half of the plant species are at risk of extinction. Thirty-five species with economic significance are already known to have become extinct. The danger to their survival is frequently caused by the impact upon the ecosystem from agriculture. In the Ararat Valley, for example, agricultural uses have displaced 65 percent of the natural ecosystem. Throughout Armenia, farmers who had relied upon imported feed for their livestock during the Soviet years found that the post-independence blockades imposed by Turkey and Azerbaijan made it impossible to continue to use imported feed. They relied upon pastures and forests for grazing, and damaged the ecosystem in the process.

The Red Data Book of Endangered Species reported in 1990 that about 37 percent of the plant species in Yerevan were endangered. In Meghri, Armenia's southernmost town, endangered plants comprised roughly 30 percent of the total plant population. Many plant species are endangered because of human encroachment on natural habitats and because of damage caused to ecosystems from improper water management.

The Armenian Red Data Book in 1988 identified 386 species of flora, or roughly 12 percent of the total present in Armenia, that are in need of conservation. The Red Book of the USSR had identified only 61 species in Armenia that were in a similar state of peril. Thirty-five plant species have disappeared from Armenia, and several plant species "of great interest" are threatened with extinction, according to a 2003 report by the Ministry of Nature Protection.

The Ancient Wheat of Erebuni

Armenia is home to hundreds of species of plants that are described as the "wild relatives of domestic crops" in Armenia's National Environmental Action Plan (NEAP). These include the "ancestors" of wheat, barley, rye and oats. Wheat is highly represented and biologically diverse in Armenia, with 13 distinct species and approximately 360 varieties. These plants are recognized as having a unique and global importance to biodiversity, according to the NEAP. These wild relatives of domestic plants also have economic value as a source for the improvement of cultivated plants. Other wild plants in Armenia are recognized for their pharmaceutical value.

Scientists believe that wheat was first cultivated in Armenia as long as 10,000 years ago. Two native Armenian species, *Triticum urartu* and *Triticum araraticum*, still exist in the Ararat Valley, and their scientific names are suggestive of the connection to Armenia. Historically, the lands of Syria and Palestine have been accepted as the birthplace of this important grain. The discovery by botanists of Armenia's wild grains in the 1930s suggests that Armenia, too, is a source of the original wheat.

The Erebuni Reserve—a state-protected nature area that was established in 1981—today protects the region in which these wild grains were discovered. [For information about Armenia's nature reserves, see "Specially Protected Areas," later in this chapter].

FORESTS OF ARMENIA

By Jason Kauffeld

At the beginning of the nineteenth century 7,500 sq km of rich forestland covered one quarter of Armenia. Since then human activities such as farming, cattle grazing and unregulated cutting have destroyed close to 5,100 sq km of these forests. There is only about 2,400 sq km of forests remaining, covering just eight percent of the land. Still, deforestation activities continue unabated. Under the current rate of cutting, Armenia's forests will be completely eliminated within twenty years. The current state of the forest is already alarming because when a nation's forest cover falls below twenty-five percent its ability to conserve soil and to store groundwater, the most basic and necessary of environmental functions, greatly decreases.

Even though Armenia has suffered severe losses to its forests, it is still blessed with an amazing diversity of woody species. Two hundred sixty species of trees and bushes are found in Armenia. Fifty-seven species are endemic, and sixty-five bear commercially valuable fruits and berries. Oak, beech, and hornbeam make up more than eighty percent of the forests. Maple, walnut, and ash are other trees commonly seen during walks through the forest.

If you are visiting Armenia and want to take a stroll along a forest path, you will have to travel away from Yerevan and its environs. In the middle of the country, where one half of the population lives, you will find only two percent of the nation's remaining forests. When Marco Polo traveled along the Silk Road through this part of Armenia in the thirteenth century, he found mostly lush grasslands. Armenia's climate has pushed most of its forests to the northern and southern parts of the country. Fifteen hundred sq km of forestland is located in Tavush and Lori Marzes of the northeast, and 900 sq km of forest is located in Syunik Marz of the far south.

If you want to impress your friends and say you have seen the majority of Armenia's forests, make sure to bring sturdy boots with good traction as well as an even sturdier heart. Most of Armenia's forestland lies at elevations ranging from two thousand to eight thousand feet on slopes of twenty-five degrees or more. Picture walking along a peaked house roof in Denver, Colorado to better understand the exertions involved with exploring a high percentage of Armenia's forests.

Clearing of land for agriculture is one of the historic activities that have forced surviving forests onto such steep slopes. Close to 600,000 Armenians live near forests and engage in subsistence farming. Each village family living near forestland is allowed by law to collect five cubic meters of wood every year. This wood is used by the villagers for the most basic of needs: for heating their homes and for cooking their food. These families require half a million cubic yards of wood every year. That is enough wood to cover an American football field to a depth of two hundred fifty feet. This seems like a lot of wood, but that is the sustainable amount that Armenia's 2,400 sq km of remaining forests can supply each year.

If the villagers are using wood at a sustainable rate, then why are Armenia's forests still disappearing? The answer is a Gordian Knot consisting of the combined effects of poverty, the lack of a national energy policy, inadequate resources to perform forest management, and illegal harvesting and corruption. The result is clear: Armenia's forests are being destroyed. Only the most inaccessible forests remain untouched.

The most disheartening aspect of the loss of Armenia's forests involves the lack of a coherent public policy to manage this renewable resource. The national government owns Armenia's forestlands while Hye Antar, the government's forestry department, is responsible for the care of these lands. From 1970 to 1980, before the republic gained independence, 50 sq km of reforestation activities took place every year in Armenia. In 2002 under Hye Antar, only two and one half sq km were reforested. Hye Antar is charged with the protection of the forests yet it must supply its own budget by cutting of trees and selling cutting permits. Hye Antar foresters earn only $20 a month, which is not a livable wage, yet they are expected to protect one of Armenia's most precious resources. These are the paradoxes driving the destruction of Armenia's forests.

Ecology

Woodlands along the southeast edge of Lake Sevan

To achieve a minimally desirable forest cover of twenty five percent, one billion trees must be planted and cared for to maturity while Armenia's remaining 2,400 sq km of forest are protected.

The government has not yet taken action to solve this problem. It is strapped for resources and is currently unequal to the task of saving Armenia's forests. Independent organizations have stepped in to help. Planting and caring for one billion trees lies beyond the ability of most organizations, however. The solution instead is within reach of the villages of Armenia. With organization, the six hundred thousand villagers whose lives depend on the survival of the forests can achieve greater successes than private organizations or the government. The villagers merely require assistance from organizations to gain the skills they need to protect and to care for the forests on their own.

A program of collaboration with the villagers has been started by the Armenia Tree Project (ATP) in the village of Aygut. This village is located north of Lake Sevan, about a two-hour drive from Yerevan. Here, ATP has formed partnerships with families and with schools to establish not only backyard tree nurseries but also environmental student groups in order to protect the future of both Armenia's forests and of Armenia's youth. At the same time, ATP is working to bring the government into the partnership. ATP was founded in 1994. It is funded by contributions from individual donors and has helped local Armenians plant and rejuvenate hundreds of thousands of trees.

Jason Kauffeld is the Deputy Country Director of the Armenia Tree Project (E-mail: jasonkauffeld@hotmail.com).

To see the village of Aygut and observe how locally led conservation partnerships can change lives, including your own, contact ATP to arrange a tour. In the US, write to ATP at 65 Main Street, Watertown, Mass. 02472 (Tel. 617-926-8733) (E-mail: info@armeniatree.org) (Internet: www.armeniatree.org). In Armenia, visit ATP at Aygestan 9th Street, Yerevan (Tel. 56-99-10) (E-mail: trees@arminco.com).

COALITION TO SAVE THE TREES

In 2002 the Armenia Tree Project and another group known as Armenian Forests collaborated to form the Protect Our Forests Coalition. The coalition consists of a diverse group of dozens of non-governmental organizations, businesses, individuals, and government agencies. Even the UNDP is a member of the Coalition. The group hopes to increase the healthy forest cover in Armenia and to encourage greater environmental awareness among Armenians. They welcome new members (Tel. 54-15-29) (E-mail: protectourforests@yahoo.com).

Since 1994, the Armenia Tree Project reports that it has planted more than 415,000 trees and has restored 450 sites throughout the country. The project operates nurseries and grows indigenous tree species that are well suited for local conditions. It also has a community tree-planting program that allows urban residents to adopt trees.

FAUNA

There are approximately 17,500 invertebrate and 500 vertebrate species in Armenia. Endemic species account for 329 of this total. Insects comprise approximately 90 percent of the invertebrate species. Birds account for approximately 70 percent of species within the vertebrate class, with an amazing 346 species present in Armenia. There hasn't been enough research regarding the status today of many of the nation's animal species, according to most experts, but with existing data the NEAP report estimates that 24 percent of Armenia's fauna are "internationally threatened species."

Biological Diversity

Bats and other mammals form a significant part of Armenia's animal diversity with 84 mammalian species recorded [see below], but it's the diversity of Armenia's bird population that probably earns it the greatest attention. Birds constitute the largest vertebrate class of animals in the country, with 346 species. Lake Sevan, Lake Arpi (in the far northwest) and the Ararat Valley are the areas of greatest importance for wetland birds and migrating species.

Reptiles are also represented with great diversity. Of the 156 reptile species recorded in the FSU, 53 are present in Armenia. Other fauna with diverse specie representation are fish (39) and amphibians (8).

Endangered Species

Armenia's International Red List of Threatened Animals lists approximately 300 species of mammal that are rare or declining in population. The Ministry of Nature Protection believes that this list, published in 1996, is outdated and that rare mammals are underrepresented on the list. The list of "internationally threatened species" that are present in Armenia includes birds (7); mammals (6); invertebrates (6); reptiles (4) and fish (1). The Armenian Red Data Book identifies 18 mammal species at risk, and 15 amphibians and reptiles.

The mammals at greatest risk are the Mehely horseshoe bat, the European free-tailed bat, the European otter, the brown bear, the Asian wild sheep, the striped hyena, and the Caucasian birch mouse. The Armenian mouflon has suffered tremendous population decline as a result of habitat loss and poaching. Fish at greatest risk are the winter bakhtak, or Salmo ishchan, which at one time represented 30 percent of the trout stock in Lake Sevan, but which has now almost disappeared. Among reptiles, the Armenian viper is threatened.

Bats

The millions of bats that live in Armenia form an important part of the country's ecosystem. They control the insect population by eating three times their weight in insects each day. They also pollinate orchards and vineyards. During the past decade, researchers have identified the presence in Armenia of seven previously unidentified bat species.

Many bat habitats in Armenia are in peril, however. Bats typically live in tree hollows, in caves, and in the crevices of mountainsides. They have suffered habitat loss from human development and also from well-intentioned hikers and cave explorers—spelunkers— who unwittingly disturb their colonies. Individual bat colonies in Armenia are known to have as many as two million members.

Armenian bats hibernate for as much as eight months each year, and generally are most active during the Summer. This is also when most people are active outdoors and therefore more likely to encounter them. Bats often frighten people, but Armenia's bat population does not present a significant risk to people. The species known to exist in Armenia are *Rhinolophus euryale, Rhinolophus mehelyi, Myotis nattereri kuhl, Barbastella leucomelas, Miniopterus schreibersi kuhl* and *Tadaria teniotis* rat.

PROTECTION THE BIRDS OF ARMENIA

By Daniel Klem, Jr.

In modern times, the increasing international growth of interest in birds has helped to spur tourism around the world. This tourism in turn is becoming a principal factor in the growth of many local and regional economies. Armenia also benefits from this, and the country is fortunate to posses a disproportionately large number of bird species (346) within its relatively modest geographic area (29,793 sq km). Several species within the republic are extraordinarily attractive. Many others, because of their rarity, are of special interest to birders.

Watching birds can be great fun. The challenge of learning about the lives of non-human creatures can be particularly enriching, even spellbinding. Doing something that makes you feel good refreshes you, and contributes to your mental and physical health in immeasurable ways. These uniquely feathered living animals are literally distributed over the entire planet and have a distinguished history of contributing to the health and happiness of people.

Figures of birds have enchanted and served as symbols of human culture. They are lavishly featured in Armenian art from the fifth century to present. Birds are some of the best symbols of freedom, spirit, and courage. All flying birds embody freedom from earthly bonds. White Storks are seen as dignified and their presence is thought to convey good luck. Doves are likened to spirits, and are often used as a sign of peace. Eagles frequently represent the courage of warriors. We admire each of these qualities. There is surprise, elation, drama, high adventure, and unlimited discovery in watching birds.

Scientists have found that birds are indicators of environmental health on local, regional and global scales. Changes in food supply, climate, habitat loss, and threats from chemical contamination and pollution, affect birds and people in similar ways.

Bird diversity and numbers are frequently at the heart of the relationship between humans and the environment because of the ability of birds to inform us about the state of the environment. In addition to their physical beauty and all the other pleasures they bestow on us, scientists use birds as tools to monitor, protect, and conserve the precious land and water which we all require for good health and survival.

In Armenia, scientists working with the Birds of Armenia (BOA) research project have studied the relationship between decreased bird diversity and environmental degradation [for more about the Birds of Armenia project, see box below]. One noteworthy study by BOA scientists highlights how waterfowl can inform the nation about the loss of wetland habitats, and about their quality and importance.

This study, published in 2002, describes current environmental conditions and encourages the local government to enact existing management plans to improve the nation's largest lake, Lake Sevan, and the surrounding waterways and wetlands that sustain it.

From 1933 to 2000, a 19.5-meter drop in the water level of Lake Sevan had a dramatic impact upon the populations of waterfowl species in the area. Moreover, the draining of nearby Lake Gilli from 1960 to 2000 caused 23 breeding birds to become non-breeders in the region. Four former breeders—the Black Stork, Glossy Ibis, white-winged Scoter, and Little Crake—have been lost to the area entirely. The research team recommends increasing Lake Sevan's water level by six meters, and taking steps to restore Lake Gilli and its productive wetlands. These actions would increase waterfowl species and numbers, and protect regional populations of globally threatened species.

At about the same time that Lake Gilli was drained, several commercial fish farm ponds were established in the arid lands of the Ararat Valley, just south of Yerevan. These ponds now attract and accommodate most of the waterfowl that once occupied Lake Gilli. The commercial fish ponds are not an adequate substitute for Lake Gilli, however. Economic conditions threaten these waters and the birds that rely on them. It is estimated that if the fish farm ponds are lost, 80 percent of the waterfowl currently breeding in Armenia would disappear. [The fish ponds are also cited as a factor that contributes to the risk of Malaria in this region. For more about this, see the "Health" section in Chapter 2, Essentials].

The celebrated organization BirdLife International studies bird habitats and designates locations all over the world as globally "Important Bird Areas" (IBA). BirdLife's objective in establishing the IBA is to encourage societies to maintain the world's natural resources for the protection of bird species and their habitats. The loss and degradation of habitats is driven by the increasing intensity of human uses of the environment. BirdLife estimates that one in eight (12 percent or 1,186) bird species worldwide are at risk of becoming extinct in the next century because of habitat loss. BirdLife identifies five IBAs in Armenia: Lake Arpi, the Pombak mountain chain, Khosrov preserve, Armash fish farms, and Lake Sevan.

The BOA and BirdLife International have identified many bird species that are at risk of extinction in Armenia. The BOA researchers report that 31 species in Armenia are considered to be endangered, 28 are "threatened," 42 are "undetermined" status and two are extirpated (lost) to the republic. Considering the distribution of each species on a global scale, the BirdLife list identifies 21 Armenian species that are at risk.

Who can we expect to address the growing need to conserve Armenia's birds and through them Armenia's environment? Individual citizens must recognize the value in learning about and documenting the nation's birdlife. Too many of us are now unaware of the value and utility of birds for the nation. Many of us see an interest in birds as ridiculous, fool-hearty, or not fitting for serious adult attention. This view is unfounded and especially harmful.

Educators should introduce and solicit the help of creative and energetic youth. Extracurricular programs such as those that exist within the Armenian Church are also

Ecology

important. The Armenian Church is committed to bird conservation and overall environmental protection and is an ally of the conservation and environmental movement. Citizens should encourage the government to implement and enforce legal protections. Visitors to Armenia should learn about its birds and other natural attractions. And Armenia's scientists should continue to study these amazing creatures.

Daniel Klem, Jr., Ph.D., D.Sc., Professor of Biology, and the Sarkis Acopian Professor of Ornithology and Conservation Biology, Muhlenberg College, Allentown, PA 18104; co-authored, along with Martin S. Adamian, Ph.D., of *A Field Guide to Birds of Armenia* (American University of Armenia, 1997) and *Handbook of the Birds of Armenia* (American University of Armenia, 1999).

Birding Areas

Armenia is internationally recognized as a significant birding—also known as bird watching—area. Britain's prestigious Birdwatch magazine has identified Armenia as the "next big birding hot-spot." "We scarcely had to leave our vehicles to appreciate how stuffed full of birds the countryside actually was," according to a feature story about Armenia that appeared in the magazine.

EURASIAN HOOPOE

Local tour organizers have begun to recognize the appeal of Armenia to birders, and are now offering bird-watching trips. The Birds of Armenia Project also organizes tours. Their primary mission is research, but one of the purposes of the research is to create greater public awareness and so it's no surprise to see that they are leading tours, too. There are several good birding locations within about a one-hour drive from Yerevan.

Lake Sevan's **Seagull Island**, which is located just off the lake's northwest shore, is home to a large colony of Armenian Gulls. These gulls are a species that is unique to Armenia. The Selim Pass, which is located south of Lake Sevan, is a habitat to Black Vultures and Griffon Vultures. The **Armash Fish Ponds**, in the Ararat Valley, are also home to a significant population of birds-of-interest. These are man-made ponds, surrounded by reeds. **Mt. Aragats** and **Garni Gorge** are also good birding locations.

The **Lake Gilli Watershed**, located in the southeastern corner of the Sevan basin, is one of Armenia's most popular birding sites. This area was once a complex wetland ecosystem. Lake Gilli was the focal point of the watershed, and had a water surface area of about 860 hectares. This had been a major habitat for migratory waterfowl and aquatic species until the early 1960s, when the lake was drained so that the lake bottom could be used for agriculture.

CASPIAN SNOWCOCK

Today the area is mostly a dry area with open peat mines and croplands. As a result, the entire Sevan basin now has fewer bird species than had previously existed in the Gilli area alone. Today, many of these bird species are registered in the Armenian Red Book of Endangered Species. Despite the loss of this wetland area, the Gilli area is still considered to be a good birding location.

Illustration of Birds reprinted with permission from A Field Guide to Birds of Armenia

The Birds of Armenia Research Project

In 1991, the year Armenia declared its independence, Mr. Sarkis Acopian, an Armenian American with a special interest in conservation, developed a plan to use birds as a means of promoting a conservation and environmental ethic among the people of Armenia. Drawing on the well-documented history of the US conservation movement, as far back as the mid-1800s, Acopian recognized that birds could serve as a tool to enhance the preservation of Armenia's nature. This plan was realized with the creation of the Birds of Armenia (BOA) project in Yerevan.

Mr. Acopian hoped that a greater awareness of birds, their beauty, richness, and environmental utility would add to the ethnic pride of Armenians living in and outside the republic's borders. He was hopeful that if the world was introduced to Armenia through its attractive birdlife, more and more people from outside Armenia would be attracted to not only the birds but other unique attributes of its culture, and by so doing invest in its economy by visiting or purchasing its many and varied products.

Operating from the American University of Armenia (AUA) in Yerevan, Mr. Acopian assembled an international research team for the Birds project. He drew upon talent from Armenia, Russia, Ukraine, the UK and the US. This research team published *A Field Guide to Birds of Armenia*, and the *Handbook of the Birds of Armenia*. The group also published, with the pain-staking precise hands-on assistance of Mr. Acopian, the first detailed and accurate map of Armenia.

These works are the most current and comprehensive treatment on the birds of Armenia, and are likely to remain so for many years to come. The Field Guide and Handbook combine to present comprehensive research data about what is known and what is needed to advance the conservation of birds and environmental awareness in Armenia.

As important for the future, the Birds project at AUA has brought together and encouraged cooperation among skilled Armenian scientists. Researchers at the project are discovering new species within the republic, studying the effects of wetland degradation, leading birding tours, and promoting the need for government policy to effectively preserve the natural resources upon which birds and humans rely. At the forefront of conservation initiatives of the Birds project is the recently created Armenian Society of Bird Protection (ASBP), which has attracted the support and cooperation of leading conservation organizations, including Bird Life International.

Gilli is located on the international flyway of many migratory waterfowl species. Thus, many species had stopped at Gilli for weeks at a time to feed on the flyway. The reed overgrowth provided an important nesting place for a number of different bird species. Specialists believe that if Gilli is restored, many bird species will return and that Gilli would once again play a major role in conserving Armenia's biological diversity. Further, Gilli's ecosystem, which had acted as a cleaning reservoir where rivers deposited their sediments, would once again act as a wetlands filter that biologically cleans the water before it flows into Lake Sevan.

Fisheries

A series of commercial fish ponds were built at Armash in the Ararat Valley in the 1960s and these ponds attracted most of the water birds that had until then been using the now-drained Lake Gilli. The opening of the fish ponds at roughly the same time that Lake Gilli was drained was fortuitous, since it mitigated the harm to migratory birds from the loss of this major water resource.

Fish production at the Armash fish ponds peaked in 1995. Production has declined in recent years because of the combined effect of foreign competition and a reduced supply of fish food. If the fish farms close for economic reasons, Armenia could lose up to 80 percent of its breeding water bird species [see "Protecting the Birds of Armenia," above].

The source of most fish production in Armenia is the Armash fish ponds and the fisheries of Lake Sevan. The decline of Lake Sevan's water level over the past several decades has hurt fish production there, however. Fish habitats deteriorated and two lake-spawning subspecies of trout are now believed to be extinct as a result. The loss of fish habitats and excessive fishing are two of the largest problems faced by the fishing industry in Armenia.

SPECIALLY PROTECTED AREAS

Armenia's Specially Protected Areas (SPAs) are classified according to their importance and are identified as National Parks, State Reserves, or Reservations. According to the National Statistical Service of Armenia, these SPAs cover an area of 310,000 hectares—roughly 10 percent of the country's surface area (one hectare is equivalent to approximately 2.5 acres). The levels of protection afforded to these areas are inconsistent and inadequate for their conservation.

National Parks

The Ministry of Nature Protection defines national parks as those areas with "special ecological, historic-cultural and aesthetic value." There are two national parks in Armenia.

Sevan National Park

Established: 1978
Area: 150,100 ha (24,900 ha land; 125,200 ha water)
Location: Lake Sevan Basin

Sevan National Park was created to protect the Lake Sevan ecosystem and its surrounding area. The Park is divided into three zones: a reserve, a recreation zone and a zone for economic use.

Conservation Issues: The Lake Sevan basin is ecologically unique and is abundant with flora and fauna. It contains more than 1,700 species of plants. More than 150 of the plant species in the basin are considered to be threatened or endangered. Only about five percent of the basin is forested. More than 10,000 ha of marshes and wetlands have been drained by the lowering of the lake [for further information, see "Wetlands," below].

Dilijan National Park

Established: 2002 (previously classified as a Reserve, 1958-2002)
Area: 28,000 ha (26,000 ha forest)
Location: North-Eastern Armenia, Ranges of Mt. Pambak, Mt. Areguni, and Mt. Ghugarat

Dilijan National Park features Beech and Oak Forests typical to the Caucasus region, and has unique natural, historical & architectural monuments. The forest is a habitat for bear, wolf, wild cats, and deer.

Conservation Issues: Uncontrolled development inside the reserve and cutting of timber. Boundaries and zoning are still being determined.

Reserves

The Ministry of Nature Protection defines State Reserves as "areas of ecological, scientific, and historic-cultural value." Reserves are established in order to protect the natural environment and the species they support. Human activities in Reserves are limited to scientific research.

There are three State Reserves covering a total area of approximately 685 sq km (39,300 ha, which is less than one percent of the national territory).

Khosrov Reserve

Established: 1958
Area: 29,200 ha
Location: Central Armenia, at the southern region of the Gheghama mountain range in the Azat and Khosrov river basins. Altitude: 1,400-2,250 m.

The Khosrov Reserve includes meadow and mountain-meadow habitats. The land-scape is dominated by dry, thick forestland with mountain and semi-desert vegetation and unique plant and animal communities. More than 50 percent of Armenia's 3,200 vascular plant species are found here. The reserve is also home to 171 animal species (60 endemic species).

Conservation Issues: This is one of Armenia's most important Protected Areas. The conservation situation is relatively good but there is a lack of equipment and human resources to ensure basic conservation activities.

Shikahogh Reserve

Established: 1958
Area: 10,000 ha
Location: Southern Armenia, in the Tzav and Shikahogh River basins. Altitude: 700-2,400 m.

Conservation issues: Conservation of Oak and Horn-beam forests with associated wildlife communities and habitats is currently not ensured because of the absence of a legal framework, an inadequate management structure, and poor resources.

Ecology

Erebuni Reserve

Established: 1981
Area: 89 ha
Location: Vicinity of Yerevan on the southwestern slope of Voghchaberd

Conservation Issues: The absence of a buffer zone in the region that is adjacent to urban development results in damage to the ecosystem. Unique ancestral vegetation, including ancient strains of wheat and other grains, are at risk.

State Reservations

The Ministry of Nature Protection identifies State Reservations as "temporary or permanent areas set aside for species conservation and reproduction." Reservations are afforded the lowest level of protection among the Specially Protected Areas. Armenia's 22 State Reservations cover an area of less than 900 sq km (90,000 ha, about 3 percent of the national territory). However, these reservations have not been fully established yet, since there is not yet legislation defining the boundaries, management responsibilities, and organizational structure for each reserve. The Ministry of Nature Protection is responsible for developing the legal basis of each reserve, in close collaboration with local authorities and other involved ministries.

Conservation Issues: Specially Protected Areas do not properly function with respect to conservation. They lack financial resources, management personnel, qualified specialists, and equipment. State reservations do not have clearly defined borders, and protection is not enforced.

Spandarian Reservoir

WATER RESOURCES

Water is the best of all things.
—Pindar, Greek poet, circa 500 BC

Water is a necessity of life, and access to basic water services is one of the most fundamental conditions of human development. Further, drinking water quality is one of the most important primary public health concerns. Providing safe drinking water should, therefore, be a priority for governments worldwide. In recognition of this, the United Nations proclaimed the years 2005 – 2015 "Water for Life," an International Decade for Action.

While human access to safe water is essential, water is also necessary to protect diverse ecosystems. Wetlands, fisheries, and other ecosystems must receive sufficient water supplies to maintain a healthy environment for the species they supports. Water quality is also important to a variety of aquatic species, birds, and other types of fauna and flora.

Water Quantity

Armenia is relatively rich in water resources; however, the water is unevenly distributed throughout the country. According to government reports, there are water shortages in the areas of the far northeast (Tavush region), west (Aragatsotn region), southeast (Vayots Dzor region), and south (Syunik region) of Armenia. It is estimated that five percent of the population lives in these areas that experience water shortages. Other parts of the country have available water resources, but they have inadequate water storage and infrastructure facilities, deficient maintenance practices to address leakage in the systems, as well as other inefficiencies.

Melting snow, rainfall, and ground water seasonally replenish Armenia's surface water resources. Because of this, river flow in Armenia fluctuates widely throughout the year. In the summer and autumn months, June through November, when the water demand is at its peak, only about one fourth of the yearly flow is available. In the winter months, December through March, the flow is around 10 percent of the yearly total, while in spring, river flow ranges between 55 and 70 percent of the yearly flow.

Reservoirs have been constructed throughout Armenia to store water in order to help alleviate seasonal shortages, to regulate river flow, and to serve the needs of the energy sector, fishing industry, and recreation. According to the Ministry of Nature Protection, there are more than 57 reservoirs, which have a total water storage capacity of about 900 million cubic meters. The largest is the Akhurian Reservoir, which has a capacity of 535 million cubic meters.

There are more than 9,000 rivers in Armenia, but only six are longer than 100 km in length. There are two main watersheds that drain the waters of Armenia: the Kur River system in the north, which drains about 23 percent of the waters, and the Araks River system, which drains roughly 75 percent. Both of these, ultimately, drain into the Caspian Sea.

The lakes in Armenia are relatively small with the exception of Lake Sevan, which now has a surface area of 1,250 sq km, about four percent of Armenia's total land area. The Lake Sevan basin, at an elevation of 1,900 meters, occupies about 4,900 sq km, approximately 16 percent of the Armenian territory. The volume of lake water is 35 billion cubic meters. Consequently, the lake has a central hydrological role in Armenia.

Despite its magnitude and importance to the nation's ecology and economy, and despite its aesthetic value, the health of Lake Sevan has been allowed to fall into great peril. Beginning in the 1930s the Soviet government embarked on a scheme to reduce the surface area of the lake as a means toward reducing evaporation and thus increasing the commercial availability of its water. The lake bottom could also be farmed, or so it was thought. For several decades, vast amounts of water were released from the lake.

By the 1970s, the water level of the lake had decreased by 19 meters (more than 62 feet), and the water volume had been reduced by more than 40 percent. There are 28 rivers that flow into the lake, but only one that flows out, the Hrazdan River. By intentionally increasing the flow into the Hrazdan River, the water generated energy by cascading through six hydroelectric stations, and then draining to the Ararat Valley for use in irrigation.

To help compensate for the excessive water withdrawals, water has been transferred to the lake through a 488-km tunnel from the Arpa and Yeghegis Rivers since 1982. Presently, an average of about 250 million cubic meters of water per year has been diverted to the lake through this tunnel. In 1981, the construction of another tunnel began. The 21-km long tunnel was designed to supply an additional 165 million cubic meters of water per year to the lake from the upper Vorotan River. However, construction stopped in the 1990s because of lack of funds.

It is not expected that the lake will, or can, be restored to its pre-1930 level. But, new policies are being implemented based on several assessments, e.g., Lake Sevan Action Program, and by adhering to international conventions such as the Convention on Biological Diversity, and the Ramsar Convention on Wetlands of International Importance. Conditions are slowly improving. As a result, Lake Sevan will remain one of Armenia's greatest natural treasures.

Water Distribution and Use

Ground water resources are also distributed unevenly in Armenia. It is estimated that 300 million cubic meters of ground water is available for use throughout the country. Deep ground water resources are generally of high quality, but the shallow aquifers, those that are close to the surface, are at risk of contamination, or have been impacted by anthropogenic activities. This is the case for large areas in the Ararat Valley, where industrial discharges and agricultural practices have impacted water resources. Fortunately, only the lower aquifer in Ararat Valley is used for drinking water.

Poor drainage and leakage of irrigation systems have flooded low-lying areas in the Ararat Valley and has led to the raising of the water table. This has provided breeding grounds for mosquitoes and has resulted in a resurgence of malaria during the past decade. This water logging is also partly responsible for the salinization and alkalization of the soils in the Ararat Valley.

Acid mine drainage near Kapan contains toxic levels of metals

Irrigation is by far the largest water use sector consuming roughly 70 percent of the water used in Armenia. During the 1980s, nearly 80 percent of the agricultural lands were irrigated. After independence, irrigation of agricultural lands decreased by an estimated 45 percent largely due to the lack of electricity, which was heavily relied on for pumping the water to higher elevations. Industrial water use also peaked in the 1980s, but decreased by as much as 60 percent during the 1990s due to the economic crisis and the associated decline in industrial operations.

Water Quality

Pollution loads entering Armenia's waters from industrial activities decreased considerably during the 1990s as a result of the economic crisis. However, waters continue to receive pollutants from uncontrolled agricultural and urban runoff, inadequately treated sewage, and increasingly from industrial discharge as productions expand and new industrial operations start up.

Mining and processing of sulfide ores in the Alaverdi and Kapan regions have occurred for centuries. Acid mine drainage in these areas has been poorly controlled. Consequently, waste discharges containing elevated levels of toxic metals have been released severely impacted waters and aquatic life.

The water quality of Lake Sevan has been deteriorating for decades due to the intentional lowering of the lake's water level and from external pollution loads. As previously mentioned, the lowering of the water level resulted in a 40 percent reduction in volume, which increased the water temperature. This disrupted the ecology of the lake and is partially responsible for the decline of fishing harvests. Further, agricultural runoff and sewage discharges have increased nutrient levels causing eutrophication of the lake.

The lake's water quality and ecosystem continue to be threatened by pollution from point sources (e.g., industrial discharges) and nonpoint sources (e.g., agricultural runoff). There are now specific laws to protect the water quality in the lake and

Ecology

Drinking Water Quality

Yerevan's drinking water comes from natural springs and other underground sources. These waters are generally high in quality. Despite this, Yerevan's water is sometimes unsafe for drinking. This is because the water distribution system has deteriorated due to the lack of resources for maintenance and monitoring, which has led to defects that cause leaks and allow contaminants to enter the water stream. As a result, waterborne diseases have sporadically occurred in Yerevan during the past decade. Other controls, such as chlorine disinfection, have been irregularly applied to the system. The health hazard from the contaminated water is compounded by the intermittent water supply. Interruptions in electricity supplies routinely decrease water pressure allowing contaminants to enter the water pipes, as well as causing an inconvenience as water cannot reach the taps in people's homes.

To assist in remedying these conditions, the World Bank has financed a project to upgrade Yerevan's water distribution infrastructure by replacing deteriorating pumps and pipes. By early 2004, 50 percent of the households in Yerevan had a 24-hour per day supply of drinking water. It is estimated that by the end of 2005, all of Yerevan's residents will have a constant supply of water. The situation in cities and villages outside of Yerevan is dire, however, because there are presently little resources for repairs and disinfection.

Consequently, travelers should drink only bottled water when traveling in Armenia and Karabagh at present, especially when in the villages. If bottled water is not available, only water that has been boiled or purified should be consumed.

environmental policies are being implemented. The condition of the lake is a matter of widespread national concern, and scientists are studying how to best restore the delicate balance of its ecology.

Deep ground water resources in Armenia are generally of high quality and well protected from contaminants due to favorable geologic conditions. These conditions include: the depth of the aquifers, which often have clay layers above them that act as barriers, and in some cases upward pressure that prevents contaminants from infiltrating. Shallow aquifers, however, may become contaminated from industrial discharges, agricultural activities (including application of pesticides), waste dumps, improper land filling, and mining activities.

In the Ararat valley, contaminants in the shallow aquifer often exceed drinking water quality limits. Fortunately, this water is used for irrigation and not for drinking purposes. Armenia does not yet have standards or water quality requirements for irrigation water, however, and these should be developed.

Ground water accounts for approximately 96 percent of the drinking water supplied to the public, therefore, the drinking water sources are of relatively high quality. However, once the water is distributed through the aging municipal piping system, it can be contaminated with sewage. There is not adequate monitoring or treatment of drinking water to prevent water-borne diseases due to the lack of financial resources.

Although water resources have received a reduction of industrial waste discharge during the past decade, they continue to receive inadequately treated sewage and surface runoff. Drinking water, ground water, and surface water quality have not been adequately monitored since Armenia's independence. And, the full extent of ground water and surface water contamination has not been accurately delineated because of lack of reliable data and insufficient environmental assessments.

Wetlands

Wetlands are transitional zones between land and water, and have been long recognized for their ecological importance. They are particularly species-rich systems and are valued because of their high biodiversity. Wetland plants also filter and cleanse surface waters by consuming nutrients, including natural and chemical fertilizers, and trapping solids, metals, and bacteria.

Human activities have severely impacted wetlands worldwide. In Armenia, water drainage and peat mining, have adversely affected wetlands. Large areas of wetlands have been drained, which threatens Armenia's biodiversity. About 140 species of vertebrates are ecologically dependent on wetlands. There are also approximately 100 species of wetland birds in Armenia.

Armenia became a signatory to the Ramsar Convention on Wetlands of International Importance in 1993. The sites included on the Ramsar list (internet: www.ramsar.org) are Lake Sevan and its basin (489,100 ha) and Lake Arpi and its surrounding bogs (3,139 ha). No other ecosystem type has an international treaty signed by more than 130 countries to ensure their protection. This attests to the importance of wetlands in water resources management and biodiversity conservation.

Lake Gilli, located in the southeastern corner of the Sevan basin, was drained in conjunction with the lowering of Lake Sevan. This area was once a complex wetland ecosystem but today the area is mostly a dry area with open peat mines and croplands. Specialists believe that if Gilli is restored, it will once again play a major role in conserving Armenia's biological diversity. They also believe that Gilli's ecosystem, which had acted as a cleaning reservoir where rivers deposited their sediments, would once again act as a wetlands filter that biologically cleans the water before it flows into Lake Sevan.

In the Ararat Valley, the upward pressure of groundwater and flooding of the Araks River created thousands of hectares of swamps and wetlands. These wetlands, which existed until about 50 years ago, were breeding grounds for mosquitoes carrying malaria. During the 1950s, the wetlands were drained and the land was transformed for agricultural use. With the disappearance of these wetlands, mosquitoes perished and malaria all but disappeared. There were undesirable consequences as well, such as the disappearance of wildlife species, and significant changes in the habitat and distribution of migrating birds.

Water Conservation

Rehabilitation of irrigation systems throughout Armenia is essential to decrease leakage, as well as to reduce the deterioration of soils from water logging, salinization and alkalization. Irrigation efficiency in the 1990s was estimated at less than 55 percent, and was much lower in some areas, reflecting the poor condition of pumps, canals, and pipes. The World Bank is currently involved in an irrigation development project that aims at increasing the efficiency of irrigation systems and improving the management of water resources, thereby reducing waste.

Leaks from water distribution pipes in municipal water supplies have been estimated to account for 30 to 55 percent of the water losses. The World Bank has also undertaken a project to upgrade Yerevan's water distribution system by installing new pipes, water pumps, and, for the first time, water meters. The meters should provide a motive for conservation of water in individual households. Outside water fountains that run continuously could be fitted with spring-loaded valves, thereby wasting very little water. Education of consumers and installation of water-efficient appliances would also greatly reduce the water demand. Finally, industrial water should be conserved, recycled, and appropriately treated prior to discharge.

Future of Water in Armenia

Historically, limited attention has been given to the ecological need for water resources in Armenia. This includes maintenance of wetlands and fisheries, and protection of ecosystems. Water resources are expected to play a key role in Armenia's continued economic development, and competition for water between hydropower, irrigation, industry, and the environment will increase. With proper water shed management, conservation, and protection from hazardous substances, Armenia should be able to provide sufficient water resources for all sectors of the economy, including residential use.

ENERGY RESOURCES

Armenia has scarce and undeveloped fossil fuel resources and it is therefore entirely dependent on oil and natural gas imports for the production of thermal energy. To utilize these imports, Armenia has built significant domestic energy generation facilities. About 40 to 50 percent of the energy is generated by thermal power plants, 30 to 35 percent by nuclear plants, and the remaining 20 to 30 percent by hydroelectric plants. The capacity for electricity generation is approximately 2,700 megawatts (MW), and electricity generation is 6.2 billion kilowatt-hours (kWh).

Nuclear Power

The Metsamor Nuclear Power Plant near Yerevan has two reactors with a combined capacity of 815 MW. The reactors began operation in 1976 and 1980 but the power plant was shut down in March 1989 because of safety concerns following the devastating earthquake that struck Armenia in December 1988. After being without nuclear power for six years, and while faced with an energy crisis due to the lack of fossil fuel and the economic blockade imposed by Azerbaijan and Turkey, Armenia resumed operation at one of the reactors at the Metsamor plant with a capacity of 440 MW, in November 1995, following upgrades and safety improvements. The plant has a design life of 30 years, but is still considered a safety risk due to region's seismic activity, and the lack of a containment dome to prevent the dispersal of radionuclides in the event of an accident.

Thermal Power

There are three major thermal power plants located in Armenia with a combined capacity of about 1,745 MW. The plants are located in Yerevan (550 MW), Hrazdan (1,100 MW), and Vanadzor (95 MW). Each of these plants has exceeded its life expectancy and is in need of further rehabilitation to increase their lifespan and improve their efficiency.

Although Armenia is reliant on fossil fuel imports, it does have great potential for renewable energy due to its geographic location. Its topography is varied and provides steep elevation reliefs and potential for hydroelectricity, it has windy conditions, and it receives a relatively abundant amount of energy from the sun.

Renewable Energy

At present, the economically viable capacity for wind energy is approximately equal to that of nuclear, about 500 MW, but wind energy development in Armenia is in its infancy. Hydroelectric capacity is currently 1,017 MW. The hydroelectric facilities, however, require rehabilitation. Most of these are installed on the Sevan-Hrazdan cascade and contribute considerably to the lowering of the water level in Lake Sevan. Small-scale hydroelectric facilities can be further exploited and estimates suggest production of an additional several hundred megawatts. Solar energy generation capacity is currently around 650 MW, but estimates for future capacity are as high as 3,500 MW.

The Engineering Research Center (ERC) at the American University of Armenia (AUA) performs a variety of solar energy related projects. Since May 1995, the AUA (Internet: www.aua.am) has operated a Solar Monitoring Station (SMS), which collects solar radiation data to assist with evaluating and developing solar energy devices. Based on data from the SMS, engineers have calculated that one square meter of land in Yerevan receives about 1,700 kWh of sun power annually.

Ecology

Yerevan Thermal Power Plant with Mt. Ararat

Additional solar data collectors are proposed for installation at several locations around the country to further research the applications of solar energy.

Another project at the ERC is the Design and Installation of a Solar Driven Desiccant Cooling Demonstration System (DESODEC). With the energy provided by the Solar Water Heating collector field installed on the AUA rooftop, and operation of the Desiccant Evaporative Cooling system, there is heating and cooling capability for the AUA. A solar photovoltaic system, also installed on the roof, will provide electricity to solar driven cooling system, making it independent from the electric grid and backing up the university internet servers. The DESODEC is the first solar driven combined system in the NIS and one of a handful in the world. This project is funded by INCO-Copernicus Program and generously sponsored by Mr. Sarkis Acopian.

Other energy research institutes in Yerevan include the Solar Energy Institute, established in 1966, the State Engineering University of Armenia, and Yerevan State University. A major alternative energy player in Armenia is SolarEn LLC (Internet: www.solaren.com). SolarEn is a private manufacturing, development, and consulting company focusing on clean energy. The company was founded by SolarEn International Corporation of Minnesota. The scope of the company includes: manufacture of flat plate solar collectors; solar water heating systems; project development for solar system design, including photovoltaic (PV) products; and development of wind energy.

The continued development and installation of alternative energy resources will help make Armenia less reliant on imported energy sources. With a renewable energy infrastructure, public education in energy conservation, and the availability of energy efficient appliances, the air quality in Armenia will improve and there will be a reduction of greenhouse gas emissions.

With an appropriate and comprehensive strategy, Armenia will have an opportunity to enter the international renewable energy market. In contrast to other already established industrial markets, the renewable energy industry has not yet matured worldwide. Armenia has the potential to take a leading position in furthering the development of the renewable energy industry.

AIR QUALITY

The air quality in Armenia has generally improved since the 1980s, the peak of industrial production and the height of pollutant emissions. With the economic crisis and the energy shortage during the 1990s there was a decrease in industrial production, estimated at 80 percent, and a corresponding reduction in air pollutant emissions. This decrease in production, combined with a switch from fuel oil to natural gas at the main thermal power plants, resulted in improved air quality.

Mobile source emissions also significantly decreased during the same period because of decreased traffic density. In recent years, automotive traffic has increased, and the relative contribution of pollutants from mobile sources has also increased. With the importation of higher quality unleaded gasoline, lead emissions have been drastically reduced. Research by Kurkjian et. al. showed that the concentration of lead in Yerevan's air in the late 1990s is three orders of magnitude lower than that of the 1980s. However, atmospheric deposition of lead during the past several decades has contaminated soil. This is a long-term problem because lead binds to particles. In certain areas of Yerevan, lead levels are highly elevated in soils where direct contact presents a significant health risk to the public, especially to children.

Emissions from industry and automobiles have been and continue to be the primary sources that impact air quality. Historically, the cities with the worst air quality have been Yerevan, Ararat, Vanadzor, and Hrazdan. These cities, along with Alaverdi, were listed among the fifty most-polluted in the former Soviet Union.

The primary source of air emissions in Alaverdi was the copper smelter and the associated mining operations. Lead and sulfur dioxide emissions were elevated several fold higher than the maximum permitted concentration. The smelter was shut down in 1989 due to economic and environmental reasons, and air quality improved. However, it was re-opened in 1998, without appropriate environmental controls.

The mountainous terrain and the physical and meteorological characteristics of these cities tend to create temperature inversions that result in stagnant conditions and trap air pollutants. During the winter months, increased burning of trash and wood adds to the hazy conditions. In summer months, when the sunlight is most intense, there is an increase in the formation of ozone, a major component of smog, particularly in Yerevan.

ENVIRONMENTAL LAW AND POLICY

Governmental oversight of the environment in Karabagh is today conducted by a State Committee of Nature Protection, just as it had been conducted during the Soviet era. In Armenia, however, the authorities have scrapped their corresponding State Committee of Nature Protection and have created an independent Ministry of Nature Protection. The government's creation of this Ministry places the protection of the environment on a ministerial footing equal to that of, for example, its Ministries of Foreign Affairs, Social Security, and Defense.

Armenia's Constitution, which it adopted in 1995, provides the basis for the Ministry of Nature Protection to create a legal framework to protect the environment. The constitution obligates the state to protect the environment and states in part that "the state shall ensure the protection and reproduction of the environment and the rational utilization of natural resources. " Armenia has built upon this foundation and has enacted national environmental legislation and has become a signatory to many international conventions.

Three years before the adoption of its constitution and just one year after establishing independence, however, Armenia participated in the Rio World Summit—a global environmental convention. Armenia joined in the Rio Pact and it signed international agreements of global significance, including the United Nations Framework Convention on Climate Change and the Convention on Biodiversity. Armenia's National Assembly ratified the Convention on Biodiversity in 1993, thereby committing the nation to the conservation of its biological diversity. Within five years, in 1998, Armenia had completed its National Environmental Action Program (NEAP), which established a strategic framework for policy and investment.

Ecology

LEGAL FRAMEWORK

The legislative keystone of Armenia's environmental framework is the Principles of Legislation on Nature Protection, which was adopted in 1991. The policy keystones are the National Environmental Action Program, Main Report, of 1999, and the Lake Sevan Action Program of 1997. The legal framework that regulates the use of natural resources and the protection of the environment in Armenia consists of (1) international treaties; (2) national codes (3) national laws; and (4) regulations.

Significant International Treaties and Conventions

(1) Convention on Wetlands of International Importance Especially as Waterfowl Habitats, the "Ramsar Convention," (Ratified 1993)

(2) Convention on Biodiversity, the "Rio Pact," (Ratified 1993)

(3) Framework on Climate Change, the "Rio Pact," (Ratified 1993)

(4) Convention on Protection of World Cultural and Natural Heritage, the "World Heritage Convention, Paris," (Ratified 1993)

(5) Convention on Environmental Impact Assessment in Transboundary Context (Ratified 1996)

(6) Convention on the Combat of Desertification (Ratified 1997)

(7) Convention on the Protection of the Ozone Layer, including the Montreal Protocol (Ratified 1999)

(8) Convention on Protection and Use of Transboundary Watercourses and International Lakes (Signed 1999, not ratified)

(9) Convention on Access to Information, Public Participation in Decision-Making and to Justice in Environmental Matters (Ratified 2001)

National Codes

(1) Underground Resources Code of 1992

(2) Forestry Code of 1994

(3) Land Code of 2001

(4) Water Code of 2002

Armenia adopted a new water code in 2002 with a legal framework for integrated basin management. Under this new code, water allocation decisions are based upon supplies and not upon demand, and for cost recovery as a basis for water management decisions.

In reliance upon the authority of this new code, the government established a National Council on Water, which operates under the direction of the Prime Minister. This water council is the highest consultative body in Armenia on issues relating to water resource management.

Significant Environmental Laws

(1) Law on Specially Protected Natural Areas (1991)

(2) Law on Atmospheric Air Protection (1994)

(3) Law on Energy (1997)

(4) Law on Protection and Use of Historic and Cultural Monuments and Historic Environment (1998)

(5) Law on Flora (1999)

(6) Law on Fauna (2000)

(7) Law on Environmental Impact (2000)

(8) Law on Lake Sevan (2001)

(9) Law on Ecological Education of Population (2001)

(10) Law on Environmental Protection and Natural Resource Use Payments (1998, revised in 2001)

Ecology

Melting snow from Mt. Aragats flows into a stream in northwestern Armenia

Transboundary Agreements

Armenia is a party to several agreements with its neighbors on matters that affect transboundary natural resources. One of the most significant of these agreements is the convention with Turkey, which governs water use from the Akhurian and Araks Rivers. This agreement, signed by the USSR and Turkey in 1928, monitors water flow and water usage from these two rivers, and provides a framework for the maintenance of the shared Akhurian Reservoir.

ENVIRONMENTAL AWARENESS

Awareness of environmental issues has existed at varying levels in Armenia during the past several decades. The National Environmental Action Program of 1999 reports that much of the population's awareness of and concern for the environment has receded during the past decade, however, because of severe economic hardship. The priority of the people, according to this government report, is economic survival.

In 2001, Armenia acted to establish a basis for environmental awareness and education. The National Assembly ratified an international treaty on Access to Information, Public Participation in Decision-Making and to Justice in Environmental Matters, and then just a few months later it adopted the national law on Ecological Education of Population. Among the principles of the national legislation is the establishment of the "compulsory character of ecological education at all levels of the educational system," and as a "component of the general educational system" in Armenia.

Non-governmental organizations (NGOs) have struggled to create greater environmental awareness in Armenia. Groups such as the Armenia Tree Project and Armenian Forests have helped to generate interest in forestry conservation, and organizations such as the Environmental Protection Advocacy Center (EPAC) have worked within the legal sector to improve awareness.

The mainstream media in Armenia have not been active in promoting environmental awareness, but domestic journalist groups such as the Investigative Journalists of Armenia (Internet: www.hetq.am) are an exception and have publicized environmental hazards and government abuses of the public trust. The online news site www.ArmeniaNow.com, which is funded by Diaspora Armenians, has championed the cause of conservation and has investigated hazardous waste disposal practices, the over-exploitation of non-renewable resources, and the abuse of public lands for private economic gain.

Ecology

ECOLOGICAL ACTIVITIES

Environmentally-Themed Tours

Avarayr, (Tel. 56-36-81; 52-40-42; Fax 56-36-81) (Internet: www.avarayr.am) (E-mail: office@avarair.arminco.com) Specialized archeological and adventure tours

Birds of Armenia Project (Tel. 51-28-18) (E-mail: boa@aua.am) Field trips to observe birds, other specialized nature tours

Zoological Institute, (Tel.15-14-13; 28-15-02) Bird watching tours. Contact Luba Balian, who participated in the Birds of Armenia project at the American University of Armenia

Hiking / Spelunking

Armenian Speleological Society, (Tel. 58-22-54; 62-02-48) Guided hikes, spelunking and mountain expeditions ranging from one day to one month

Botanical Tours, (Tel. 56-86-90) Field trips to observe flora and fauna, with hikes in the nature preserves that can be arranged with government permission

Eco-tours, (Tel. 39-75-52 Fax: 15-17-95) (E-mail: info@ecotourismarmenia.com; zhanna@freenet.am) Specialized nature tours

IRCS Services, (Tel. 34-23-49; 35-83-41) (E-mail: alexan@arminco.com; archo-tel@freenet.am) Rock Climbing, hiking and horse expeditions. Lodging is available

Mountaineering Sports Union (Tel. 53-49-61; 35-27-02; 39-75-52) Adventure tours: mountain climbing, sailing, surfing, skiing, horseback riding, camping and hiking tours

Ecology

YerevanArmenia

four

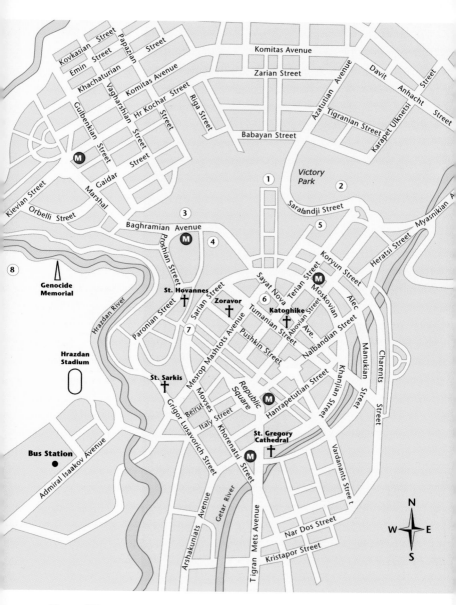

Central Yerevan

1 Cascade; 2 Mother Armenia Statue; 3 Presidential Palace; 4 Parliament;
5 Matenadaran; 6 Opera Square; 7 Yerevan Brandy Factory; 8 Sports Complex

Map of Yerevan © 2004 Stone Garden Productions

INTRODUCTION

Yerevan is a modern city that traces its lineage to 782 BC. It is situated just north of Armenia's fertile Ararat Valley beside the ancient Urartian settlement of Erebuni. For a city with historic roots that extend so deeply, however, its infrastructure and buildings are surprisingly youthful. With too few exceptions, the architecture that has survived in Yerevan is from the twentieth century.

Yerevan was just a frontier village until a century ago. Its population was just 14,000 in 1897 and it covered an area of just one square mile. Most of its development occurred during the Soviet occupation, when it was on the frontline of the Cold War. Today Yerevan is still on the frontier between East and West. Political conditions are more tranquil now, however, and this once sleepy village is now a bustling city and Armenia's largest urban center.

Yerevan became heavily industrialized during the twentieth century, and its population swelled. Today more than one million people live here, and in the summer and early autumn it sometimes seems that everyone is out at once. Sidewalk cafes are abuzz with customers, and streets are jammed with people and cars. There's actually a rush hour now—something that would have been unthinkable just a few years ago. And in the center of the city it would be difficult now to walk more than a block or two without passing a new clothing boutique or some new restaurant with an international cuisine.

The focal point of the central city is **Republic Square**, which is the location of many government offices, the state museum, and the country's grandest hotel—the one where the foreign visitors stayed during Soviet times. This square, which was once known as Lenin Square, was presided over by an imposing statue of the revolutionary leader during Soviet times. The massive statue was promptly pulled down in 1991 when Armenia re-established its independence. The spot where the statue stood had also been the location of the viewing stands when Yerevan hosted

Note About Getting Around in Yerevan

Pedestrians must use caution to avoid being hit by oncoming cars. Drivers in Yerevan rarely (if ever) yield to pedestrians, even when the pedestrian is in a crosswalk. Driving can be unnerving, too. If you are operating a car in Yerevan, be careful to avoid hitting the pedestrians who fearlessly (it seems) walk in the street and cross amid heavy traffic. Be careful at night, when the lack of streetlights makes it difficult to see darkly clad pedestrians.

Taxicabs are abundant, and generally park at street corners while waiting for passengers. The standard minimum fare for short distances within the city is 600 to 1,000 drams ($1 to $1.75). The subway operates 6 am to 11 pm and is popular for connections that span the center, thereby avoiding its congestion, with its fare of only 50 drams (about eight cents). Vans and mini-busses, which the locals call "*marshrutni*," (100 drams) are the most commonly used means of transport among locals.

Photograph, previous page: Victory Park, Yerevan

military parades on holidays such as May Day. The era of military pageantry is over, and this part of Republic Square has been put to varied uses over the years. In 2001 a large cross was erected there in recognition of the 1,700th anniversary of Armenia's adoption of Christianity. The Square was extensively renovated and redesigned in 2003, and a video billboard was erected. The concrete island at its center features the design of an Armenian rug.

Opera Square is another of the city's great meeting places, and it was until recently a popular site for political rallies and stump speeches. Today the square's new discotheques, cafes, and bars have displaced the political discourse. A major new boulevard that is under construction will link the two squares, probably by the end of 2005, thereby fulfilling the original architectural plan for the city.

On a clear day it would be difficult to deny that the geographic focal point of Yerevan is Mt. Ararat, a twin-peaked mountain that dominates the southwest skyline. Its rival for the affection of the Armenians, Mt. Aragats, is visible along the horizon north of Yerevan.

BACKGROUND

Yerevan derives its name, as well as its history, from the ancient Urartian capital of Erebuni. Today, a fortress and other remains from the Erebuni settlement are preserved at its original site on a hilltop just south of the modern city. It is generally accepted by historians that the Armenian people themselves are descendant from the ancient Urartians of Erebuni, and that they are an indigenous people who arose after the fall of Urartu. About one century after settling Erebuni, historians say that the citadel there was abandoned and the settlement was moved to Karmir Blur ("Red Hill"), just a few km to the west. Sovereignty over Yerevan was transferred from the Persian to the Russian Empires in 1828, but it remained a small garrison town until about 80 years ago. As recently as the 1890s it had a population of only about 12,500. The development and growth of the city did not begin in earnest until after its incorporation into the Soviet Union.

Living conditions in Yerevan were dismal immediately following independence in 1991. Industry declined by more than 80 percent, and there was massive unemployment, which persists to this day. Economic problems in Yerevan, as well as in the rest of Armenia, have been compounded by a decade-long blockade by neighboring Turkey and Azerbaijan.

POPULATION

According to the most recent census, more than one million people live in Yerevan. Anecdotal evidence about empty apartments and emigrant friends suggests that the population may be a bit lower, as unemployed residents seek work elsewhere. The population of the city is almost entirely ethnic Armenian. There is also a prominent expatriate community of several hundred, most of whom are the American and European employees of international organizations, as well as Diaspora Armenians who have moved to Yerevan.

ARCHITECTURE

Yerevan's street design dates back only to the 1920s, when architect Alexander Tamanian was called upon to create a modern Soviet city. He opted for broad avenues and expansive public spaces. As a result, there are none of the narrow and winding roads that you might expect in an ancient settlement with such hilly environs. The streets in the central city are instead arranged in concentric circles that are crossed by major avenues.

In 1827, on the eve of the Russian conquest, Yerevan was a town of 1,736 mud-brick houses, and Czar Nikolai I would later refer to the settlement as a "clay pot." In the 1890s, a Russian travel writer described Yerevan as a city of "clay houses with flat clay roofs, clay streets, clay squares, clay surroundings, in all directions clay and more clay." Practically nothing of this earlier town remains today. Most of the buildings that are now standing in Yerevan date only from the twentieth century, although homes in some neighborhoods date back to the early 1800s.

Construction in the city during the past fifteen years suggests a disregard for zoning. Tall buildings with glass facades sit beside the historic stone edifices of Abovian Street. Neon-lighted cafes compete garishly with the stately Opera House. And throughout Yerevan, noisy bars and restaurants have occupied sidewalks and parklands, displacing the public and blighting the environment. Yerevan's greatest zoning success of the past decade has been its banishment of casinos to the outer perimeter of the city. Many of the old casino buildings have been converted to cafes or to other retail purposes. Its greatest loss has been the relentless conversion to commercial use—usually for cafes and bars—of its green public spaces.

USEFUL INFORMATION

Safety

Violent street crime is unusual in Yerevan, and there are no areas that one needs to avoid in order to avoid crime, even at night. Still, you should take the same precautions that you would take in any city anywhere. Probably the greatest risk of injury is from the automobile traffic.

Wild dogs have been a problem in Yerevan, especially late at night when they sometimes travel in packs. Their numbers have decreased in the past several years, but you should still use caution to avoid these dogs if you are walking alone at night.

Petty and nonviolent theft is probably the city's most common crime. Don't become paranoid, but don't leave valuables laying around unattended, either.

Traveling with Children

Families with children can safely travel to Yerevan. There is no safety or security reason to discourage families from doing so. The greatest safety concerns for parents are probably the lack of seatbelts in most cars and hazards similar to those in any city in developing countries.

Electricity and hot water are available in the city's tourist hotels without interruption. Don't expect to find diaper changing tables in public rest rooms, or high chairs in restaurants, however. Elevators are also luxuries that are not available in many public buildings, including at some hotels, resulting in inconvenience to families with babies in strollers or young children.

Baby formula and other items that babies need, such as pacifiers and spill-proof bottles, are available at many of the Western grocery stores. Try Aroma, at the corner of Sayat Nova Avenue and Nalbandian Street; or Europe Market, 4 Vardanants Street, near Nalbandian (Tel. 58-68-08). Disposable diapers are difficult to find in Armenia. Bring them with you.

MONEY

Yerevan has a cash economy, but there are some limited opportunities for using the major bank-issued credit cards, mostly at the larger hotels. Visitors should bring enough cash for their entire stay, or make arrangements for wire transfers for lengthy visits. If you bring an ATM bank card, you can limit the amount of cash you will need to carry. US dollars are widely accepted in Armenia, and are readily exchangeable for Armenian currency.

ATM Machines

ATM machines are no longer a novelty in Yerevan. There are many of them now, mostly in the city center, and many of them offer a choice of US or Armenian currency. In addition to the local banks, international financial institutions such as Converse Bank and HSBC have ATM's (as well as branch offices) in Yerevan.

Converse Bank has 24-hour machines at: (1) 49 Komitas Avenue; (2) 1/1 Abovian Street; and (3) 26 Vazgen Sargsian Street.

HSBC Bank Armenia has 24-hour machines at: (1) the lobby of the main office of the HSBC bank, which is located at 9 Vazgen Sargsian Street, next to the Armenia Marriott Hotel (Tel. 58-70-88; 58-70-95); (2) the lobby of the Komitas branch of the HSBC bank, which is located at 3 Komitas Avenue (Tel. 22-25-96; 22-87-57); (3) a kiosk on the corner of Baghramian Avenue and Moskovian Street; (4) near the Yeritasardakan (Youth) metro station at 27 Abovian Street; and (5) at 11 Abovian Street near the intersection with Sayat Nova Avenue. GlobalAccess and PLUS cards are accepted, but CIRRUS is not. You can also get a cash advance on a MasterCard or Visa credit card.

Banking and Wire Transfers

Accounts can be maintained in US dollars or in Armenian dram at the Yerevan branches of Converse and HSBC. Converse is located at 49 Komitas Avenue (Tel. 54-54-52). HSBC is located at 9 Vazgen Sargsian Street, next to the Armenia Marriott Hotel (Tel. 58-70-88; 58-70-95).

Wire transfers are available to and from Yerevan through the offices of Western Union, which are located throughout the city, including at 2 Nalbandian Street, near Republic Square.

TELEPHONE

Placing International Calls from Yerevan

To place a direct dial international call from Yerevan to the US that you bill to your calling card, use either the ATT, Sprint, or MCI lines. For **ATT**, enter **08-00-111** to reach the English-speaking international operator. To use your Sprint calling card, call the international **Sprint** operator by entering **08-00-155**. For the **MCI** operator, enter **08-00-122**. You can use these numbers to make collect calls, too.

For a direct dial international call from Yerevan to any other country, enter (00) + (country code) + (local area code) + (local phone number).

To pay cash on the spot for a call, use the business center that many major hotels operate. The business centers at some of the better hotels charge as much as $3.75 per minute for calls to the US.

Long-distance calls can also be made from post offices, where they are a little less costly. Try the large post office at Republic Square, the main office at 22 Sarian Street, or the branch located at the corner of Abovian Street and Sayat Nova Avenue. These post offices also sell international phone cards, and the blue phone cards that allow you to make local calls from the new pay phones on the street. To use one of the old-style pay phones for a local call, you'll have to purchase a token from a nearby street vendor.

Prepaid phone cards from AlexServ offer rates as low as about 18 cents per minute for calls from Yerevan to the US. Purchases must be made in person at their office, which is located behind the Erebuni Hotel, near Republic Square.

Placing International Calls from Other Cities

To make an international call from a city in Armenia other than Yerevan, you will usually need to go to the main post office. In some cases you may also need to go to the post office to make a city-to-city call within Armenia.

Placing Calls to Yerevan from Abroad

To reach Yerevan from outside Armenia, enter (011) and then Armenia's country code (374) plus the Yerevan city code (1). If you are calling a cell phone, enter (09) immediately before you enter the local phone number.

Placing Calls to Other Cities in Armenia from Abroad

To reach cities other than Yerevan from outside Armenia, connect to an international line (In the US, enter 011) and then Armenia's country code (374) plus the code for the city you are calling. City codes for many locations in Armenia are listed below.

Armenia-to-Armenia Long Distance Calls

To call a city or town in Armenia, from another location within Armenia, enter (0) and then the city code, plus the local phone number. City codes for many locations in Armenia are listed below.

City Area Codes

Abovian (22); Alaverdi (53); Aparan (520); Aragats (570); Ararat (38); Armavir (37); Ashtarak (32); Dilijan (680); Echmiadzin (31); Goris (84); Gyumri (41); Ijevan (63); Jermuk (87); Kapan (85); Meghri (860); Noyemberian (66); Sevan (61); Sisian (830); Spitak (550); Stepanakert (7-1); Stepanavan (56); Tsaghkadzor (23); Vanadzor (51); Yeghegnadzor (81); and Zvartnots (31).

Cell Phones

Because of the poor service offered by landlines, many people in Yerevan have turned to cellular service for relief. When calling a cell phone in Yerevan, enter (09) and then the mobile phone number. Cellular telephone service is reliable, and the phone service works throughout Yerevan and also along the major roadway up to Gyumri. Because of a monopoly held by the local phone company ArmenTel, your cell phone from the US will not work.

Short-term visitors can rent a mobile phone, with pre-paid service, from a business called Rent-A-Phone (Tel. 55-99-80) (E-mail: info@rentaphone.am) (Internet: www.rentaphone.com). Daily rates vary in cost from roughly $5 to $15 per day depending upon length of service. Rent-a-Mobile offers phones for about $5 per day (Tel. 59-99-95). Phones are also available for rent from a shop at Sil Plaza on lower Abovian Street. Service is also available directly from ArmenTel, 22 Sarian Street (Tel. 54-94-54).

EMERGENCY MEDICAL CARE

European Medical Center is located at 3 Vazgen Sargsian Street (Tel. 54-00-03; 54-05-40). This modern clinic offers Western-style medical care, with English-speaking doctors and nurses, and 24-hour ambulance service. Emergency dental care is available at Deluxe System Dental Clinic, 31 Moskovian Street (Tel. 53-95-38). The American Embassy can offer a list of doctors in general practice and also in various specialties (Tel. 52-16-11; Fax 15-15-50). If the Consulate is closed, you can still get help in an emergency at any time of day or night by calling the Embassy switchboard (Tel. 15-15-51).

Armenia's equivalencies of the "911" emergency number that most Americans are familiar with are 1-01 (Fire); 1-02 (Police); and 1-03 (Ambulance). Operators may not speak English, however, and we suggest these numbers to foreign visitors only as a last resort. If you need hospitalization, the Ministry of Health Hospital #4, located at 21 Paronian Street, usually has an English-speaking doctor or nurse on staff.

COMPUTERS AND INTERNET

Short-term visitors who want access to the Internet can use their own laptop computers. Dial-up access to your Internet service provider is available through the local telephone line. This means that disconnects are common, and it may take several attempts before you can even get online. When surfing the web, expect slow connections to US-based servers.

If you are dialing from a hotel room, you can probably use a standard US-style phone jack. From an apartment or an older office, you may need an adaptor. If you can't find one in the US, try one of the Zig Zag electronics stores located at either 22 Abovian Street (Tel. 52-65-54) or at 24 Mesrop Mashtots Avenue (Tel. 53-76-75). Most electrical outlets use European-style plugs, so you'll need an adaptor for this as well. Most laptop computers can operate on either the US standard of 120 volts or the European standard of 220 volts. If your computer can operate only on the standard US current, then you'll need a voltage converter to handle the Armenian standards of 220 volts and 50 amperes.

You can also get access to the worldwide web from one of the many **Internet cafes** in the city. These businesses tend to come and go, but you should be able to find a few to choose from on Mesrop Mashtots Ave, Abovian Ave, and near Opera Square. Rates are usually less than $2 per hour. The hotel business centers usually have internet access, but with charges of up to 120 dram per minute, which is the equivalent of approximately $12 per hour.

Long-term visitors may prefer to get their own local ISP (Internet service provider). X-ternet offers monthly dial-up service for about $40. 19 Sayat Nova Avenue (Tel. 54-80-41; Fax 54-80-45) (E-mail: support@xter.net) (Internet: www.xter.net). High-speed connections are available from AATV Communications (Tel. 54-54-54; 56-29-92) (E-mail: aatv@arminco.com) but are too expensive for most non-commercial use. Arminco also offers ISP service (www.arminco.am).

BOOKS

Bookstores

Artbridge Bookstore Café, at 20 Abovian Street, sells new and second-hand books, including art and photography books, as well as magazines and maps, in both English and Armenian. Open 8:30 am to midnight (Tel. 52-12-39) (E-mail: artbridge@netsys.am). **Noyan Tapan Bookstore**, on Republic Square, sometimes has some English-language books, as do the vendors each weekend at the Vernissage. The selections are extremely limited, and English-language texts are usually expensive.

Libraries

The **Armenian Tourism Development Agency** allows visitors to use its library, but it does not lend or sell books. This is a good source for books about Armenian culture and travel. You can also pick up free tourist maps and brochures advertising many sites of interest to visitors. Open daily 10 am to 7 pm. Located at 3 Nalbandian Street near Republic Square (Tel. 54-23-03) (E-mail: info@armeniainfo.am).

The **US Information Service** (USIS) library at the US Embassy is available to US citizens, but only by appointment and only at limited times. Located at 18 Baghramian Avenue (Tel. 52-98-25). The **Papazian Library** at the American University of Armenia (AUA) is the largest English-language library in Armenia. You do not need an appointment to visit, and it's open daily except Sunday. Located on the ground floor of the AUA building at 40 Baghramian Avenue (Tel. 51-27-60) (Internet: www.aua.am/aua/library).

NEWS

Newspapers and Magazines

Noyan Tapan Highlights is the leading English-language newspaper in the city. It is published weekly in Yerevan, and costs 1,000 dram (about $2). Two tabloid weeklies, the **New Yerevan Times** and the **Yerevan Courier**, were introduced in 2004. The **Armenian International Magazine** (AIM) is a monthly English-language magazine that covers news from Armenia. It's published in Armenia, and it is distributed in both Armenia and the US. Single copies are 1,600 dram (about $3).

Street vendors generally sell only Armenian and Russian language periodicals. It is sometimes possible to buy months-old English-language magazines, at full cover price (or higher) from some vendors. There's such a scarcity of English-language periodicals that month-old copies of the New York Times, for example, can sometimes be found on sale for 2,500 drams (about $5).

TELEVISION AND RADIO

There's an English-language broadcast of CNN that you should be able to receive in the Yerevan area. The local broadcast stations are in Armenian or Russian, but satellite television provides access to CNN, MTV, and to the BBC World Service.

AATV Communications is a wireless cable television provider that rebroadcasts several English-language channels, including CNN, BBC, ESPN, Discovery and others. The service is roughly $20 per month, with an installation fee of about $60 (Tel. 54-54-54; 56-29-92) (E-mail: aatv@arminco.com).

Radio Hye FM 105.5 FM is Armenia's first non-political entertainment radio station. It offers eight hours of Voice of America news, plus regional news in English. At the time of research this was the only station with regularly scheduled English language programming.

MAIL

Letters and postcards sent to the US directly from a post office in Yerevan generally arrive within about two weeks. The rate for a first-class letter is 250 dram (about fifty cents), and the rate for a post card is 170 dram (about thirty-five cents). Sending packages to the US, however, is less reliable. Don't be surprised if a local resident asks you to carry a letter back to the States, so that you can mail it to a US destination from a US post office.

Mail delivery to addresses within Armenia is not reliable. Don't expect the Armenian post office to make local deliveries within Armenia, regardless of whether the origin of the letter or package is local or foreign. Still, if you wish to try, use Yerevan's main postal code, 375000, for general delivery.

To make it simple for tourists to purchase stamps as souvenirs, the postal service operates a special office called Namakaneesh where you can purchase, at face value, individual or complete sets of mint stamps and other postal items. The supply here is greater than at any post office, and includes issues dating back several years. Located at 43 Mesrop Mashtots Avenue, near the Matenadaran.

SHIPPING

When shipping heavy packages that do not require immediate delivery, it is economical to use a cargo company such as **Jet Line**. Contact them in Los Angeles at 307 East Beach Avenue, Inglewood, California 90302 (Tel. 310-419-7404; Fax 310-419-8957) (Internet: www.jetlineaircargo.com) or in Yerevan at 15 Sarian Street (Tel. 58-06-40; Fax 54-31-98) (E-mail: cargojetline@netsys.am). Another option is the local Armenian company **Saberatour-Sevan**, 37 Hanrapetutian Street (Tel. 52-54-48). The private shipping company **DHL** was among the first entrants to the Armenian market, and they offer reliable and fast delivery both in and out of the country. Delivery time for a letter is about five days. 6 Demirchian Street (Tel. 58-66-88). **UPS**, the huge US-based shipping company, has a local office at 1 Kievian Street and offers worldwide delivery of documents and packages (Tel. 27-30-90; 27-32-93). **Federal Express** also provides service. 1 Charents Street (Tel. 57-46-86).

Seaborne International ships cargo and has offices in both Los Angeles and Yerevan. The charge for shipping airport-to-airport between Armenia and California, usually on a British Airways flight, is about $6 per kilogram. In the Los Angeles area, they are located at 11222 La Cienega Boulevard, Suite 470, Inglewood, California 90304 (Tel. 310-216-4225) (E-mail: sarlax@aol.com). In Yerevan they can be reached at (Tel. 56-66-99; 56-65-99).

United Armenian Fund flies humanitarian aid from the US to Armenia and sometimes accepts commercial cargo on the return trip from Armenia to the US when it has room. Contact them at 126 South Jackson Street, Suite 205, Glendale, California 91205 (Tel. 818-241-8900; Fax 818-241-6900).

If you are in the US and wish to ship a package to Armenia, you can simply go to your neighborhood post office. The US Postal Service has a service agreement with DHL and offers delivery in as little as four days.

CAR RENTAL

Lower Abovian Street appears to have become Yerevan's car rental district, with three agencies within shouting distance of each other. **Lemon** Rent-a-Car is open every day, with a wide selection of good cars that are rented for roughly $30 per day. 4 Abovian Street (Tel. 54-55-47). Weekly and monthly rates are available, too. **Elitar Travel Company**, agent for **Hertz** Rent-a-Car, has a small selection of cars for roughly $60 to $80 per day. Closed Saturday and Sunday. 7 Abovian Street (Tel. 54-33-77; 58-48-18) (E-mail: hertz@arminco.com). **Aspera** Rent-a-Car is also worth a try. Sil Plaza, Abovian Street (Tel. 54-77-66; 52-26-36) (E-mail: rent@netsys.am). The cars at these three rental agencies are

Yerevan, as seen from the top of the Cascade

all rented without drivers, just as you would expect to rent a car in the US or Europe. The cars are insured, too, but each company requires a cash deposit before they'll let you drive away. **Euro East Tour** Rent-a-Car offers rentals of sedans, SUVs and vans with or without drivers, as well as an 18-seat mini bus. Credit cards accepted. 15 Tumanian Street (Tel. 54-42-05) (E-mail: eet@netsys.am) (Internet: www.eet.net).

TAXI CABS

Taxi service can be arranged in advance by telephone. These companies offer radio-dispatched cabs: **Doka Taxi** (Tel. 55-55-55); **Dream Taxi** (Tel. 55-00-00); **Glorius Taxi** (Tel. 53-73-10); **Franse Park Taxi** (Tel. 28-77-33; 28-35-53); **Taxi Avis** (Tel. 44-00-02; 44-00-22); **Yerevanian Taxi** (Tel. 58-10-10). Taxi cabs can also be hailed on the street [see "Note About Getting Around in Yerevan," above for details]. Doka Taxi operates Mercedes Benz cars and uses meters and offers receipts. Its fares are also the most expensive in this unregulated business.

MAPS AND INFORMATION

Pocket-sized tourist maps of Yerevan are widely available from hotels and gift shops, as well as from the visitor information center of the Armenian Tourism Development Agency at 3 Nalbandian Street, near Republic Square. This visitor center is also a good source for information about exhibitions and events in Yerevan.

Yerevan's English-language newsweekly, Noyan Tapan Highlights, prints a map and a list of tourist services in its center spread. There's also a color map of the city in each edition of Yerevan Guide, an advertising brochure that is distributed for free at most hotels.

LAUNDRY

Most of the professional laundry services will wash and fold your clothes for about 500 to 800 drams (roughly $1 to $1.50) per kilogram. The services usually require two days, but you may be able to get same day or next day service for a premium. Try **Dzyunik** Laundry, 26 Amirian Street (Tel. 53-88-43); **Masis Taraz** Laundry, 3 Grigor Lusavorich Street (Tel. 52-79-21); **Selena Service**, 4 Zakian Street (Tel. 53-65-08); **Spitak Lavanda** ("White Laundry"), 51 Tigran Mets Avenue (Tel. 55-24-34). Most hotels now offer laundry services, as well, although at much higher rates. There are no self-service laundromats in Yerevan.

BEAUTY SALONS

Beauty salons are plentiful in Yerevan, and can be found throughout the central city. For unisex haircuts and styling: **Elina**, 37 Mesrop Mashtots Avenue (Tel. 53-13-51); and **Ross Beauty Salon**, 31 Moskovian Street (near Sarian Park). For women's facials and skin care: **Vitak Skin Care Center**, 10/6 Pushkin Street (Tel. 56-63-59) (E-mail: vitak@xter.net); **Vivien Beauty Salon**, 46 Pushkin Street (Tel. 53-71-21).

ATTRACTIONS AND SIGHTSEEING

It is easy to walk to just about everything within central Yerevan. The streets are arranged in a compact and concentric pattern that makes it easy to get around. And those locations that are difficult to reach by foot are still only a 600 to 1,000-dram (roughly $1 to $2) cab fare away. The subway is convenient, too, especially for cross-town trips. Subway stations are listed below whenever one is located near one of the sites.

The statue of **Mother Armenia** is a good place to start your tour. This statue is perched high above the city, and from here you will be able to see all of Yerevan laid out before you. The statue seems to stand sentry over Yerevan, and it sometimes appears to be directly in line with Mesrop Mashtots Street. This 34-meter-tall statue was erected in 1950 to replace a statue of Stalin, who was out of favor by that time. Mother Armenia was dedicated as a World War II memorial. The statue is actually located in **Victory Park**, which occupies a hilltop overlooking the center of the city. This park is also worth a visit. There's a Ferris wheel and several carnival rides at the park, as well as a small artificial lake where you can rent a rowboat, and lots of cafes. Inside the base of the Mother Armenia monument is a museum dedicated to war veterans.

To get there, start at the base of the Cascade on Tamanian Street and climb the stairs to the top. Be sure that you do not confuse tiny Tamanian Street with the grand Tumanian Street. Tumanian is a major artery that crosses the city center. Tamanian, the street you're starting from, is just a short connector at the Cascade. At the top of the stairs, cross the street and enter Victory Park at its main entrance. You can avoid most of the steps by taking a recently renovated Escalator that is tucked out of sight beneath the marble steps. Or you can cheat by taking a cab to the top and then starting your foot tour (all of it downhill!) from there. The escalator operates until 11 pm and you can ride it for free

Armenia commemorated its fiftieth year as a Soviet Republic with a nearby monument at the top of the Cascade. To reach the monument from Victory Park, cross Azatutian Avenue at the park's main entrance and walk south about 50 m. The city center is located hundreds of steps below. Athletes sometimes run up the steps for exercise, but the greatest attraction of these steps to tourists is the view of Mt. Ararat and the city from the top, especially at sunset.

Construction of this Cascade of white steps was halted many years ago when money ran out, and the top quarter has remained unfinished for years. A comprehensive project to complete and restore the Cascade steps began in 2002, privately funded by Armenian American businessman Gerard L. Cafesjian and is expected to be completed by 2006.

The restoration project includes the construction of a modern art museum on an adjacent parcel of land. This museum, The Gerard L. Cafesjian Museum of Contemporary Art, will become Armenia's largest repository of modern art when it opens in 2006. Its first object of art, a larger-than-life sculpture of a black cat, is displayed at the base of the steps.

At the base of the Cascade's 553 steps you can rest at one of several cafes under the gaze of the black cat, and visit the statue of Alexander Tamanian, the architect of Yerevan. At the base of the statue you'll see a street map of Yerevan engraved in stone. The office of the Cafesjian Museum Foundation is located nearby, at 2 Tamanian Street (Tel. 54-19-32; Fax 56-85-50). **Subway:** Yeritasardakan (Youth) station.

The **Matenadaran** houses an impressive collection of ancient manuscripts and is probably Armenia's most famous museum. The building is just a five-minute walk from the base of the Cascade. The documents at the museum provide insight into Armenia's historical, scientific, literary and artistic development over the ages, and make the Matenadaran the most important site on any city tour.

The building is also home to the Matenadaran Scientific Research Institute, an important library for academic research. There are more than 14,000 Armenian manuscripts at the museum, and another 2,500 manuscripts from foreign sources. Only about one percent of them are on display to the public at any time, but even that one percent is enough to make this a world-class museum that warrants a special visit.

Self-guided tours are permitted, but you're apt to overlook the significance of many items if you rely only upon the signs for guidance. English-speaking tour guides are available, and will make your visit more meaningful. Admission and the tours are free, but donations are accepted. Reservations are not needed, but large groups should call beforehand. Open 10 am to 4 pm daily except Sunday and Monday. Located at 53 Mesrop Mashtots Street, at the top of the street (Tel. 56-25-78; 58-32-92) (Internet: www.matenadaran.am). **Subway:** Yeritasardakan (Youth) station.

Azatutian Hraparak (Freedom Square), which is also called the **Opera Square**, is a short walk from the base of the Cascade, across Moskovian Street, at the corner of Mesrop Mashtots Street and Sayat Nova Avenue. This is a popular public gathering place, in addition to being the location of the National Opera House. In summer months, children on skates and roller blades fill the park, competing for space with others who are playing ping-pong, or sipping Cokes at one of the square's many cafes. This is the largest public space in the city center, and it was the location of many political rallies during the closing years of the Soviet Union and throughout the 1990s.

Ever since the nation's independence in 1991, the Opera House had been closing down each winter because it lacked fuel for its central heating. An extensive $1.9 million renovation in 2003 and 2004, funded by the US-based Lincy Foundation, has restored the heating and made it possible for it to resume a 12-month schedule. Renovations also included new lighting and wiring, and structural repairs.

The "yard" of the Opera House, which is actually paved asphalt, features monuments to the writer Hovhannes Tumanian (at left) and the composer Alexander Spendarian. At the street-side of the Opera House, near the intersection of Sayat Nova Avenue and Mesrop Mashtots Avenue, there is a monument to the musician Aram Khatchatourian. At the opposite end of Azatutian Hraparak (Freedom Square), near the corner of Terian Street and Tumanian Street, there is a concrete pond and a bizarre-looking statue of the pianist Arno Babajanian. The statue was

Museum of Contemporary Art

The Gerard L. Cafesjian Museum of Contemporary Art hasn't opened yet, but already it is destined to become one of Armenia's most prominent and internationally-known facilities. The Gerard L. Cafesjian Collection of Contemporary Art will form the core of the museum's permanent collection. Cafesjian, an Armenian American businessman, has personally funded the entire project and is contributing his own extensive collection of fine art.

Cafesjian is known throughout the art world for his collection, which includes diverse media, such as large-scale works in bronze by the Latin American artist Fernando Botero. The Cat that is prominently displayed at the base of the Cascade is a Botero. Among the many other artists whose works are featured in the Cafesjian Collection are Arshile Gorky, Pablo Picasso and Andy Warhol.

The Museum is widely expected to become a national center for artistic expression, and it is probably the most eagerly anticipated museum opening that Armenia has ever experienced. The 2006 opening will also be significant for its impact on the world art community. This will be the first major museum in Armenia with a stated objective of fostering and exchange of contemporary culture between Armenia and the world.

Museum benefactor and namesake Gerard Cafesjian intends for the museum building itself to be a work of art. The building will occupy a commanding site at the top of the Cascade in central Yerevan. The Cascade is essentially a grand granite staircase that rises to the height of a 30-story building.

Museum facilities will include an outdoor sculpture garden, an auditorium for educational programming and performance art, a gift shop, and a restaurant. Repairs to the existing structure of the Cascade are part of the project, and include landscaping, refurbishment of the fountains, and structural repairs. Construction and site preparation are budgeted at approximately $25 million. Cafesjian has pledged to donate $100 million to establish the museum. More information about the museum is available from the Cafesjian Museum Foundation, 2 Tamanian Street (Tel. 54-19-32; Fax 56-85-50) (Internet: www.cmf.am).

controversial when first erected because many thought, incorrectly, that it mocked the artist. Unfortunately, cafes have been crammed into too much of this public space all around the Opera House in recent years. The public's misfortune in losing this public space to private enterprise is compounded by the loud music that the café owners blast at all hours of the day. **Subway**: Yeritasardakan (Youth) station.

From the National Opera House, walk southeast one block on either Sayat Nova Avenue or Tumanian Street until you reach the intersecting Abovian Street. Here on Abovian Street you'll find many of the city's better shops and cafes. You'll also find the last vestige of a thirteenth century monastery—its **Katoghikeh chapel**—tucked away behind an office building that houses the state Linguistics Institute at 15 Abovian Street. This is Yerevan's oldest religious center.

There had been a basilica on this site from 1693 until about 1936, when the Soviet authorities decided to raze it as part of their urban renewal plan for the city. While they were razing the basilica, they discovered that this small Katoghikeh chapel was inside the basilica—the basilica had been built around it. Its historical value was immediately apparent, and the authorities declined to destroy it. This surviving relic is the tiny chapel that now abuts the new office building on the site. Private litigants are seeking to acquire the office building now. They allege that it is built on church property, and that it should be restored to the Armenian Church. If the litigants prevail, they would raze the office building and rededicate the site for religious purposes.

Today, the surviving remnant of the church is so small that many parishioners stand outside of it during the daily church services. If you visit, remember that this is a functioning church, so behave accordingly. Katoghikeh is not visible from the street. To find it, you walk behind that twentieth century office building, on Abovian Street.

From Katoghikeh, walk south on Abovian Street toward Republic Square. Just before reaching the Hotel Yerevan you pass **Zodiac Square**, a pedestrian zone that is so-named because it features at its center a fountain with sculptures of the various zodiac signs. The square was renamed **Charles Aznavour Square** in honor of the French-Armenian actor. There's also a Charles Aznavour Square in the city of Gyumri.

Republic Square is the heart of the city, and it's the point from which all distances are measured in Armenia. There's a massive road construction and urban redevelopment program underway that will link a new street, to be called Northern Avenue, with the square. Construction of this major new avenue fulfills an original, and now 80-year old, design for the city. It also forced the relocation of about 400 people from their homes. The avenue will be 24 meters wide and will be lined with stately new buildings.

During the Soviet era, military parades crossed the square and passed viewing stands that were filled with the country's elite. The square underwent a comprehensive reconstruction in 2003, and a large concrete island was built in its center. There's a carpet pattern in the concrete. During the reconstruction, workers discovered the ruins of what was at first believed to be an ancient settlement beneath the asphalt surface. Forensic architects and historians determined the ruins to be more modern and of little historical value, however, and the construction was resumed after a brief delay.

The National Museum at Republic Square

Today, the square is still the site of national parades, although floats and balloons have replaced guns and rockets. This is also a popular gathering spot for young people, especially after sunset during the hot summer months.

This square, which is actually shaped more like an oval, is flanked by some of Armenia's most prestigious buildings. **The National Museum** occupies the most prominent location [see museum listings for details], and the fountains at the front of the building attract large crowds.

Across the square, a green lawn occupies the spot where a statue of the atheist revolutionary Lenin had once stood. Ironically, a 40-foot-tall cross was installed here in late December 2000 for ceremonies commemorating Armenia's 1,700-year history of Christianity. More recently, a large artificial Christmas tree has been installed at the center of the Square for the holiday display. Behind the green lawn there's a park filled with fountains and cafes. In early 2004 a large Times-Square-sized video billboard and loudspeakers were installed on the spot where Lenin once stood. **Subway**: Hanrapetutian Hraparak (Republic Square) station.

Just a five-minute walk from Republic Square is Yerevan's newest and largest cathedral. **The Cathedral of St. Gregory the Illuminator** is a massive structure that was consecrated in September 2001. It's located near the crossroads of Tigran Mets Avenue and Khanjian Street, south of Republic Square. In a nod to Armenia's celebration in 2001 of the 1,700th anniversary of its adoption of Christianity, the church is designed to accommodate 1,700 parishioners. This modern cathedral has a design that is unusual for an Armenian church. It is one of the few churches in the country with pews, and it is brighter than most, too, with its abundant windows. Traditional churches in Armenia have few windows and are usually dark, which contributes to the feeling of mysticism of the church.

A large monument to Armenian hero Vardan Mamikonian flanks the left side of the cathedral. Mamikonian led the Armenians to battle against Persia in AD 451, at the battle of Avarayr. The Armenians lost the battle, but celebrate it nevertheless because they prevailed in their fight to preserve their cultural and religious identity. The statue was erected in 1975, roughly 25 years before the cathedral was built. Today, it looks a bit out of place, but it's actually an appropriate location, considering that Mamikonian had fought for religious freedom. **Subway:** Zoravar Andranik metro station.

Just a few steps down the street from the cathedral is one of the city's largest outdoor markets. Vendors set up here on both sides of Tigran Mets Avenue, but the more interesting location for visitors is the market on the east side of the street, which includes a huge indoor shuka (food market) as well. This isn't a tourist attraction, but is instead a genuine market that local residents use every day. It offers a fascinating glimpse of one part of daily life in Yerevan. And, since this is the end of your walking tour, you can purchase some items to bring back to your hotel.

Off the walking tour, but of interest nevertheless, is a trio of religious sites. **St. Zoravar Church** is hidden from the street, and located inside the block bounded by Moskovian, Pushkin, and Tumanian streets. The church and its small yard are an oasis of calm in the midst of a busy city.

The **Blue Mosque** on lower Mesrop Mashtots Street, which was built in 1765, is almost modern by comparison to the antiquity of many other sites in Armenia. It had fallen into ruin during Soviet rule, but has been carefully rebuilt by Iranian benefactors and was reopened in 2003. The building and grounds are closed to visitors, but the minaret and the blue tile roofs are visible from the street, behind a new brick wall and an ornately and colorfully tiled facade. The religious site is a reminder that the rule of the Persian Empire had once been extended as far north as this city. Yerevan had served as a garrison town for the Persians beginning in about the seventeenth century, and it was a key strategic point at the convergence of the Russian, Ottoman and Persian Empires. Today, Yerevan's leaders point out that the five-year renovation of the mosque and its current revival are symbolic of the strong ties and friendly relations between Armenia (the world's first Christian nation) and Iran (a fundamentalist Islamic republic). The Mosque has a small information center for tourists on Mesrop Mashtots Street, just to the right of the arched entrance.

The third site in this trio of religious sites is actually the oldest church complex in Yerevan today. Still, we are reluctant to let it steal the distinction from Katoghikeh (mentioned above) as being Yerevan's oldest. This is because Avan, the old village in which it is located, has only recently been incorporated into Yerevan's city limits. This church, **St. Astvatsatin**, was built from AD 591 to AD 603 and is hidden in a secluded neighborhood just a bit beyond the city zoo and the new water park. This site cannot be part of any walking tour—it's just too far from the center.

To get there, drive to the top of Abovian Street and then continue uphill past the zoo on Myasnikian Street. Avan is located just past the new Water World complex.

After passing the Water World, turn right onto Haik Avenue, which is the main boulevard for the Nork housing complex. Just a couple of hundred meters up this road, on the left side, there's a statue in honor of the legendary father of the Armenian nation, **Haik**, with a stretched bow and aiming an arrow toward the sky. Haik is believed to have been a direct descendant of Noah, of Noah's Ark fame. At the far end of Haik Avenue, also on the left side, is a statue that looks something like Atlas except that the man is carrying rocks, instead of the world. The statue depicts the "Strong Man," which is a mythic figure from the writings of Hovhannes Tumanian.

There are two other functioning Armenian churches in central Yerevan. Both are from the nineteenth century, but neither is of great architectural or historic significance. **St. Sarkis** is perched above the Hrazdan Canyon, near the confluence of Mesrop Mashtots and Grigor Lusavorich Streets. This is the seat of the Diocese of the Armenian Apostolic Church in Yerevan. **St. Hovhannes** is located on Paronian Street, just south of the barbecue stands of Proshian Street. Elsewhere in Yerevan, other new churches have been built during the past several years. Still, there are surprisingly few churches serving this capital city of the world's first Christian nation.

Outside the City Center

The Yerevan Brandy Company is one of the most prominent sights that greet visitors when they are arriving from the airport. This is the maker of the famous Ararat brandy that is exported throughout the world and advertised extensively in Yerevan. The neon sign on the roof of the distillery announces simply "Ararat," although they recently added a smaller Armenian language sign beneath it. Free tours of this famous distillery are available to those who call ahead to make arrangements. One of the highlights of the tour is their reserve room of 24,000 bottles, some of them a century old. There are no free samples, but visitors are invited to a tasting room where all of the new brandies are available for purchase. Or you can skip the tour and just visit the tasting room and gift shop. Located five minutes by car from the city center, on Admiral Isakov Avenue, directly opposite the large bridge that spans the Hrazdan River. Call for a tour schedule before you visit (Tel. 52-68-91; 54-00-00) (E-mail: inform@ararat.ru).

That large bridge that leads directly to the Yerevan Brandy Company (mentioned above) is **Victory Bridge**. This majestic bridge was completed in 1945 and was named to honor the nation's victory in World War II. Standing on the bridge, you have a great vantage of Mt. Ararat, as well as the Hrazdan River Valley. Several meters from the bridge there is a stairway that descends to the valley floor. There's a roadway along the narrow and shallow Hrazdan River, with several cafes and parks lining the route. In summer, this is Yerevan's greenest and coolest oasis, and it's a popular area for joggers and picnickers.

Tsitsernakaberd, site of the Genocide Memorial, is too far away to include in a walking tour of the city. Visits to this memorial and museum are reverent, and should be made separately. The memorial is outdoors and may be visited at any hour. The memorial consists of twelve massive blocks of stone and an obelisk that stands off to the side. The twelve blocks of stone lean inward and they surround an eternal flame which is recessed in a pit (see photo previous page). These stones represent the provinces of western Armenia that were emptied of their native Armenian population. The obelisk stretches high to the sky in two parts that are separated by a fissure. The obelisk symbolizes the union of western and eastern Armenia.

Tens of thousands of Armenians make a pilgrimage to this memorial each year on April 24, which is a national day of commemoration and mourning. The **Museum of the Armenian Genocide** is located nearby and is open Tuesday through Sunday (Tel. 39-09-81). The memorial and museum are located at Tsitsernakaberd Park, on a hill overlooking the city, just west of the Hrazdan Canyon. Although the Memorial was dedicated back in 1965, the Museum is more recent and was not constructed until 1995. Plans are underway to add a new museum dedicated to the history of the

The Armenians have had a Matenadaran—a book depository—since the fifth century AD. Today's Matenadaran in Yerevan thus has a lineage of 1,600 years. For centuries, scribes have painstakingly created manuscripts that told of religious or historical events, and they lavishly illustrated the pages with their original paintings. Today many of these manuscripts are preserved at the Matenadaran, and scholars at the Matenadaran's Scientific Research Institute study the documents not only for their artistic merit, but also as contemporary accounts of history and of scientific achievements. The manuscripts often serve as primary research for historians.

Scribes often used parchment for these creations, and their sources for inks ranged from dead insects to genuine liquefied gold. The insects—small worms, actually—were pulverized to create a rich red ink. The gold was combined with garlic juice to make it adhere to the page. Some of the qualities and shades of these colors have eluded synthetic duplication, even today.

The oldest of the remnant pages date back to the fifth century, which is perhaps no surprising. After all, the unique Armenian alphabet was developed in AD 405, at right about the same time. The oldest intact manuscript that has survived is a seventh century Gospel. Museum curators mention a collection of historical and scientific work from AD 981 as one of their most significant holdings, however, and they cite the Gospel of Lazarus, from AD 887, as a unique and priceless gem. There has also been an AD 1477 Armenian gospel from Karabagh on display in recent years.

The museum also houses the largest Armenian manuscript in the world—the Homilies of Moush. This 800-year-old manuscript (it was inscribed during the years 1200 to 1202) measures roughly 55 x 70 centimeters and weighs 27.5 kilograms. Its 603 parchment leaves contain a collection of biographies, sermons, and historical passages. The book is divided into two halves that are kept separately. The division of the book into two halves was not done for archival reasons, however. In 1915, after having survived for seven hundred years, it had been cut in two by two women in the village of Moush who were trying to escape the Genocide. The book was too heavy for either woman to carry off alone, so they broke it in two and managed to save it—and themselves—from destruction.

The collection at Yerevan's Matenadaran was originally gathered together in the 19th century at the seat of the Armenian Church in Echmiadzin. These documents were protected, but it's estimated that tens of thousands of rare manuscripts in Turkey were intentionally destroyed by Turkish authorities during the Genocide. The preservation of the Homilies by those two women was an uncommon event.

The surviving Armenian manuscripts remained at Echmiadzin until 1959, when they were moved to their present location. Their modern home in Yerevan is a museum that looks like a giant vault that is built into the side of a hill. The museum is a shrine to the Armenian language and the soul of the nation. A statue of Mesrop Mashtots, the inventor of the Armenian alphabet, and the man who made it all possible, greet visitors at the front entrance. Several khatchkars are displayed here, as well.

Stored deep in vault within the adjoining hill, most of the museum's 14,000 Armenian manuscripts and 2,700 foreign manuscripts have been preserved, and are awaiting further study. The rest, about 200 at any given time, are on display to the public.

Statue of Sasuntsi Davit at Yerevan's Central Train Station

Armenian communities of the Diaspora, and a gallery for art that is related to the Genocide. Officials hope to have everything completed by 2005, in time for the commemorative services honoring the 90th anniversary of the Genocide.

Also too far to walk to, but right on the subway line, is a statue of the legendary hero and leader **Sasuntsi Davit** and the city's major transportation hub for buses and trains. Sasuntsi Davit, also known as David of Sassoun, is a tenth century folk epic hero who fought to defend the Armenian nation against Arab invasions. **Subway**: Sasuntsi Davit station.

On the outskirts of the city are the ancient settlements of **Erebuni** and **Karmir Blur**, each of which comprises an essential part of Yerevan's history. Erebuni is the original settlement of Yerevan, and Yerevan's name is derivative of Erebuni. The excavated ruins and rebuilt segments of the citadel on the Erebuni hilltop are today open to visitors, and there's a museum on the site too. The citadel had been founded by Urartian king Argishti in 782 BC. This was the year of the first Urartian conquest on the east side of the Araks River. The Urartian Kingdom, from which Armenia derives, was centered on Lake Van in eastern Anatolia. **To get there**, (Erebuni), drive south on Tigran Mets Avenue from its starting point on Republic Square. The settlement is just past the train station.

Historians believe that Erebuni was used for about one century, and that its inhabitants then relocated to the nearby Karmir Blur. There is some dispute among historians about the reason for the relocation. One theory is simply that Karmir Blur was considered to be less vulnerable to attack. The English language translation of Karmir Blur is Red Hill, and the settlement takes its name from the red clay on the hill. There really isn't too much to see here now. Very little of this ancient settlement is preserved.

Indeed, very little has been preserved from Yerevan's more recent pre-Soviet days as well. Just one hundred years ago, and before the modernization program that began during Soviet times, Yerevan was just a small town of mud-brick houses set among gardens likewise walled with mud. Practically nothing of this earlier town remains today, except in the neighborhood of Kond, which is wedged between Moskovian Street and Proshian Street. This was an Armenian neighborhood during the Persian era, and today it is a neighborhood that preserves a taste of the city's oriental past. Aside from these precious pockets, Yerevan's architecture is mostly a product of the twentieth century, and the capital of this ancient nation is a modern city.

Pantoon Memorial is located at **Komitas Park** on Arshakuniats Avenue. This reverent site includes the graves of famous writers and artists such as William Saroyan, Aram Khatchadourian, and Sergei Parajanov. Located 2 km south of Republic Square.

NATURE AND CONSERVATION

Nature habitats for people, as well as for birds and other small animals, are inadequate in many urban communities. But when Alexander Tamanian designed the city of Yerevan in 1920, he had the foresight to include a generous expanse of parkland at the perimeter of central Yerevan. This greenbelt, which extends from the Cascade at the north of the city, all the way to the new Cathedral at the southern end of Yerevan, has been an oasis of nature in an otherwise crowded city.

The greenbelt, and many of the city's other parks, has been destroyed in recent years. Public lands have been parceled out for private business purposes. The public response has been mostly limited to shrugged-shoulders. The new business owners are usually those with political connections, according to investigations by news organizations such as Radio Free Europe, and by local journalists and lawyers.

Green zones made up close to 12 percent of the city until 1990. Today, trees cover less than three percent of Yerevan's land, according to the city's environmental groups, and the coverage continues to shrink. For example, at Opera Square in the heart of the city, cafes and discos have displaced nature and public space. The Armenian Forests Coalition, which is a collective of environmental organizations in Yerevan, has protested but to little avail.

Yerevan's chief architect says there will be a new master plan for Yerevan in 2006. The plan designates six forest zones that will supposedly be immune from further so-called "privatization." But there's no plan for recovering the parkland that has already been exploited, or for removing the private businesses that have usurped the open space.

Information about the conservation of Yerevan's parkland is available from groups such as the Yerevan Environmental Association (Tel. 58-55-78) (E-mail: sona@transparency.am). See the Appendix for a list of other environmental organizations in Armenia that are working to conserve Armenia's nature.

Erebuni Reserve was established in 1981 as a nature conservation area. Within the reserve's protected lands are the ancestors of modern wheat—plants that scientists believe to have played a significant role in the development of modern grains. This reserve was established to help preserve the genetic heritage of the region's wild cereals, but it has been criticized for its lack of a buffer zone to limit disruptions of its natural habitat by humans. With an area of only 89 hectars, this reserve is the country's smallest [for more about the ancient wheat of Erebuni, see Chapter 3, Ecology].

MUSEUMS

Major Museums of History

Yerevan's museums have all undergone major renovations and repairs during the past couple of years. They were closed during the construction work, disappointing tourists and residents alike. Today they are now mostly open to the public once again.

Erebuni Fortress Museum, located next to the Erebuni citadel, features Urartian metal crafts and artifacts from the ancient site. 38 Erebuni Avenue. Open 11 am to 4 pm daily. Closed Monday (Tel. 45-82-07)

Matenadaran, features an extraordinary collection of 14,000 ancient Armenian manuscripts of which up to 200 or so are usually on public display. The oldest dates back to the fifth century. This building also houses the Matenadaran Scientific Research Institute, where scholars study the many documents that are not on display. This is certainly Armenia's most significant museum and you would be foolish to miss it. English-speaking guides are available and we recommend that you use one so that your visit will be more meaningful. 53 Mesrop Mashtots Avenue. Open 10 am to 4 pm daily. Closed Sunday and Monday (www.matenadaran.am) (Tel. 58-32-92)

Middle East Museum, micro-museum with carpet weaving display and items of interest about Middle East history. 1 Arami Street, at the corner of Abovian Street. Entrance at the rear of the State History Museum (Tel. 56-36-41)

Museum of the Armenian Genocide, documents the Genocide and honors its victims. The museum building is built into a hillside in a dark, tomblike structure that evokes the unfathomable darkness of this national tragedy. It would be unthinkable to visit Armenia without making a pilgrimage to this hallowed site. Closed on Monday. Tsitsernakaberd Park, near the Genocide Memorial (Tel. 39-09-81)

State Museum of Armenian History, features an archaeological exhibit on the main floor that includes engraved stone crosses, or *khatchkars*, and artifacts from the Stone Age through the medieval period. There are also native costumes, ancient coins, some interesting models of Yerevan and of the Zvartnots Cathedral, and a collection of maps. Of particular interest is a wall-sized map of Van that was hand-drawn in 1920 by the artist and cartographer Martiros Kheranyan. A visit to this museum should be high on your Yerevan itinerary. Open 10 am to 5 pm daily. Closed on Monday. Republic Square between Abovian and Nalbandian Streets (Tel. 58-27-61)

Selected Art Museums

Cafesjian Museum, international collection of modern art. Cafesjian Museum Foundation office, 2 Tamanian Street, Suite 48, modern art (Tel. 54-19-32)

Composer Aram Khachaturian Museum, home of the composer has been preserved as it was when Khachaturian lived here. Museum includes a concert hall. 3 Zaroubian Street. Open 11 am to 4 pm daily. Closed Monday (Tel. 58-94-18)

Hovhannes Tumanian Museum, house museum of the poet and writer. 40 Moskovian Street (Tel. 56-00-21)

Yerevan

The statue of Mesrop Mashtots in front of the Matenadaran

Martiros Sarian Museum, features the studio of the famous painter, which has been preserved on the second floor of the museum, and a gallery of his work on the main floor. 3 Sarian Street. Open 11 am to 4 pm daily. Closed Thursday (Tel. 58-17-62)

Modern Art Museum, one of the two leading modern art museums in Yerevan. The other, of course, is the Cafesjian Museum. 7 Mesrop Mashtots Avenue. Open 11 am to 4 pm. Closed Monday (Tel. 53-53-59)

Poet-Writer Yeghishe Charents Museum, home of the poet, who lived and worked here until his arrest during Stalin's purges. Displays feature his works, his studio. 17 Mesrop Mashtots Avenue (Tel. 53-55-94)

Sergei Parajanov Museum, honors the famous movie director. Displays include sketches and materials pertaining to the films that Parajanov directed. Perhaps his most famous was "The Color of Pomegranates." The museum opened shortly after Parajanov's death in 1990, and it has since become one of Yerevan's most popular, with more than 9,400 visitors in 2003. 15/16 Dzoragyugh Street, overlooking the Hrazdan Gorge (Tel. 53-84-73)

State Folk Art Museum, featuring Armenian woodwork, carpets, pottery and more. 64 Abovian Street. Open Noon to 4 pm daily. Closed Monday (Tel. 56-93-83)

Yervand Kochar Museum, paintings and sculptures in an intimate setting. 39/12 Mesrop Mashtots Avenue. Open 11 am to 4 pm daily. Closed Monday (Tel. 58-06-12)

SELECTED PUBLIC ART GALLERIES

Children's Art Gallery of Armenia, original artwork by children. Large windows facing the street allow even passers-by the opportunity to view some of the artwork on display here. 13 Abovian Street, near Tumanian. Open 11 am to 4 pm. Closed Monday (Tel. 52-09-02)

National Art Gallery, the third largest collection in the former Soviet Union, and a rival to the Hermitage. Republic Square, located on the top floors of the State Museum of Armenian History. Open 10 am to 5 pm daily. Closed Monday (Tel. 58-43-12) There are also many privately operated art galleries in Yerevan, where artists sell their work. Two of the larger galleries which are open to the public are the First Floor Gallery, 75 Koghbatsi Street (Tel. 53-37-99) and the National Centre of Aesthetics, 11 Abovian Street (Tel. 52-09-53). An outdoor gallery of paintings is set up each weekend at Sarian Park, near the Opera House.

MUSIC HALLS

Aram Khachaturian Music Hall, 46 Mashtots Avenue (Tel. 56-06-45)
Komitas Chamber Music Hall, 1 Isahakian Street (Tel. 52-67-18)
Municipal Music Hall, 2 Abovian Street (Tel. 58-28-71)
Sports and Concert Complex, Tsitsernakaberd Park (Tel. 39-99-13)

THEATERS

Chamber Theater, 58 Mesrop Mashtots Avenue (Tel. 56-63-78)
Hamazgain Theater, 26 Amirian Street (53-94-15)
Hovhannes Tumanian Puppet Theater, 4 Sayat Nova Avenue (Tel. 56-32-43)
Hrachia Ghaplanian Dramatic Theater, 28 Isahakian Street (Tel. 52-47-23)
Metro Theater, Garegin Njdeh Metro Station
National Opera and Ballet Theater of Armenia, 54 Tumanian Street (58-63-11)
Stanislavsky State Russian Drama Theater, 54 Tumanian Street (Tel. 56-91-99)
State Musical Chamber Theater, Marshall Baghramian Metro Station (Tel. 56-60-70)
State Theater of Musical Comedy, 4 Vazgen Sargsian Street (Tel. 58-01-01)
Yerevan State Chamber Theater, 58 Mesrop Mashtots Avenue (Tel. 56-63-78)

There are, of course, many other cultural opportunities in Yerevan. This listing covers only the major sites that will appeal to most visitors. For additional listings, and for show times for the performing arts, pick up a copy of the Noyan Tapan weekly newspaper or check the current edition of the "Yerevan Guide," which is available at most hotels and gift shops.

SHOPPING

The best places to shop for souvenirs and gifts are the outdoor markets that operate each weekend. The biggest of these is the **Vernissage**, which sets up in the pedestrian mall that starts at Republic Square and runs all the way down to Khandjian Street. Here you will find artisans selling handcrafted backgammon boards, engraved stones, original paintings, woven dolls, and lace, from 10 am until about 4 pm each Saturday and Sunday. Other vendors offer old stamps and coins, samovars, used books and jewelry.

A group of artists have set up a specialty market just for original paintings at **Sarian Park**, which is located just across from Opera Square at the corner of Sayat Nova

Avenue and Mesrop Mashtots Avenue. Every weekend here you'll find a large selection of original oil, acrylic, watercolor, and pastel paintings. Paintings rarely carry a sticker price, so you'll be expected to negotiate for each purchase. The artists are of uneven abilities, but some of the work is outstanding.

For a more traditional shopping experience, there are several gift shops throughout the city offering souvenirs and carpets, generally at fixed prices. Try Gabeh Carpet Shop, 28 Moskovian Street (Tel. 52-13-18) (E-mail: gabeh_am@yahoo.com). Other shops that specialize primarily in carpets are located on Amirian Street near the Armenia Marriott, and also on Tumanian and Abovian Streets.

Some of the better shops are: Armenian Souvenirs, tourist gift shop. 14 Abovian Street (Tel. 56-45-73); **Gor Souvenirs and Art Works**, hand crafted gifts and original sculptures. 28 Moskovian Street (Tel. 52-32-50). **Salon of Souvenirs**, hand crafted gifts, locally owned. 6 Tamanian Street near the Cascade (Tel. 52-52-61) and also at 3 Arami Street at the intersection with Abovian Street in the Sil Plaza (Tel. 52-20-69) (E-mail: barev@acc.am); **Salt Sack**, hand crafted gifts and souvenirs. 3/1 Abovian Street near Republic Square (Tel. 56-89-31); **Sharan Crafts Center**, handcrafted gift items. 57 Arshakunyats Street, south of French Embassy (Tel. 09-40-13-76); **Stone Gallery**, hand crafted items made from indigenous stones and minerals. 10 Abovian Street, next to the Geological Museum (Open 11 am to 4 pm. Closed Monday) (Tel. 56-45-04).

Made in Armenia Direct Gift Shop is located in the Marriott Hotel Armenia. If you return home having forgotten to buy any souvenirs, you can purchase Armenia-made crafts by mail order from this US-based company (Internet: www.MadeInArmeniaDirect.com) (Tel. 866-381-6423).

Collectible souvenir coins of Armenia are available from **Hushadram Shop**, 3 Vazgen Sargsian Street, near HSBC (Tel. 01-56-36). Collectible postage stamps of Armenia are available from **Namakaneesh**. Located at 43 Mesrop Mashtots Avenue, near the Matenadaran.

For movies on videotape and DVD, for audio CDs and for computer software, there are several stores that come and go on Abovian Street, Mesrop Mashtots Avenue and throughout the center of the city. You'll frequently find traditional and modern music from Armenian and Russian artists for as little as 1,000 dram (about $2) for each CD. Computer software, some of it in English, is also available for as little as $10, and the DVDs are about $5. Most of these items are obviously bootlegged, and you should purchase them at your own risk. We have not been able to locate vendors who offer non-bootlegged discs.

If you want to experience shopping the way the many locals do, check out the daily outdoor market near the Hrazdan stadium. Most of the vendors offer inexpensive clothing, but there are some electronics and kitchen appliances for sale, too. There's also an indoor bazaar that sells clothing on the top floor of the Hayastan Market. The market is located at the top of Baghramian Avenue near the intersection with Kievian Street, at the Barekamutiun metro stop.

Several boutiques and specialty shops have opened in recent years, selling Levi's jeans, famous brands of sneakers, designer fashions and cosmetics. There's even a

Hugo Boss boutique now. Many of these stores are located along fashionable Abovian Street and Mesrop Mashtots Avenue, which are the primary retail strips. Prices at most of these stores are higher than one would pay in the US, and the selection is usually quite limited.

Specialty stores selling Armenian brandy seem to have popped up everywhere. Beware, because some retailers may offer counterfeited brands, whether knowingly or unknowingly. You can avoid this problem by shopping at an outlet authorized by the Ararat Brandy factory. One of the larger outlets, and one which has been in business for several years, is the **Yerevan Brandy Company Shop**, located at 45 Mesrop Mashtots Avenue, just north of Isahakian Street and close to the Matenadaran (Tel. 56-59-94). A distributor of the Yerevan Brandy Factory, the Agulis Brandy Shop, is located at 29 Mesrop Mashtots Avenue (Tel. 53-11-01).

ENTERTAINMENT

Yerevan's two movie houses show mostly Russian language films, but English language films are sometimes shown, too. **Nairi Cinema**, 50 Mesrop Mashtots Avenue, offers English language films on most Saturday nights. Call on Saturday afternoon to learn what that night's film will be— the film is usually not known until the day it's shown (Tel. 54-28-29); **Moscow Theater**, 18 Abovian Street, usually has American movies dubbed in Russian (Tel. 52-12-10).

For live classical entertainment, check with the box office at the Opera House, which is located at the Opera Square. There you will learn about scheduled performances of the **Yerevan Ballet Company** and the **Armenian Philharmonic Orchestra**. The ballet company performs on Sundays, as does the symphony orchestra. The **National Chamber Orchestra** performs at the Komitas Chamber Music Hall, located at 1 Isahakian Street (Tel. 52-67-80).

Jazz is popular in the city, and you'll find an abundance of bars and cafes that offer live performances. Some of the more popular spots include: Crystal Bar and Café, 24 Sayat Nova Avenue; Luxor Café and Crystal Bar and Café, which are both located just across the street; and the Paplavok Jazz Café, in the park near the corner of Abovian and Moskovian Streets. Lady Blues, on Amirian Street near Republic Square, offers live entertainment from 8 pm to midnight every night.

Folk music and the music of the Armenian duduk are also popular. The duduk is a double-reed woodwind instrument which is carved from Apricot wood. Performances are often scheduled at the **Komitas Chamber Music Hall**, 1 Isahakian Street (Tel. 52-67-30) and at the **Aram Khachaturian Music Hall**, 46 Mesrop Mashtots Ave (Tel. 56-06-45). Call for current schedules, or check the current edition of the "Yerevan Guide," which is available at most hotels and gift shops.

Dance clubs come and go with regularity, but one that has survived for several years is the Relax Dance Club, 31 Moskovian Street (no cover, couples only)(Tel. 53-21-72). If you would rather watch others dance, try the Omega Club, on Terian Street near Sayat Nova Avenue. They offer 'R' rated dance performances and a full bar. There's usually a cover charge (Tel. 58-25-49; 52-79-93). Pioneer Club, 2 Baghramian Avenue, also offers risqué dance performances (Tel. 58-18-19), as does Charlotte Cabaret, 25 Baghramian Avenue, across from the British Embassy (Tel. 27-70-20).

A young man rows a boat in the lake at Victory Park, Yerevan

Gambling casinos are now restricted to a zone at a distance of several kilometers outside the city center. You'll see Yerevan's version of the Vegas Strip just outside the prohibited zone, on the Admiral Isakov Highway—the road that goes out to the airport. Most of these casinos are limited to a small room with slot machines that accept only tokens and pay out tiny jackpots. Larger halls may also offer card games and roulette.

The Khagheri Ashkhar **Video Arcade**, on Abovian Street between Sayat Nova Avenue and Moskovian Street, has a large selection of games. Tokens are sold for 100 dram (about 20 cents) each.

SPORTS AND RECREATION

Athletic facilities in the capital and throughout Armenia are limited, and many are in poor condition. The reason is not a lack of interest but rather a lack of funding. In recent years, many new opportunities have become available for visitors in Yerevan, including these indoor activities:

Bowling is available at the Arena Bowling Center in central Yerevan. Genuine duck-pin bowling, five lanes, 24 hours, for 12,000 dram (about $24) per hour, with discounted rates on weekdays. 8 Mesrop Mashtots Avenue (next to the Blue Mosque) (Tel. 53-61-01); There's a larger and slightly less expensive 24-hour facility at the aptly named "Bowling Center" just outside the city center at 18 Halabyan Street (after the Kievian Street Bridge) (Tel. 39-36-37); **Target Practice**, at the Tasits Tas ("Ten out of Ten") Shooting Range. Target practice with real weapons. Yeghvard Highway, in the north end of the city (Tel. 36-10-10); **Weightlifting and Aerobics**, at DDD Sports

Club, 1,400 drams (less than $3) per visit. 54B Komitas Street (Tel. 23-70-40); **Weightlifting and Swimming**, at the Hotel Yerevan Sports Center, weightlifting and aerobics, rooftop swimming pool. $80-$140 per month. 14 Abovian Street (Tel. 58-94-00; Fax 56-46-77) (E-mail: yerhot@arminco.com) (Internet: www.hotelyerevan.com); and also at the Congress Hotel Sports Center for $80-$140 per month. 1 Italia Street (Tel. 58-00-95; Fax 52-22-24) (E-mail: congress@arminco.com) (Internet: www.congresshotelyerevan.com); **Swimming** is available indoors, and at limited times, at the International Committee for the Red Cross. Limited public access to a modest exercise room, gym, and sauna, as well. Located on the Ashtarak Highway, just across the road from the new driving range (listed below).

There are many seasonal activities at outdoor facilities, as well:

Rooftop Swimming, at the Hotel Yerevan. This rooftop swimming pool and sun-deck is the best rooftop swimming pool and sundeck in the entire country. Daily admission about $15, monthly membership fee about $80. 14 Abovian Street (Tel. 58-94-00; Fax 56-46-77) (E-mail: yerhot@arminco.com) (Internet: www.hotelyerevan.com). Outdoor swimming is also available at the Congress Hotel for similar daily or monthly membership fees (Tel. 58-00-95); **Water Amusement Park**, at Water World offers swimming and water sports at its vast outdoor park. In addition to the main pool, this Western-style facility offers water slides, a separate wading pool for children, beach chairs, showers, and a pavilion where live entertainment is sometimes scheduled. Admission prices are determined by one's height, but figure 6,000 dram (about $12) for an adult, 1,500 dram ($3) for a child, and free for toddlers. Located five minutes by car from central Yerevan, on Miasnikian Avenue, also known as the Nork roadway. Seasonal. Open 11 am to 7 pm (Tel. 63-34-30; 64-97-30) (E-mail: valensia@acc.am) (Internet: www.accc.am).

Miniature Golf and Chip and Putt Golf, at the Ararat Valley International Golf Course. Facilities include a 150-meter driving range. Long-term plans call for a par-3 nine-hole course, and two tennis courts, as well as an upscale suburban US style housing development [see "Apartments and Homes," below, for more about the housing development]. This is the only known golf facility in the Caucasus, and it has a spectacular view of Mt. Ararat. Located ten minutes by car from central Yerevan, on the Ashtarak Highway.

Tennis courts are available for hourly rental at the Ararat Tennis Club, located at 2 Alek Manukian Street near Nalbandian Street, in the park across from Yerevan State University (Tel. 55-56-30) and also at the Hrazdan Tennis Club, near the Genocide Memorial (Tel. 56-56-65). There's also a sport center located near the soccer stadium at the city's edge, where courts and playing fields are sometimes available to the public. **Table tennis** and **Billiards** are available outdoors at parks throughout the city, from private vendors who rent tables by the hour. "American-style" **pool tables** are available for hourly rental at the Arena Bowling Center, 8 Mesrop Mashtots Avenue (Tel. 53-61-01).

Horseback riding is available at the Ayrudzy Riding Club at their stables in Ashtarak, which is located about 20 minutes outside Yerevan. In addition to riding classes, the club offers excursions throughout Armenia on their purebred and trained Arabian horses. Arrangements can be made at their central Yerevan office.

21 Paronian Street (Tel. 42-45-70; Fax 58-36-30) (E-mail: ayrudzy@ayrudzy.am) (Internet: www.ayrudzy.am). Their stables are located at 3 Bagratouni Street in Ashtarak (Tel. 032 + 3-46-28).

If all of this sporting activity results in routine muscle aches and pains, you can get a sixty-minute **therapeutic massage** for 8,000 dram (about $16) from Christa-life Massage, 54 Pushkin Street (Tel. 53-65-25); for a massage of 20 minutes for 2,500 drams (about $5) try the masseuse at the DDD Sports Club, 54B Komitas Street (Tel. 23-70-40). There are also several locations throughout the city where you can rent a private sauna by the hour.

CHILDREN'S ACTIVITIES

For children, the best **playgrounds** and carnival style kiddie rides are available at the Hrazdan Canyon Park, at Victory Park, and at the Carnival near the new Cathedral. The park at the Hrazdan Canyon can be reached by a road opposite the Hotel Dvin, or through a tunnel that passes under Sarian Street, at the main post office. The cooling effect of the Hrazdan River makes this a great place to escape the heat of the city. It's also popular with early morning joggers. During the summer, an amusement-park-style tour mobile carries passengers from the Malibu Café on Mesrop Mashtots Avenue, through the tunnel and into the children's park in the Hrazdan Canyon. The fare is 100 dram (roughly 20 cents).

Victory Park, however, offers more amenities. The playground there is Yerevan's biggest, and has a Ferris wheel, bumper cars, rowboat rentals and slow rides for children. Victory Park is located near the top of the Cascade on the hilltop overlooking the central city. The park is also home to the statue of Mother Armenia, and it offers great views of the city.

There are also many carnival rides in the park that is next to the new Cathedral of St. Gregory the Illuminator, southeast of Republic Square at the corner of Tigran Mets Avenue and Khandjian Street. There's no Ferris Wheel, but the bumper cars are the best in Yerevan and the rides are just a short walk from the subway or from Republic Square. There's also a hamburger joint nearby—Yerevan's closest facsimile to McDonald's. **Subway:** Zoravar Andranik (Commander Andranik) metro station.

The outdoor swimming pool at the Congress Hotel includes a wading area that is suitable for younger children. The Water World complex also has pools for youth of all ages [see listings above at "Sports and Recreation" for further details].

Children may enjoy watching performances at the **State Puppet Theater** (4 Sayat Nova Avenue, Tel. 56-32-43). Go-Karts and Paintball are featured at Fast Kart. 35 Acharian Street (Tel. 28-82-77) (E-mail: fkart@arminco.com); and there is miniature golf at the Ararat Valley International Golf Course, and bowling [see listing above at "Sports and Recreation" for further details]. A video arcade is located on middle Abovian Street (between Sayat Nova Avenue and Moskovian Street).

For educational children's activities, the **Botanical Gardens**, located on the Nork roadway near Water World is a worthwhile stop. The **National Zoo**, which is located just a little closer to the city center, but on the same road, should be avoided, however. It is really more of a prison for most of the animals—especially for the caged lions and the bears that beg for bagels—than it is a zoological park.

HOTELS AND PLACES TO STAY

Many of Yerevan's hotels still do not accept credit cards, so you would be wise to inquire in advance. Hotels listed here have both electricity and hot water 24 hours per day, and their prices include the government's 20 percent VAT, unless stated otherwise. These are the city's major hotels, categorized according to price and level of service, and then listed alphabetically within each category. Room prices are listed as a guide only, and are not guaranteed. Rates may be higher during the high season. Prices are listed in US dollars for those hotels that quote US dollars when advertising their rates. Otherwise, prices are listed in Armenian drams.

High End Hotels ($100 and up)

The high end hotels listed below offer business centers with telephone, fax, photocopying and internet services. The prices at these business centers are usually much more expensive than the prices that are charged at the post office, internet cafes, and at many other privately owned locations.

Armenia Marriott, which until late 2003 was known as the Hotel Armenia, faces Republic Square in the heart of the city. The hotel operates 115 rooms. Amenities: private bath, air conditioning, satellite television and phone in each room. Renovated rooms have queen size beds. In-room high-speed internet available. Facilities include two restaurants, café, bar, health club and business services. Double $175. MasterCard/Visa/Amex. Includes breakfast buffet. Handicapped accessible. Frequent flyer miles awarded. 1 Amirian Street, at Republic Square (Tel. 59-90-00; Fax 59-90-01) (E-mail: armenia.marriott@hotelmail.r.am) (Internet: www.marriotthotels.com/EVNMC).

A child playing at Republic Square, Yerevan

Astafian Hotel is luxuriously appointed, although with a décor that is a bit nouveau riche. There are only 10 rooms, but they're massive suites that are designed for entertaining guests. One even has a large boardroom style table and a china-filled cabinet. Amenities: private bath, air conditioning, café, bar, health club. More than half the hotel is devoted to a dance club and banquet facility, and the atmosphere is geared toward adults rather than families. Suite $120-150. No credit cards. No handicapped access. 5/1 Abovian Street, across from the Yerevan Hotel (Tel. 52-11-11; Fax 56-45-72) (E-mail: astafian@netsys.am) (Internet: www.astafian.com).

Avan Villa Yerevan offers 14 designer-rooms located high above the city center in a residential neighborhood. The luxury accommodations are designed to pamper guests with all of the traditional Western amenities, while also providing traditional Armenian décor. Amenities: private baths, fitness and business centers, air conditioning. Single $105; Double $125; Suite $162. MasterCard/Visa. No handicapped access. 13 Nork St, Building 16 (Tel. 54-78-77; Fax 54-78-88) (E-mail: hotels@tufenkian.am) (www.tufenkian.am).

Metropol has reduced its rates and is no longer expensive, while remaining quite luxurious. Its location near the Cognac factory isn't the best, but views of Mt. Ararat from this 40-room hotel compensate for the location. Amenities: private bath, air conditioning, mini-bar, telephone, satellite television in each room. There's also in-room coffee and tea, and in-room internet access. Facilities include indoor swimming pool, sauna, jacuzzi, restaurant, bar, conference rooms, underground parking garage. Single $110; Double $125. MasterCard/Visa/Amex. No handicapped access. 2/2 Mashtots Avenue (Tel. 54-37-01; Fax 54-37-02) (E-mail: information@metropol.am) (Internet: www.metropol.am).

Yerevan Hotel is one of Armenia's finest but priciest hotels. There are 104 rooms, many of them fairly small, and 20 spacious suites. This is a good hotel to select if you want an overpriced room in a great location that has no view. Amenities: private bath (no tubs), air conditioning, satellite television and phone in each room. Facilities include a spacious atrium lobby and lounge, as well as an (excellent) Italian restaurant, bar, exercise room, business services, and the best rooftop swimming pool and sundeck in the country. If you're not a hotel guest, you can use the swimming pool for a monthly membership fee of about $90, which is a fair price for this rare commodity. Single $180; Double $240; Suites as high as $700. MasterCard/Visa. Handicapped accessible. 14 Abovian Street, in the heart of the city (Tel. 58-94-00; Fax 56-46-77) (E-mail: yerhot@arminco.com) (Internet: www.hotelyerevan.com).

Moderate Hotels (Less than $100)

Ani Plaza Hotel had operated for years as the dismal Hotel Ani. A major renovation made it acceptable to Westerners, and its management has made it a good value, as well. Amenities: private bath (no tubs), air conditioning, satellite television and phone in each room. In-room high-speed internet available. Facilities include a comfortable lobby with a lounge, gift shop and travel agency, as well as business services. The travel agency can also help you find a short-term or long-term apartment. Economy Single $90; Deluxe Double $145. MasterCard/Visa/Amex. Includes breakfast. No handicapped access. 19 Sayat Nova Avenue, at the corner of Abovian Street in the city center (Tel. 59-95-00; Fax 56-53-43) (E-mail: info@anihotel.com) (Internet: www.anihotel.com).

Ararat Hotel is a bit far from the action, just beyond Republic Square at the southern edge of the city-center. This newly opened (2002) hotel is convenient to the French Embassy. Fifty-two modern rooms. Amenities: private bath, air conditioning, mini-bar, satellite television and phone in each room. Facilities include a business center, swimming pool, and an atrium lobby. Single $85; Double $100; Presidential Suite $900. MasterCard/Visa/Amex. 7 Grigor Lusavorich Street (Tel. 54-11-00; Fax 54-11-01) (E-mail: info@ararathotel.am) (Internet: www.ararathotel.am).

Arma Hotel is located on a hillside above the city in a quiet neighborhood. 34 rooms. Amenities: private bath, air conditioning, cable television and phone in each room. Facilities include exercise room, swimming pool. Single $70; Double $110. MasterCard/Visa/Amex. Includes breakfast. No handicapped access. 275 Nork Ayginer Street (Tel. 54-60-00; Fax 54-41-66) (E-mail: hotel@arma.am) (Internet: www.arma.am).

Hotel Aviatrans is new and clean, but a bit dark in mood. Amenities: private bath, air conditioning, satellite television and phone in each room. Single $75; Double $75 to $140. Includes breakfast. Handicapped access: one step to main lobby, elevator to all floors. Abovian Street, just steps from Republic Square (Tel. 56-72-26; 56-72-28; Fax 52-22-24) (E-mail: hotel@arminco.com).

Hotel Bass was the first of the new hotels to open in Yerevan. In just a few years it has earned a solid reputation for service and comfort, and it has become a favorite choice among people traveling on business for the US government. The hotel is small, with only 14 rooms, but the rooms are spacious. Amenities: private bath, air conditioning, satellite television for an extra fee, and telephone in each room. Facilities include restaurant, bar, sauna and business services. Single $70; Double $90. MasterCard/Visa/Amex. Includes full breakfast. No handicapped access. 3 Aigedzor Street, just off Proshian Street (Tel. 26-10-80; 22-13-53) (E-mail: bass@lans.am) (Internet: www.bass.am).

Congress Hotel is a clean and modern four-star facility with 126 rooms. Amenities: private bath, air conditioning, satellite television, and phone in each room. Facilities include an outstanding Italian restaurant, a bar, the best and largest outdoor swimming pool of any hotel in Armenia, and a fitness center. If you're not a hotel guest, you can use the swimming pool for a monthly membership fee of about $90. Single $95; Double $125. MasterCard/Visa. No handicapped access. Located just south of Republic Square, not too far from the French Embassy, at 1 Italia Street (Tel. 58-00-95; Fax 52-22-24) (E-mail: congress@arminco.com) (Internet: www.congresshotelyerevan.com).

Europe Hotel boasts that its rooms are built to French specifications. This modern 47-room hotel is located on a quiet street between Republic Square and the new cathedral. Opened Summer 2003. Amenities: private bath, air conditioning, mini-bar, satellite television included, internet access, and phone in each room. Facilities include restaurant and piano bar. Single $70; Double $85. MasterCard/Visa. Includes breakfast. No handicapped access. 32 Hanrapetutyan Street (Tel. 54-60-60; Fax 54-60-50) (E-mail: europhtl@arminco.com) (Internet: www.europehotel.am).

Hotel Olympia is located at the edge of the Hrazdan River Canyon, and it boasts of its views. In addition to the hotel's 12 rooms, there are also suites and apartments. Facilities include a restaurant and an outdoor cafe. Single $50; Double $70.

No credit cards. No handicapped access. Located near the Kievyan Bridge at 56 Barbus Street (Tel. 27-18-50; Fax 27-18-26) (E-mail: manager@olympia.am) (Internet: www.olympia.am).

Hotel Sil is located in a commercial zone just outside the center of the city. The location is not ideal, but the extravagantly appointed rooms, all at reasonable rates, are an appropriate consolation. Amenities: modern bath (no tubs), remote controlled air conditioning, television, phone, terry bathrobes. Facilities include a tiny spa-like swimming pool in the basement, sauna, exercise room, and a restaurant. Single $80; Double $94; Deluxe $150. No credit cards. Includes breakfast. Handicapped access: several steps to main lobby, but elevator to all floors. 20 Tigran Mets Avenue, near the outdoor markets (Tel. 54-07-08; 54-07-09; Fax 54-50-00) (E-mail: silhtl@arminco.com) (Internet: www.sil.am/hotel/index.htm).

Hy Business Hotel attracts business travelers with its emphasis on business services such as rooms with large desks, reading chairs and Internet access. Its suites with kitchenettes are convenient for families with children. Amenities: fully applianced kitchen, large desk, and a separate bedroom with private bath, air conditioning, cable television and phone. Single $75; Deluxe $90. Villa $130. No credit cards. Handicapped access: stairs to all rooms, no elevators. 8 Hanrapetutian Street (Tel. 56-75-67; Fax 54-31-31) (E-mail: hybus@arminco.com) (Internet: www.hybusiness.com).

Valensia Hotel is located at the Water World complex, near the Nork district of Yerevan. Facilities include 58 standard rooms and cottages and a view that overlooks Water World. Single $70; Double $100. No credit cards. Breakfast included. 40 Miasnikian Avenue (Tel. 52-40-00; 54-35-73) (Fax: 54-35-71) (E-mail: valensiahotel@valensiahotel.com) (Internet: www.valensiahotel.com).

Budget Hotels ($50 and less)

Areg Guesthouse, Single $24; Double $34. No credit cards. 80 Burnazian Street (Tel. 45-62-13; Fax 45-61-27) (E-mail: anazo@web.am) (Internet: www.areg.am)

Crown Hotel, Single $35. No credit cards. 8 Abovian Street, near Republic Square (Tel. 58-98-79)

Erebuni Hotel, Single $28; Double $40. No credit cards. Breakfast included. No handicapped access. 26 Nalbandian Street, behind Republic Square (Tel. 56-49-93; Fax 54-43-23)

Hotel Hrazdan, Single $50; Double $100. No credit cards. Handicapped accessible. 72 Dzorapi Street, just off Paronian Street and astride the Hrazdan Canyon. (Tel. 53-53-32; Fax 53-84-28) (E-mail: hrazdan@aviatrans.am) (Internet: www.aviatrans.am)

Senior Hotel, Double $40. No credit cards. No handicapped access. 26 Vazgen Sargsian Street (Tel. 54-15-55; Fax 52-56-84)

Shirak Hotel, Single $30. No credit cards. No handicapped access, but there is an elevator. Hot water twice each day. 13 Movses Khorenatsi Street, one block south of Republic Square. (Tel. 52-99-15; Fax 58-35-93) (E-mail: shirak_hotel@infocom.am) (Internet: www.shirak-hotel.am)

Yerevan

Guest Houses

Yerevan State University Guest House offers dormitory-style lodging with no frills. Each room has as many as five beds, each of which is rented out individually for about $20. 52 Mashtots Street, in the center of the city (Tel. 56-00-03) (E-mail: pr-int@ysu.am)

For an excellent value try the small housing compound on the grounds of the **International Committee for the Red Cross (ICRC) Hospital**. The location just outside Yerevan on the Yerevan-to-Ashtarak highway is inconvenient, and you'll need a driver or a taxi for everything. But the accommodations are modern and European, and fairly priced. Studio $18; 2-bedroom $30. Also available by the month for short-term rentals starting at $150 monthly (Tel. 34-23-49; 35-32-97) (E-mail: archotel@freenet.am)

Apartments and Homes

Apartments are available to visitors for both short and long term rentals. Rates typically are as low as about $20 each night for an apartment with two or three rooms. Electricity is generally included in the rental, but if there's a satellite television you will be expected to pay for the service. The quality of the apartments varies widely. Many will not have 24-hour supplies of water, and air conditioning is unlikely. Usually no handicapped access. The elevators in many buildings are broken, and those that have been repaired are generally located at the top of at least one-half flight of stairs.

Many local travel agents can help you locate a suitable apartment. For assistance, try: Odette Aghabegians of **Menua Tours** (Tel. 52-73-72; Fax 58-39-01) (E-mail: info@menuatours.com) (internet: www.menuatours.com); Sisak Abramian of **Tourism Management** (Tel. 22-41-11; 27-73-44; Fax 27-73-44) (E-mail: sabramyan@hotmail.com) (Internet: www.armasta.am); Gayaneh Madatyan of **Madatyan and Sons Realty** (Tel. 54-46-66) (E-mail: madatian2002@yahoo.com) (Internet: www.mrealty.nt.am); Shakeh Petrossian of **Yerevan Rentals Company** (Tel. 53-11-65) (Internet: www.yerevanrentals.com); and Hyur Service (Tel. 56-04-95) (Internet: www.hyurservice.com).

If you want to buy or rent an apartment, check with Bars Real Estate Agency (Tel. 56-85-89) (Internet: www.realestate.am); or VVP Real Estate (Tel. 58-09-01). Yerevan Apartments is an American-Armenian-owned business that finds and renovates residential properties (Internet: www.yerevanapartments.com). Newly-constructed free-standing homes are offered for sale and timeshare by Hovnanian International (Tel. 39-01-02; Fax 39-97-80) (Internet: www.hovnanianinternational.am).

RESTAURANTS AND PLACES TO EAT

Khorovats, which is a meal of barbequed pork, is certainly the most popular food in Armenia. There's even a street that the locals have dubbed Khorovats Street because there's a *khorovats* stand every few feet. Its real name is Proshian Street, and this is a good place to look for a genuine barbecue dinner, prepared in a local atmosphere. *Khorovats* tastes great, but as with any food that you purchase on the street, you should use care when selecting a vendor, and ask for meat that is cooked thoroughly. **Subway**: Marshal Baghramian Station.

Reservations are neither needed nor accepted in Yerevan. Tipping is catching on, thanks to the Westerners who live or visit here. The norm for good service is about ten percent of the bill, and many restaurants simply add the gratuity onto the check. Dining out is a leisurely activity. You will not be rushed. You won't even get the check, unless you ask for it, even if you sit at your table all night. It would simply be too rude for most servers to encourage you to leave. Of course this doesn't mean that you'll necessarily enjoy prompt or attentive service. The waitress who keeps stopping by your table to ask "how's everything" is not someone you're likely to encounter in Yerevan.

There are plenty of traditional restaurants to choose from and they offer international fare as well as traditional Armenian and Eastern dishes.

Guide to prices: *Very expensive (more than $20 per person); Expensive (approximately $12 to $20 per person); Moderate (approximately $6 to $10 per person); Inexpensive (approximately $5 per person); Very inexpensive (less than $5 per person).*

Traditional Eastern and Armenian

Ararat, Armenian and Near Eastern cuisine. Expensive. Republic Square; **Avan Villa Yerevan**, Western Armenian cuisine. Very expensive. 13 Nork Marash Street (Tel. 54-78-88); **Dolmama**, Armenian cuisine. Excellent food, popular with foreigners. Very expensive. 10 Pushkin Street, near Abovian Street (Tel. 56-13-54); **Eastern Cuisine**, indoor/outdoor seating. Kebobs, spas (yogurt-based soup that is served hot) and eastern entrees. Local clientele. Inexpensive. 16 Komitas Street; (Tel. 27-16-20); **Lagonid Middle Eastern Cuisine**, Hummus, taboule, full meals. 37 Nalbandian Street (Tel. 58-49-93); **Lebanese Cuisine**, Lebanese and Arabic cuisine. Lahmahjoun, kebobs. Inexpensive. 8 Khordarani Street (Tel. 58-42-32); **Old Yerevan Tavern**, Armenian cuisine. Entrees include kuftas, dolmas and kebobs. Live entertainment. Moderately priced. 23 Tumanian Street; **Our Village** (Mer Gyoogh), Village ambience and music. Home-cooked food. Moderately priced. 5 Sayat Nova Avenue (Tel. 54-87-00); **Shahrazad**, Arabic cuisine. Hummus, taboule. Inexpensive. 5 Amirian Street.

International

AMERICAN: Marriott Armenia offers a Sunday brunch buffet that will make you feel as if you are back in the States. Expensive, 1 Amirian Street at Republic Square (Tel. 59-92-48); **Mr. Toaster Sandwich House**, American-style hot oven grinders and authentic American-style pizza. Inexpensive, 25 Koryun Street, near the Matenadaran (Tel. 56-64-44).

BULGARIAN: City Restaurant, limited menu of Bulgarian cuisine, plus other European fare. Inexpensive. 34 Mesrop Mashtots Avenue (Tel. 53-50-01)

CHINESE: Lotus Restaurant, moderately priced. 33 Sayat Nova Avenue (Tel. 52-24-63); **Great Wall Restaurant**, moderately priced. Prossian Street, near Baghramian Avenue (Tel. 26-10-07).

GEORGIAN: Old Tbilisi Restaurant, traditional Georgian cuisine such as Hinkali and Khatchapouri. Inexpensive. 7 Alek Manukyan Street, near the intersection of Sayat Nova Avenue and Khandjian Street, not far from Yerevan State University (Tel. 57-33-44); **Caucasus Tavern**, traditional Georgian cuisine. Moderately priced. Accepts credit cards. 82 Hanrapetutyan Street (Tel. 56-11-77).

FRENCH: Monte Christo, French-Levantine cuisine. Expensive. 20 Vazgen Sargsian Street (Tel. 54-50-07)

INDIAN: Hindakastan, Traditional Indian cuisine. Expensive. 23 Komitas Avenue (Tel. 22-72-20)

ITALIAN: Al Leoni, Gourmet Italian entrees, cappuccino. Upscale and expensive. 40 Tumanian Street (Tel. 53-83-31); **Cucina** (at the Marriott Armenia Hotel). Genuine Italian-style pizza and pasta. Moderately priced. Republic Square (Tel. 59-90-00); **Hotel Yerevan**, Fine Italian cuisine. Expensive but worth it. 14 Abovian Street (Tel. 58-94-00); **Pizza Di Roma** and **Diamond Style Restaurant**, Armenian-style pizza. Inexpensive. 1 Abovian Street near Republic Square (Tel. 58-7-0-54); **Raffaello's Restaurant** (at the Congress Hotel), fine Italian cuisine. Upscale and moderate to expensively priced. 1 Italia Street (Tel. 58-00-95).

MEXICAN: Cactus, Armenia's best Mexican restaurant. Tex-Mex menu, semi-frozen margaritas. 42 Mesrop Mashtots Avenue. Moderately priced (Tel. 53-99-39)

THAI: Mark's Thai Cuisine, traditional Thai food. Inexpensive. Proshian Street, near Baghramian Avenue

OTHERS: Phoenicia Restaurant, varied menu. Very expensive. Not worth it. 3 Tamanian Street (Tel. 56-18-94); **Sayat Nova**, its full restaurant menu includes fondue. Inexpensive. 33 Sayat Nova Avenue (Tel. 58-00-33)

Fast Food

Armenian Pizza, genuine Armenian food. Lahmajoun, Qufta. Very inexpensive, fast. 21/1 Tumanian Street, near Abovian Street (Tel. 58-01-06); **California Pizza**, an Armenian interpretation of Italian-American pizza. Inexpensive. 21 Abovian Street (Tel. 58-63-95); **Armenian Style Khatchapouri,** Very inexpensive, fast, take-out window only. Lower Abovian Street next to Salt Sack; **Queen Burger**, American-style burgers. Inexpensive. Tigran Mets Avenue, near the new cathedral (Tel. 56-01-22).

None of the Western franchises are here, which makes Armenia one of the few countries in the world where the native cuisine hasn't been pushed aside by Ronald McDonald or the Taco Bell crowd.

Take-out And Delivery

It's now possible to order food for take-out and for delivery to your hotel or apartment in central Yerevan. We've found that orders are usually delivered within about 30 minutes. For home delivery, try: **California Pizza**, 21 Abovian Street (Tel. 54-31-00); **Great Wall Chinese Restaurant**, Prossian (Tel. 26-10-07); **Lotus Chinese Restaurant**, 33 Sayat Nova Avenue (Tel. 52-24-63); **Mr. Toaster Sandwich House**, 25 Koryun Street (Tel. 56-64-44); **SAS Grocery Store**, Mesrop Mashtots Avenue (Tel. 56-33-99); **Southern Fried Chicken Express**, 12 Tigran Mets Avenue (Tel. 52-42-32).

Eating, drinking and toasting, Yerevan

Coffee and Dessert

COFFEEHOUSES: Artbridge Café, 20 Abovian Street, offers espresso, cappuccino, and light meals and sells books and magazines, too (Tel. 52-12-39); **Café de Paris**, 23 Abovian Street, sells gourmet coffee by the kilogram, and Armenian coffee by the cup, at their sidewalk café (Tel. 52-26-48); **Coffee Man**, 28/20 Tumanian Street, offers Irish Coffee and other desert coffees in its basement shop (56-73-24); **Jazzve**, Isahakian Street, across from the Nairi Cinema, serves Armenian style coffee and light snacks; **Lagonid Bistro Cafe**, 37 Nalbandian Street, offers coffee and pastry in addition to its main courses (Tel. 58-49-93); **Yum Yum Donuts**, 40 Mesrop Mashtots Avenue, near the Cascade, and a second shop at the intersection of Marshal Baghramian Avenue and Kievian Street near the Barekamutiun metro stop, offers American-style coffee and donuts. Delivery service available (Tel. 56-19-84).

TEA HOUSES: For English tea, there's **Natura Gold**, 11 Abovian Street, which is an authentic teahouse that sells tea leaves by the kilogram and brewed tea by the pot or cup (Tel. 56-90-91; 58-21-86); **Ronnefeldt Tea House**, 12 Abovian Street, offers gourmet tea by the pot (Tel. 58-06-58); **Thomas Tea** at 22 Abovian Street is a basement teahouse just up the street from Artbridge and Natura Gold, which is popular with young people (Tel. 54-33-30).

PASTRY SHOPS: For take-away pastries, three of the city's best bakeries are **Granatas Bakery** (Tel. 58-37-47); **Sona Bakery** (Tel. 56-08-67), and **Lakomka Bakery** (Tel. 56-05-15). These three independent stores are conveniently located side-by-side in the same building at 49 Mesrop Mashtots Avenue, near the Matenadaran.

GROCERIES

If you're shopping for food to prepare in your hotel room or guesthouse, there is an abundance of small grocery stores to choose from throughout the city. Regardless of where you shop, always check the expiration dates on perishable items. Some of the better choices are:

Anoush, 32 Tumanian Street (Tel. 52-13-01); **Aragast**, open seven days, 24 hours. 1 Tamanian Street near the Cascade (Tel. 58-04-01); **Aroma**, at the corner of Sayat Nova Avenue and Nalbandian Street; **Europe Market**, 4 Vardanants Street, near Nalbandian (Tel. 58-68-08); **Partez**, the first of the Western-style markets, 16 Vagharshian Street, near Komitas Avenue. **Parma**, large selection of Western goods. 79A Baghramian Avenue near the Barekamutiun metro station (Tel. 27-33-60); and SAS, home delivery available, 18 Mesrop Mashtots Avenue near Amirian Street (Tel. 56-33-99).

Two large food markets, known as *shukas*, feature vendors who sell fresh produce, meat, dried fruit, fresh bread and homemade *matsun* (yogurt). There's usually someone selling live chickens and turkeys, too. These markets are still the primary food sources for most local residents, despite the recent arrival of the small Western style grocery stores. The main *shuka*, located at 3A Mesrop Mashtots Avenue, is open 8 am to 6 pm. There's another huge *shuka*, on Tigran Mets Avenue that is thriving and worth a visit even if you're not shopping for anything. Look for it across the street from the Zoravar Andranik (Commander Andranik) metro station, and near the Cathedral of St. Gregory the Illuminator.

The ancient Vardavar water festival is celebrated each year in Armenia. For details, see "Water Festival," p. 47

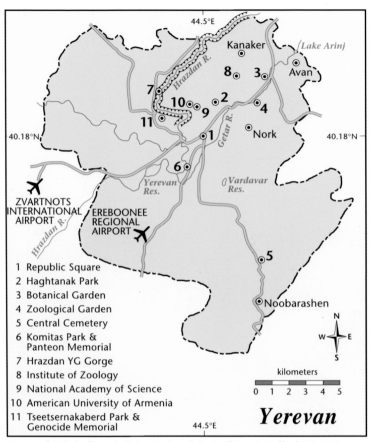

Yerevan

1 Republic Square
2 Haghtanak Park
3 Botanical Garden
4 Zoological Garden
5 Central Cemetery
6 Komitas Park &
   Panteon Memorial
7 Hrazdan YG Gorge
8 Institute of Zoology
9 National Academy of Science
10 American University of Armenia
11 Tseetsernakaberd Park &
   Genocide Memorial

Yerevan

Courtesy of the Birds of Armenia Project, American University of Armenia, Oakland, CA, 1999

CentralArmenia

five

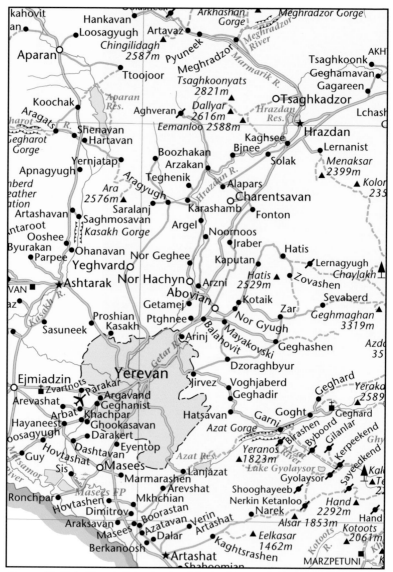

Courtesy of the Birds of Armenia Project, American University of Armenia, Oakland, CA, 1999

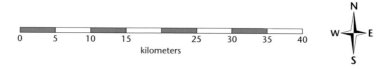

The monasteries have been the pillars of the country, the fortresses against the enemy, and shining stars.

—Nerses the Gracious

INTRODUCTION

Our choice for the most scenic roadway in Armenia is the road that winds its way from Yerevan through Ashtarak and then north to Spitak. The proximity of this road to Yerevan makes this an easy trek that you can complete, round tip, in about three or four hours.

For months on end, the fields along this road are saturated with the yellows, reds, and purples of wild flowers. Mt. Aragats forms the backdrop along the west side of the road, and orchards are common sites along the other. During the summer, this excursion is a quick escape from the heat of Yerevan, but this is also a drive that you'll enjoy in every season.

YEGHVARD, ASHTARAK, MT. ARAGATS AND NORTH OF YEREVAN

Yeghvard

There's a clearly sign-posted (in Armenian) turnoff for the village of Yeghvard, immediately before you reach Ashtarak. In the center of the village there is a two-story-tall tower-like church, **St. Astvatsatsin**, which was built in 1301. There are some other ruins of church buildings nearby, but you'll need to ask the villagers to help you locate them because they are hidden behind the walls of private homes. The village itself is compact and the people here are quite friendly.

Note About Traveling Outside Yerevan

It is difficult to find bottled drinking water for sale outside Yerevan, so when traveling outside the city always take enough bottled water for the entire trip. If you forget, you will probably be able to purchase only warm beer or soda from the roadside vendors, neither of which is appealing on a hot day. Bring food, too. You should always expect that the only thing you'll have to eat on any trip outside Yerevan is whatever you bring with you, or roadside *khorovats* (barbecue). If you purchase vegetables or fruit while traveling, peel them or wash them with bottled water.

There are no super-highways in Armenia, and many of the roads, although in relatively good condition, wind through mountains, or pass through villages, resulting in slow going. Mileage will not always be an accurate indicator of travel time. To guide your travel decisions, we have therefore listed approximate travel times, based on our own experience, for most destinations.

This section treats Yerevan as a launching point for your travels, and lists the nearby regional sights that you can easily see in a day or less, and still return to your hotel or apartment in Yerevan.

Photograph, previous page: Mt. Ararat as seen from the foothills of Mt. Aragats

If you travel northeast of Yeghvard to the village of **Zoravan**, you'll find the ruins of a circular church—only half of the walls remain—off by itself in the center of a large rocky field. You can see **Mt. Ara** in the background and the setting is quite stark. Mt. Ara is named for an Armenian king who, according to legend, was killed and then brought back to life by a queen. From the Yerevan-to-Ashtarak road, the ridge of the mountain supposedly takes the form of the king's nose, arms and body. All that we have been able to discern, even after hiking the entire length of the ridge, however, is a large nose.

If you've got the stomach for it, and a rugged jeep, you can try to continue north of Zoravan all the way to the village of Buzhakan. The village is the site of the **Teghenyats Monastery**, with buildings that date back to the twelfth and thirteenth centuries. There are some interesting tombstones that are shaped like horses.

To get there, from Yerevan take the right turnoff immediately before Ashtarak. There is a signpost in Armenian for Yeghvard. The village of Yeghvard is approximately 9 km from the turnoff.

Travel time from Yerevan to Yeghvard is about thirty minutes. Travel time from Yerevan to Zoravan is about forty-five minutes. Travel time from Zoravan to Buzhakan is another forty-five minutes because of the horrible roads.

Ashtarak

The town of **Ashtarak** is the second stop (after visiting Yeghvard) that you will want to make along this Yerevan-to-Spitak road. Ashtarak is just 20 km north of Yerevan, and is worth a separate visit for all its ancient monuments. From the new double-span bridge that crosses the Kasakh River, and which bypasses the town, you can see three of the town's churches all at once. The most famous is the **Karmravor Church**, which was built in the seventh century. Karmravor is a tiny chapel, and it can accommodate only a few parishioners at a time. The church takes its name from its red tiled roof. The Armenian word for the color red is *karmir*.

Within a two minute walk of Karmravor are the less interesting ruins of **Tsiranavor** and **Spitakavor**. The churches have apparently all been named for the colors that they are associated with. *Tsiran* is the Armenian word for apricot, and *spitak* is the word for white.

Also noteworthy in the center of Ashtarak is the church of **St. Mariane**, which was built in 1281. This church is located just west of Karmravor, and you'll see it in the distance from the Karmravor churchyard. The newly built church of **St. Sargis**, on the top of the gorge, was constructed on the foundation of its ruined predecessor. St. Sargis is even smaller than Karmravor and its shape resembles a rocket on a launch pad.

To get there, from Yerevan take the left turnoff for the Ashtarak exit immediately before the large twin-span bridge that crosses the Kasakh River Gorge. Follow the road down into the center of town.

Travel time from Yerevan to Ashtarak is about thirty minutes. Hire a driver for about $20 for the half day, or combine this visit with stops at Aragats, Amberd and Saghmosavank (which are described below).

The town of **Oshakan**, located just five km south of Ashtarak, is a popular field trip destination for Yerevan school children who have just learned the Armenian alphabet. This is because Mesrop Mashtots, the inventor of the Armenian alphabet, is buried beneath the modern (1875) St. Mesrop Mashtots church here. So every year, teachers take their young pupils here to visit his grave as a way of acknowledging Saint Mesrop Mashtots and celebrating their accomplishment. This is a good side trip after visiting Ashtarak and Karmravor. But it is probably not worth a separate trip.

Farther along the roadway that leads from Yerevan to Spitak, northeast of Ashtarak but still in the Ashtarak region, there are a trio of sites that can be visited in one half day. All three sites are located on the east side of the road, within a 10-kilometer span. Mughni is the first town that you will reach when driving from Ashtarak. Here you will see the fourteenth century monastery of **St. Gevorg**, which is unusual for the stripes that circle the drum of the church, and the checkerboard designs that highlight its gables. The monastery is also quite small by Armenian standards, and has only one church.

Ohanavank is the second of the trio, and is located in the village of Ohanavan. Parts of the monastery date back to the seventh century. The church and hall (gavit) are from the thirteenth century, and the ruins of a fortified wall surround part of the facility. There are also many *khatchkars* in the churchyard, which sits atop the Kasakh River Gorge. St. Gregory the Illuminator is believed to have visited this site with King Trdat, and to have laid the foundation stone. Although the existing structures date only to the seventh century, the monastery is much older. The first chapel of Ohanavank was probably built in the fourth or fifth centuries on the remains of a pagan temple that had been destroyed. A restoration and reconstruction program has been underway for several years.

The most popular of the three sites along this span, however, is **Saghmosavank**. The monastery of Saghmosavank has been called the twin of Ohanavank, and it also stands atop the gorge of the Kasakh River. Saghmosavank is a dramatic example of thirteenth century architecture and its style is considered to be a faithful reflection of significant trends in Armenian art from the Middle Ages. A wall of red volcanic stones encloses most of the monastery, and there are apple orchards nearby. The two surviving churches of the monastery, which were built in 1215 and 1235, were restored in 2001. Services are now held there each Sunday.

To get there, from the Yerevan-to-Spitak highway, drive across the large double-span bridge that crosses the Kasakh River near Ashtarak. The turnoff for Mughni is on the right side of the road immediately after this bridge (hidden between a couple of stores and a gas station) and before the sign-posted turnoffs for Gyumri and Vanadzor.

To reach Ohanavank, from the main highway drive about two km farther north of Mughni, in the direction of Spitak, and take the right turnoff to the village of Ohanavan. Then follow the road downhill toward the gorge until reaching Ohanavank.

To reach Saghmosavank, from the main highway drive about five km farther north of Ohanavan and take the right turnoff at the village of Artashavan. Take the first left and then turn right onto the sign-posted road, which leads straight to the village of Saghmosavank and to the monastery.

Travel time from Yerevan to Saghmosavank is about 35 minutes. Hire a driver for about $20 for the half day. For a full day of touring, combine visits to these churches with a stop at Amberd and Aragats.

Central Armenia

Amberd

Amberd Fortress is located on the slopes of Aragats at roughly 2,300 m. The fort and an adjoining church sit on a promontory that was formed by the steep valleys of the Amberd and Arkhashian rivers. The gorges formed by these two rivers are about 100 m deep, with vertical drops of up to 50 m in places. Historians point to the sharp surfaces of the stones that formed the fortress, and to their black color, as psychological deterrents that abetted the defensive terrain. Still, Mongol invaders conquered Amberd in 1236, and destroyed it. The fort was never rebuilt.

Amberd is believed to have been one of the primary defenses for the perimeter of the Armenian capital of Ani—which is located about 100 km to the west. Historians theorize that no invader would dare penetrate the territory towards Ani and leave behind a well-equipped fort that at any moment could strike at its rear flank by means of quick sorties.

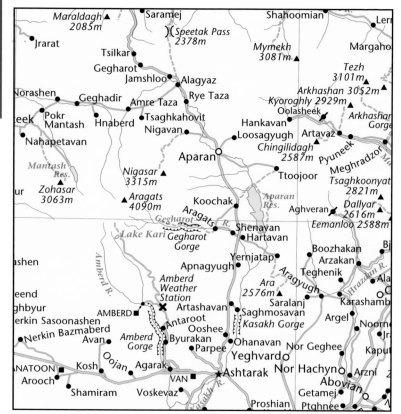

Courtesy of the Birds of Armenia Project, American University of Armenia, Oakland, CA, 1999

Amberd Fortress

The fortress and its adjoining church were probably originally built in the tenth and eleventh centuries, although there is some evidence they may be older. Regardless of their age, they offer magnificent vistas and an example of a fortress that is a contemporary of the golden era of Ani.

To get there, from the main Yerevan-to-Spitak highway, drive past Saghmosavank and take the paved left turnoff, from which you head west toward the mountain. This road is not printed on many maps, but it is the most direct route to Amberd and then to the top of the mountain. At a fork in the road, there is a directional arrow and sign spray-painted on the asphalt road.

Travel Note: it is also possible to drive to Amberd from the south slopes of Aragats, through the village of Byurakan. This alternate route will also arrive at the same fork, with the same spray-painted sign. To use this alternate route, drive across the double span bridge at Ashtarak, but then take the left turnoff (west) that is sign-posted for Gyumri.

Travel time from Yerevan to Amberd is about one hour. Hire a driver for $30 for the half day.

Mt. Aragats

Visits to Mt. Aragats (elevation 4,090 m) are especially rewarding during the summer, when temperatures here can be ten or twenty degrees Fahrenheit cooler than in Yerevan. This is Armenia's tallest mountain, and non-professionals can climb most of it in four or five hours, after first driving to the man-made Lake Kari. This small lake is situated at 3,190 m, next to a weather station and the Cosmic Ray Institute, at the end of the mountain access road.

Hiking shoes and stamina are almost the only essential gear for much of the hike. Weather can change quickly at this altitude, so hikers are advised to start early in the morning, to allow enough time for the return hike. It is also prudent to dress warmly, and to wear a hat and sunscreen to protect from the ultraviolet radiation.

There's snow cover on the mountain's four peaks year-round, and the air is thin, so go slowly. The best time to visit is in the summer when there is the least snow cover. Access roads are usually obstructed by snow until June.

To get there, from the main Yerevan-to-Spitak highway, drive past Saghmosavank and take the paved left turnoff, from which you head west toward the mountain.

Travel time from Yerevan to Amberd, and the rest of the way to Aragats, is about ninety minutes because of all the switchbacks. Hire a driver for $30 for the half day. If you wish to hike at Aragats, plan to spend the entire day there.

Place to Stay

Pine Tree House is a small bed and breakfast lodge located in the village of Byurakan, on the south side of Mt. Aragats and not too far from the Byurakan Observatory. Hot showers and modern baths. Ask proprietor Mary Panian about a horseback riding tour. Single $25. Breakfast included (Tel. 52-16-25).

Place to Eat

Dzor Restaurant is a sprawling outdoor café, located in the canyon along the Kasakh River near the town of Ashtarak. *Khorovats* (barbecue). Live entertainment. Take the turnoff into the canyon immediately before the new double-span bridge at Ashtarak, and follow the (Armenian language) signs.

Aparan

Continuing north roughly 15 km past Saghmosavank along the Yerevan-to-Spitak highway, one reaches Aparan Reservoir. On the drive up, you'll see fields of flowers in bloom in April and May, as well as several apricot orchards. The reservoir is an interesting place for a picnic or for hiking. North of the reservoir, the town of Aparan is perhaps best known for its people, called Aparantsis, who are the object of many jokes told by the people of Yerevan.

Just after passing through Aparan there's a monument at the top of a hill on the left (west) side of the road honoring a 1918 military victory against the invading Turkish army, and field after field of grasslands and wild flowers. Alongside the road there's a tiny Yezidi village named **Rya Taza** which has an old and fascinating cemetery. The Yezidi are an ethnic minority in Armenia, and as is the custom with so many ethnic groups in this part of the world, they have formed a village of their own. The cemetery is located on the right (east) side of the road, and it features tombstones that are shaped like horses and other animals. Beyond Rya Taza, there is nothing of great interest to tourists until reaching Spitak [information about Spitak is included in Chapter 8, Northwest Armenia].

Photograph: Mt. Aragats, 4,090 m

Central Armenia

ARARAT VALLEY AND SOUTH OF YEREVAN

Khor Virap

Khor Virap Monastery is a shrine to Armenian Christianity. The church complex was built atop the pit where St. Gregory the Illuminator had been imprisoned roughly 1,700 years ago for the crime of preaching Christianity. According to the legend, sometime around AD 288, give or take a year, King Trdat III had imprisoned a Christian proselytizer by the name of Gregory. Armenia was a pagan nation at the time, and the king did not appreciate Gregory's disruptive conduct. Gregory languished in his prison pit for 13 years until, upon miraculously curing the king of a loathsome disease, the king freed him and converted Armenia to Christianity. This conversion in AD 301 forever distinguished Armenia as the world's first Christian nation.

Access to the prison pit has been preserved. Today, visitors can descend into the pit through a long and narrow shaft that is accessible from one of the small monastery chapels. The top of the shaft is located on the right side of the chapel's altar. To get to the bottom of the pit you have to climb straight down 27 steps on a metal ladder that has been bolted to the wall of the shaft, so this is not a descent that young children or anyone with claustrophobia will be able to take. There's a separate underground chamber nearby that serves as a chapel, access to which is from another opening in the floor of the same building. The underground chapel is tiny, measuring only about eight feet wide and fifteen feet long, with a low arched ceiling. Access is by a metal ladder, but the climb down is not as long or as difficult as the climb down into St. Gregory's pit.

Although the Khor Virap site is ancient, the large church of **St. Astvatsatsin** dates back only to the seventeenth century. The monastery complex is surrounded by tall walls, and sits atop a small hill in the flat Ararat plain, near the Araks River. This river forms the international boundary between Armenia and Turkey, so you won't be permitted to approach its shallow banks. The monastery gates are closed each day at 5 pm, but this shouldn't deter you from visiting at dusk, when the orange glow of the sun setting behind the monastery and the backdrop of Mt. Ararat combine to make this one of the most spectacular sights in the country. If you visit on a Sunday morning, you may be able to observe church services. This is also the busiest time of the week for the aggressive beggars, most of whom are children, who line the pathway to the monastery.

The hills surrounding Khor Virap are the site of the ancient Armenian capital of Artashat, which was founded by King Artashes I sometime around 180 BC. There are extensive excavations on the hillside located northwest of Khor Virap, and visitors can still find old pottery shards. King Khosrov III moved the Armenian capital to nearby Dvin in AD 330. On a small hill just south of Khor Virap, close to the village of Lusarat, there's a large statue of Gevorg Chavoush, an Armenian war hero. Chavoush was killed by Turks while defending Armenian villagers in western Armenia (eastern Anatolia) in 1907.

To get there, from Yerevan drive south on Arshakuniats Street and then to the Artashat Highway. Shortly after passing through the town of Artashat, there's a signpost for Khor Virap at the village of Pokr Vedi. Turn right onto this paved road and travel through the village until the road ends (about three km). There is no admission fee to the monastery, but you might be asked for 100 dram (twenty cents) for parking.

Khor Virap Monastery at sunset

Dvin remained a cultural capital of Armenia for several centuries, even after having been plundered by Arab conquerors in the seventh century. It is believed to have had a population of 100,000 at its zenith. **To get there**, from the Artashat Highway take the turnoff to the modern village of Dvin, and drive south through the village to the gate of the old capital.

This region is the closest point to Mt. Ararat from within the borders of modern Armenia, and Khor Virap is just about as close as you can get to this mountain without going to Turkey. The view from the Turkish side is actually not as good so enjoy the view while you are in Armenia.

Ararat, of course, is the mountain that snagged the bottom of Noah's ark, and it is the spiritual heart of Armenia. The Armenians make a legendary claim that they are descendants of Noah and so Ararat is central to Armenian self-identity. The mountain is depicted on Armenian currency, its postage stamps, and its peaks adorn the republic's coat of arms. Ararat is the tallest mountain of historic Armenia, at 5,165 m, and it soars in the national consciousness as well. The mountain loomed large when National Geographic magazine published an article about Armenia in its March 2004 edition: "Armenians have been pondering Mount Ararat and its neighbor, Little Ararat, since the birth of civilization," according to their report. In Armenia, the large peak of Ararat is usually identified as **Masis**. The small peak is known as **Sis**.

The **Ararat Valley** is reputed to be the hottest and driest place in Armenia. If you visit during the summer this is an extra incentive to go at sunset, after the hottest part of the day has gone. Go early in the morning if you want to walk inside the Khor Virap compound.

The hot weather is great for the watermelons that are grown here, which farmers sell on the roadside in August and September. If you hesitate about a purchase, the farmer will cut out a core of the fruit to show you how fresh it is! The fertile soil and hot weather here also help produce some of the reddest and juiciest tomatoes that we've ever tasted. Sweet apricots are also grown here in great abundance, as are grapes. This is the largest, richest and most productive agricultural area of the country.

There's a military base nearby, and several watchtowers throughout the valley, which are manned by Russian soldiers, pursuant to a mutual defense treaty between Armenia and the Russian Federation. Don't point your camera at the towers. Photography of the soldiers or of the military stations is forbidden. At the south-ernmost end of the valley, near the frontier with Nakhijevan, there are several **fish farms** where trout are produced. You'll see fish for sale at the roadside here, too. The marshes around these fish farms are great birding locations.

The town of **Surenavan**, which is located near these fish farms, at approximately 55 km from Yerevan, is a major nesting site for cranes. You can see their giant nests at the top of the utility poles throughout the area. There's an interesting little café here along the main highway—the Suren Bistro—which is run by a friend-ly man named Suren. The café has a fantastic view of the mountain, and it is a great place to stop for some coffee and a snack while you're watching the birds.

Just beyond Surenavan and the fish farms is the village of Yeraskh, the last Armenian village before the Nakhijevan border [for more about fish farming, see Chapter 3, Ecology].

Grapes, Ararat Valley

Travel time from Yerevan to Khor Virap and the Ararat Valley is about 45 minutes. Hire a driver for about $20 for a stay lasting a couple of hours. Travel time from Yerevan to Surenavan, at the southern end of the Ararat Valley, is about one hour.

GARNI-GEGHARD AND EAST OF YEREVAN

Garni and Geghard

Garni Temple is located just off the roadway before you reach Geghard, and you should stop here as part of your excursion to this region. The temple was built in the first century AD by an Armenian king, and dedicated to a sun god. The site was probably also used as a summer home by Armenian kings. Today it is the site of the oldest known *khatchkar* extant, dating from AD 879.

The temple was just one of many buildings on this site, which comprised the **Garni Fortress**. The fortress is situated on a triangular cape, two sides of which adjoin a steep gorge. Only the third side required a fortress wall. This wall was reconstruct-ed in 2004 as part of a major restoration of the site. The Garni complex included a palace, bathhouse, servants and guards' residences, a church, and a meeting hall. The remains of the bathhouse have been preserved and a protective shelter and vis-itors' center was recently built around it. There are remnants of stone mosaics on the floor, the theme of which draws upon Greek mythology. Against the light-green background, representing the sea, are inlaid pictures of gods of the Ocean and Sea.

Photograph: Monument to Gevorg Chavoush on a hilltop near Khor Virap.

A Greek inscription over the heads of the gods says "Work and gain nothing," according to the translation written by scholar O. Khalpakhchian in the text "Architectural Ensembles of Armenia." The inscription suggests that the craftsmen had not been adequately paid for their services.

Earthquakes throughout history have ruined the site, most recently in 1679, but the temple building was reconstructed in 1975. There are still many ancient *khatchkars* here, as well as the tile ruins of the King's bathhouse, palace, and a seventh-century church. Comprehensive renovations to the rest of the site—including construction of a new gateway, visitor center and an outbuilding to protect the remnants of the bathhouse—were completed in 2003. The temple overlooks a deep canyon, which is known as Garni Gorge and which offers great hiking. The village of Geghard is compact and interesting, and features a basilica-style church from the twelfth century, just behind one of the main squares.

Geghard Monastery is a fascinating complex of buildings that are built into the side of a mountain, just a bit beyond Garni. This is probably the most popular tourist site in Armenia, after Echmiadzin. The buildings are considered to represent a high point in Armenian Medieval architecture, and UNESCO (the UN Educational, Scientific and Cultural Organization) recognizes the complex on its list of World Heritage sites.

The complex has also been called **Ayrivank**, meaning the Monastery of the Cave, and its surviving buildings date from the thirteenth century. The monastery has been literally carved into the side of the mountain, and more than half of its floor area is located within the mountain itself. Water that seeps into the various cavernous chapels (there are many) through their porous mountain walls is removed in a series of shallow, six-inch wide drains. In one chapel, this drainage system feeds

a shallow pool of water. According to local lore, if a visitor throws a coin into the pool, it ensures that he will return. In addition to the chapels that are located within the mountain, more than 20 rooms have been hewed at various levels into the exterior of the mountainside. Most of them were built as chapels.

The common name Geghard refers to its legendary status as the repository of one of the spears that was associated with the crucifixion of Jesus. Geghard is the Armenian word for spear. The legendary spear is now housed at the museum at the Echmiadzin Cathedral.

There is no architectural evidence on the site, but historians believe, from other sources, that the Monastery of Ayrivank (Geghard) may have been founded as early as AD 300 to 400. Documentary evidence dates the monastery as far back as the seventh century. The main cathedral that survives on the site was built in 1215.

The grounds are home to several magnificent *khatchkars*, and there is frequently a trio of musicians performing folk music in the parking lot, which adds to the magical ambience of this wonderful site. There is no admission fee to Geghard, but foreign visitors to Garni are sometimes charged 200 dram (about forty cents).

To get there, from Yerevan drive north (uphill) on Abovian and then Miasnikian Street. Turn right after passing the Water World amusement park. This road will take you all past the Nork housing complex. At the end of this road, turn left at the "T" intersection. This road dead-ends at Geghard, roughly 40 km from Yerevan.

NATURE AND CONSERVATION

Khosrov Preserve

The Garni Gorge is popular with hikers and it provides a potential access point to the **Khosrov Reserve**, which is home to many endangered plants and animals. Officially, access is prohibited. A cobblestone and gravel road leads down to the gorge from a point not far from the temple. Tall basalt columns stretch upward from the canyon floor.

Khosrov Reserve was established in 1958 and it covers an area of approximately 29,200 hectares (approximately 70,000 acres), which is slightly larger than the area of Dilijan National Park. Khosrov is considered to be one of the most important protected areas in Armenia. There are meadow and mountain-meadow habitats within the reserve, and the area is distinguished by its mountain dry vegetation, semi-desert landscapes, and its unique plant and animal communities [for more about Armenia's nature reserves and specially protected areas, see Chapter 3, Ecology].

Azat Reservoir

On your return trip to Yerevan, stop at **Azat Reservoir**. The lake is west of the main road (on the left if you are returning to Yerevan from Garni) and is a great setting for a picnic with a spectacular view of Mt. Ararat. You may not be able to see the lake from the roadway, but there's a narrow paved road that will take you right up to its shores.

Travel time from Yerevan to Geghard and Garni is about 45 minutes. Hire a private driver for about $20 for the entire half-day trip. If you plan to hike in the gorge, add several hours to the trip, and an extra fee for the driver, who will wait for you. Travel time from the main roadway to the Azat Reservoir is about 30 minutes.

dzin (originally established in AD 301) is the seat of the Armenian ᴜh, and is the holiest of religious sites in Armenia. And, at more than 1,700 yᴇ ᴜs old, it is also the oldest surviving Christian site in the country. The town in which the church is located was also known as Echmiadzin, until just recently when it was changed to Vagharshapat in honor of Armenian King Vagharshak who founded the town roughly 1,900 years ago. The name change is actually a restoration of the original, pre-1945 name of the town (see city map above).

The Echmiadzin complex consists of several buildings, including the main cathedral on the church campus and two other churches nearby. UNESCO recognizes the Echmiadzin complex, together with Zvartnots (below), as a World Heritage site.

There have been several modifications and additions to the main cathedral over the centuries, including a major reconstruction in AD 484. The cathedral's original wooden dome was replaced in the seventh century with the stone dome that is in place today. The most modern components are the cathedral's cupola and three-story bell tower, which were attached to the front of the western entrance in 1658. A bulky stone gateway, built in 2001, greets visitors at the street. Opposite the main entrance to the cathedral, the Trdats Gate offers photographers a much more attractive vantage though which they can frame the cathedral's bell tower.

Ornate murals cover the interior walls and ceilings, and there is a museum within the cathedral that contains the **Treasures of Echmiadzin**. The campus is filled with ancient *khatchkars* and religious monuments. The old pagan altar, over which the cathedral was built, can be viewed by entering a small room at the rear of the building. The spear from the monastery of Geghard [see above] is on display in the room here.

In the yard of the monastery are several buildings, including the offices and residence of the leader of the church, the Catholicos, a school, a hostel, and two refectories, all of which were built during the seventeenth through nineteenth centuries. Off campus, but nearby, are the three churches of **St. Gayaneh, St. Hripsimeh**, which were each built in the seventh century, and **St. Shogokat**, which was built in 1694. Art historians point to the St. Hripsimeh church as having greatly influenced the future course of Armenian architecture. The simple structure, which was constructed in AD 618, was adorned with a two-tier bell tower in 1790. The architectural style is much different from its contemporary, the AD 630 church of St. Gayaneh. The structure of St. Gayaneh is a domed basilica, with an interior that is divided into three naves. The more modern St. Shogokat, which is located just west of St. Hripsimeh, features only modest architectural and decorative detail.

Zvartnots Cathedral is located along the Yerevan-to-Echmiadzin roadway and can be visited during the same trip. Zvartnots was completed in AD 661, and so it is from the same era as St. Gayaneh and St. Hripsimeh. Still, the architecture of Zvartnots—it looks like a grand wedding cake—is unique among Armenian churches. The site is now a ruin of pillars, and records show that it has been in this

Photograph: Garni Temple

state since at least the tenth century. The destruction is commonly attributed to an earthquake, but there's no historical record. A reconstructed model of Zvartnots is on display in Yerevan at the State Museum of Armenian History.

To get there, from Yerevan travel west past Zvartnots Airport on Admiral Isakov Street (also known as the Yerevan-to-Echmiadzin road). The origin of this road is located in Yerevan near the Ararat Brandy factory.

Travel time from Yerevan to Echmiadzin and Zvartnots is about 30 minutes. Don't take the slow #111 bus. Instead, hire a private driver for the entire trip, for about $15 to $20 for one half day.

Sardarapat and Metsamor

Roughly 30 km west of Echmiadzin (60 km west of Yerevan), near the village of Araks, just past the town of **Hoktember** (October), is the battle monument of **Sardarapat**. A monument and an archaeological and folk art museum mark the location of what is certainly Armenia's most significant military victory of the modern era. In 1918, Kemalist Turkish forces internationalized the Genocide by invading the Armenian regions of what was then part of the Russian Empire. The Turks were turned back at Sardarapat, however, and the Armenian nation survived. It is unlikely that the current Armenian Republic would exist if this battle had been lost. The stone statues of two massive winged lions flank a bell tower. Relics from the battle are among the items at the nearby **Sardarapat Museum** (Open 11 am to 4 pm daily; closed Mondays). This museum is certainly one of the best in Armenia. Admission is 500 dram (less than one dollar).

To get there, from Echmiadzin travel west through Armavir, and then south past Hoktember until reaching the village of Araks.

On the way to Sardarapat, you will pass the town of **Metsamor**—famous both for a modern nuclear power plant and for a bronze-age settlement and the adjacent **Metsamor Museum** (Open 11 am to 5 pm daily; closed Mondays). There is a row of phallus stones just outside the front entrance of the museum. The stones were created as part of a fertility rite. Excavations at the site demonstrate that there had been a vibrant cultural center here from roughly 4,000 to 3,000 BC, and many artifacts are housed in the museum. The settlement persisted through the Middle Ages.

A modern settlement was built nearby, at the town of Metsamor, to house workers from the Metsamor Nuclear Power Plant. The power plant was closed in 1989 after an earthquake prompted officials to reconsider the safety of the location. The plant reopened in 1996 after being retrofitted to make it earthquake-resistant. Today, it generates roughly 30 to 35 percent of Armenia's energy needs. The balance of Armenia's energy use is fueled by thermal and hydro-generated power [for more about alternative energy sources, see Chapter 3, Ecology].

Travel time from Echmiadzin to Sardarapat is about 30 minutes. Travel time from Yerevan to Sardarapat is about one hour.

LakeSevan

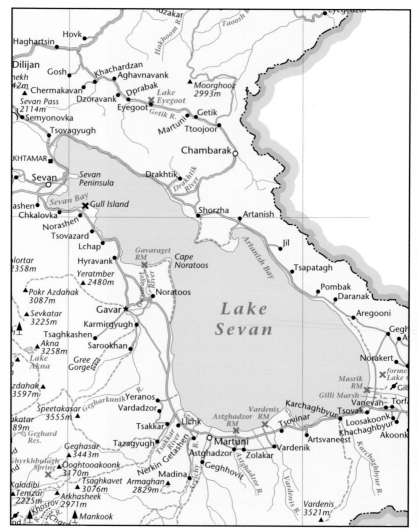

Courtesy of the Birds of Armenia Project, American University of Armenia, Oakland, CA, 1999

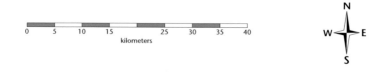

0   5   10   15   25   30   35   40
kilometers

INTRODUCTION

Lake Sevan forms the centerpiece of **Sevan National Park**, which is one of Armenia's greatest natural resources. The lake is probably the country's greatest recreational resource, too. Every summer Lake Sevan lures thousands of visitors away from the heat of Yerevan and into its cold, fresh, water.

The park contains a treasure trove of birds and plants, making the region as popular with **bird-watchers** and botanists as it is with swimmers and sunbathers. The region of the park that includes the wetlands of the **Lake Gilli** area is rich with bird-watching opportunities. [For more about birding and about Lake Gilli, see Chapter 3, Ecology.]

There are also several ancient historic sites of great significance here. Sevan is an easy day-trip from Yerevan. But this is really a great spot for an excursion of two or more days, especially for travelers who want to combine outdoor recreational activities with traditional sightseeing.

ON THE ROAD TO SEVAN

Tsaghkadzor and Hrazdan

The road from Yerevan to Sevan climbs steadily upward in elevation through a bucolic agricultural area of rolling hills, scattered villages, and the beautiful **Tsaghkadzor** mountain resort. As you begin your journey to Sevan just outside of Yerevan, on a clifftop on the west (left) side of the road you'll see a large memorial called **The Eagle of Vaspurakan**. The pewter-colored statue is dedicated to "the heroic struggle of Van," a reference to the Armenians' defense of Van during the 1915 Genocide. Farther along on the route to Tsaghkadzor there is a roadside statue of a maiden, and a Soviet-era monument to laborers. Tsaghkadzor (which means valley of flowers) was once popular with skiers, and it was an Olympic training ground during Soviet times. It has fallen into disuse, however, since the re-establishment of Armenia's independence in 1991.

Lake Sevan

Note About Traveling to Sevan

Most of the road from Yerevan to Sevan is a four lane divided highway that is very well maintained. There are services available near the north shore of the lake and at a couple of points along the way from Yerevan. If you are driving from Yerevan to the popular north shore, you need take only the standard preparation that you would take for a trip anywhere.

The roadway that circumscribes the lake is mostly rural, however, and you should expect that services will only be available along a short stretch of road near the Sevan Peninsula, and on the south shore near Martuni. The entire length of the east shore road south of Tsapatagh was in very poor condition at time of research. If you want to drive all the way around the lake, start with a full tank of gasoline, some food, and a supply of bottled drinking water.

Photograph, previous page: Lake Sevan at sunset

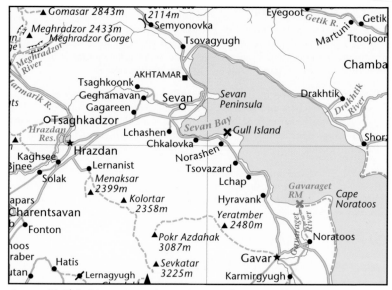

Courtesy of the Birds of Armenia Project, American University of Armenia, Oakland, CA, 1999

There's a chair lift that still operates at Tsaghkadzor, and which will cost you 500 dram (about one dollar) for each ride. To get to the top of the mountain, you need to take rides on three lifts, and pay 500 dram each time. There are no daily passes, so you'll need to bring plenty of 500-dram banknotes. Skis and boots are available for rental at the parking lot near the first lift, and you may even be able to rent a snowboard.

At the top, there are some rough trails that you can ski. But don't expect special amenities such as hot chocolate and Jacuzzis. Still, the slopes are open. And with an elevation here of more than 2,000 meters, the ski season is long. Snow usually arrives by November and then stays on the ground until spring—which for Tsaghkadzor is usually late May. Many of the hotels in town offer ski and boot rentals. This forested zone is more than just a winter get-away. It's also popular in early autumn for its beautiful orange and yellow foliage. And it's a popular resort for hiking and picnicking when the snow cover is gone.

The thousand-year-old **Kecharis Monastery** draws sightseers, too. Kecharis has three churches, two chapels and a hall (gavit), all compactly arranged and facing a verdant courtyard. The main building, and the oldest at the complex, is the church of **St. Gregory**, which was built in 1033. The newest of the structures dates from the thirteenth century.

There's no fortress wall around the monastery, as is seen at many others in Armenia. There are no surviving buildings of a non-religious nature here, either, although historians say it is likely that there were other buildings at the site through the ages. There are a couple of plausible explanations for this. First, the minor buildings of the monastery complexes, such as libraries, dining halls, and housing, may have been built with materials and designs that simply could not survive many centuries, as did the stone churches. A second theory is that, during the repeated plunder of Armenia, the churches may have been spared, while the secular buildings were not. Either of these theories might explain why some of Armenia's monasteries seem to be so isolated, with no neighboring buildings. Apart from destruction by plunder during ancient times, an earthquake in 1927 destroyed part of the Kecharis Monastery. A full restoration was completed in 2001.

Travelers to Tsaghkadzor and Kecharis will first go past the relatively modern town of **Hrazdan**. It's impossible to miss Hrazdan. There's a thermal power plant here, with massive cooling towers. Nearby you can see the Hrazdan Reservoir—a small lake that is filled with water that has been tapped from Lake Sevan. The water gets here by way of aqueducts and the Hrazdan River, and the reservoir forms part of the Hrazdan hydroelectric cascade.

To get there, from Yerevan there's a sign-posted turnoff to Hrazdan, roughly 40 km from the city. This is not the best turnoff for Hrazdan and Tsaghkadzor. Instead, take the second turnoff, which is seven km farther north (i.e. 47 km from Yerevan), and which is unmarked. Travel straight off the exit for five km through two rotaries. At the second rotary, either turn right and drive one kilometer for Hrazdan, or continue straight and drive four km for Tsaghkadzor.

Travel time from Yerevan to Tsaghkadzor is about 45 minutes. Travel time from the main road turnoff to Kecharis is only about 10 minutes, on a well-paved road.

Hotels and Places to Stay

Adi-Gaz Hotel opened in 2000, but was nevertheless built to the finest Soviet-era specifications. 32 rooms, some of which have views of Kecharis. Hot water in morning and evening only. Double 12,000 drams (about $22). Located two km beyond Kecharis monastery (Tel. (0-23) + 5-23-90).

Alik Hotel is the best of Tsaghkadzor's hotels, and also its newest. It first opened in 1999 and then in 2003 added a new hotel building and a restaurant. 39 rooms, each of them well furnished, clean, with 24-hour hot water. The better rooms are in the newer building, but all of them are a good value. Double $30; Deluxe $50-80. Ski rentals available. Located immediately before the center of town in Tsaghkadzor, near the Nairi Hotel, eight km from the main Yerevan-to-Sevan road.

Nairi Hotel, a Soviet-era building with 75 musty-smelling rooms. 24-hour hot water in private, but primitive, baths. Probably OK for one night. Single $14; Double $28. No handicapped access. Located in Tsaghkadzor, 8 km from the main Yerevan-to-Sevan road (Tel. 28-28-91).

Nkarichneri Toun (Painter's House) in the center of town, opposite the main square, has seven dismal rooms that are dirty and overpriced even at only 3,000 drams (about $6) per night. Not recommended (Tel. (0-23) + 5-23-04).

Splendor Hotel, located one kilometer beyond Kecharis Monastery. Eight cottages with kitchenettes in a quaint campground-like setting. Double $30 (Tel. (0-23) + 5-24-25; Yerevan Tel. 56-38-99).

Writer's House of Creativity, another Soviet-era hotel, has 77 rooms that are modest but clean. Site of frequent conferences. 24-hour hot water. Single $18; Double $36. No handicapped access. Rent ice skates and skis for 1,500 drams (about $2.80). Not so bad for a night or two. Tsaghkadzor (Tel. 28-10-81).

Prices are listed in US dollars for those hotels that quote US dollars when advertising their rates. Otherwise, prices are listed in Armenian drams.

Telephone: The area code for Tsaghkadzor is 23. When calling Tsaghkadzor from Yerevan, enter (0) + (23) + (local phone number).

SEVAN'S BIRDS OF PREY

By Keith L. Bildstein

Armenia is home to 38 species of raptors, a group of charismatic predatory and scavenging birds that includes hawks, eagles, falcons, and vultures. One of the most conspicuous and easily seen of these dramatic birds of prey is the Kestrel. A colorful, dove-sized, scaled-down version of the Peregrine Falcon, Kestrels feed mainly on small mammals, birds, and insects. Like other birds of prey, Kestrels have keen vision, hooked beaks, and sharp talons.

The species, which is sometimes called Eurasian or Common Kestrel, are found in open and semi-open habitats across much of its European, Asian, and African range. In Armenia, they are found throughout the countryside, especially in semi-deserts and open steppes. Unlike many birds of prey, Kestrels are not particularly wary of people, and one of the best places to see them on your travels is along the road between Yerevan and Lake Sevan. A one-hour drive along this four-lane route in spring through autumn is likely to produce sightings of dozens and, possibly, a hundred or more Kestrels with many of the tiny falcons hovering gracefully above grassy fields searching for their prey, and others perched stately on utility lines and poles, and on trees planted along the roadside. In May, breeding Kestrels can be seen in their nests incubating their eggs and shortly thereafter feeding their young.

Male and female Kestrels have different plumages and it is possible to tell them apart. Males have a gray head and tail, a brick-red back, and a tan breast and belly with a few dark spots. Females and juveniles are brick-red above and tan below with heavier spotting and streaking throughout. Both adults and juveniles are vocal (a high-pitched klee… klee… klee… is the most common call) and are easy to locate near their nests. Seeing these birds in the wild is a special treat for anyone with an interest in nature. Unfortunately, it is not clear how long this exceptional facet of Armenian bird-watching will continue.

As recently as the late 1990s, the road from Yerevan to Lake Sevan provided hundreds of pairs of Kestrels with the combination of resources that pairs of Kestrels need to raise young: grassy fields rich in mice and insect prey to serve as a kitchen, and roadsides lined with trees to serve as a bedroom and nursery. Although the grassy fields and abundant prey remain, the stately rows of ornamental poplars and groves of pines that had been planted in the 1970s and 1980s, and that once provided nesting sites for an important breeding population of Kestrels are now being cut for their wood, both to cook the meals and to heat the homes of thousands of Armenians that live in towns and villages lining the route.

A recent survey by members of the Birds of Armenia Project revealed that 87 pairs of Kestrels were still hanging on, but that long stretches of the once tree-lined causeway were devoid of trees, and that in most of the areas where trees remained, recent cutting was obvious. At the time of the survey, it appeared that more than half the trees that had been planted in this, otherwise, treeless region had been cut to the stump and carried off. Without nest-sites, all the food in the world is not enough for successful breeding. And at the rate that trees are now being cut, all of them will be removed within three years.

As if the loss of the trees were not enough, another problem looms for the roadside Kestrels. Like other falcons, Kestrels do not build their own nests, but rather lay their eggs on cliff ledges and in abandoned nests built by other birds. On the road to Lake Sevan, most Kestrels breed in the abandoned nests of Black-billed Magpies and Carrion Crows. Although both of these species construct their nests mainly from twigs and small branches, both also frequently incorporate decorative items, including discarded nylon bailing twine, into their constructions.

Like many of the world's predatory birds, Kestrels are especially sensitive biological indicators, species whose declining populations offer an early warning signal of troubled environments. The no longer "common" Kestrels on the road to Lake Sevan are telling us that something is wrong. We would be wise to listen.

Although it is evident that many of Armenia's conservation challenges will take decades to reverse, the plight of Kestrel need not be one of them. Discarded bailing twine needs to be removed from the roadside and adjacent fields. Replanting and protecting trees along the road needs to begin as soon as possible. Of course, the trees will take time to grow. In the mean time, nest-boxes for Kestrels should be placed on utility poles in the area. None of this will work without community involvement and support. Public meetings and a practical grade-school curriculum in environmental education will help, as will solving the region's episodic fuel shortages.

The tragedy of Armenia's roadside Kestrels can and should be turned into an example of how such problems can be solved. Restoring the region's Kestrels could become a flagship project for natural resource conservation throughout the country.

Keith L. Bildstein, Ph.D., is coauthor of *Raptorwatch: a global directory of raptor migration sites* (Birdlife International, Cambridge, England) and Director of Conservation Science at the Acopian Center for Conservation Learning, Hawk Mountain Sanctuary, Pennsylvania, USA.

LAKE SEVAN

Lake Sevan National Park is Armenia's first, and most famous, national park. It was established in 1978 and it held the distinction as the country's only such park for nearly 25 years—until the elevation of the Dilijan Reserve to national park status in 2002. Sevan is a somewhat large lake by any standard—it is one of the largest freshwater alpine lakes in the world— but for a tiny country such as Armenia, the lake looms huge. The lake occupies five-sixths of the park's area. The surface area of the lake (1,250 sq km) covers four percent of the country and its watershed extends to an area four times that size, giving a good indication of how important Sevan is to Armenia's ecology. The region is habitat to approximately 1,700 species

Lake Sevan

of flora and 270 species of birds. More than 150 of the plant species in the Sevan basin are considered threatened or endangered. The surface level of this mountain lake currently rests at an elevation of about 1,890 m, and there are beaches of sand and fine gravel along many stretches of the shoreline.

Mountains encircle Lake Sevan and form a huge basin for the lake's ice-cold water while also having a dramatic effect upon the local climate. It's not unusual to discover that there's cool and stormy weather in Sevan when it's hot and dry in Yerevan, just 60 km away. From north to south, the lake stretches roughly 78 km. At its widest point from east to west, it spans approximately 58 km.

The park was created with the intention of protecting the Lake Sevan ecosystem and its surrounding area. It is divided into three zones: a reserve, a recreation zone, and a zone for economic use.

Swimming and Recreation

For recreation, many of the better beaches are on the northwestern shore, near the **Sevan Peninsula**. These beaches are close enough to Yerevan that you can easily visit them and also see the nearby historic sites in a day trip. If you are spending only one day at Sevan, then you should start with a visit to this peninsula and then go south as far as Noraduz, which is at the midpoint of the western shore.

Protecting Lake Sevan

Lake Sevan is one of Armenia's greatest natural treasures, and it is also in great peril. Its troubled history dates back to the 1930s. That's when the Soviet government embarked on a scheme to reduce the surface area of the lake by approximately 80 percent. Their objective was to reduce evaporation and thereby increase the commercial availability of the lake's water. Those areas of the lake's floor, which would thereby become exposed, were to have been devoted to agriculture. Vast amounts of water were diverted for irrigation and for hydroelectric generation.

By the early 1960s, the water level of the lake had decreased 19 meters, and the water volume had been diminished by more than 40 percent. More than 20,000 hectares or marshes and wetlands that formed part of the Sevan ecosystem had been drained. The cancelled project hadn't put an end to all commercial use of Sevan's waters, which were still available for irrigation and hydroelectric power.

The more shallow waters were warmed by the sun. Fishing harvests declined. Eutrophication increased. The survival of the lake was threatened. Commercial needs continue to threaten Lake Sevan, but scientists are today studying how to restore the delicate balance of its ecology, and the condition of the lake is a matter of widespread national concern. An aqueduct was built during the 1970s and 1980s in order to redirect water from the Arpa River into the lake. In 2003, scientists actually registered a modest rise in the surface level of the lake. No one expects that the lake can be restored to its pre-1930 level. But there is hope that conditions will slowly improve, and that Lake Sevan will remain one of Armenia's greatest treasures [for more on conservation of Lake Sevan, see Chapter 3, Ecology].

Horse and cart at a village near Lake Sevan

There are historic sites elsewhere around the lake, but they are few and far from the popular north shore beaches, making them sites that you will probably want to explore only after you have seen everything between the northwest shore and Noraduz. If you plan to venture beyond Noraduz, and to go all the way around the lake, you could do it with a private driver in one long and tiring day. It would be better to stay overnight and make the trip in two days.

You can swim for free at many of the beaches located along the northwestern shore, near the Sevan Peninsula. The better beaches have been privatized and "improved" with amenities such as showers, umbrellas and cafes, and they usually charge for parking. They may also charge a separate admission fee per person. Whichever beach you select, the water is clear and cold, and in the summer it acquires a turquoise hue that can fool you into thinking you're in the Greek Isles.

Several private beaches offer hourly rentals of paddleboats and rowboats. To charter a catamaran sailboat with a captain by the hour or by the day, check with the manager of the Blue Sevan Motel, or with the manager of one of the private beaches. There are no rentals available at the lake for bicycles, or for equipment for diving and fishing. Hotel Hasnakar, located near the turnoff to the Sevan Peninsula (see hotel listings below), maintains a sandy beach and swimming pool, as well as a water world amusement park on its grounds. If you are not a hotel guest, you can pay a daily rate of 3,000 drams (about $5) to use the recreational facilities.

There are several *khorovats* (barbecue) stands along the north shore road where you can purchase a meal of kebob and roasted vegetables. We have found that they often don't have bread or cold drinks, so treat these places as a supplement to the provisions that you bring with you from Yerevan. Be sure to request well-cooked meat.

Hairavank Monastery on the western shore of Lake Sevan

Birders and others will want to stop near **Seagull Island**, located about eight km south of the town of Sevan, along the west shore road. The seagulls that gather here are unique to this area. During the summer it is sometimes possible to rent a paddleboat that will take you to this tiny and just-off-shore island, but most rentals are available at the larger beaches of the northwest shore (see above) which is a bit farther.

Fishing is popular at the lake, but you will not be permitted to keep any of the *Ishkhan* trout that you might catch. The *Ishkhan* is unique to Lake Sevan, but its harvest has been restricted by the government for nearly 30 years because of its endangered status. *Ishkhan* were once plentiful. Today their survival is imperiled because of the introduction several decades ago of predator fish and because of environmental changes that have accompanied the lake's declining water level. Eutrophication and increased water temperatures, along with decreased habitat areas, are the primary environmental reasons for the decline of the *Ishkhan*.

Travel time from Yerevan to the northwest beaches is about one hour. Travel time from the main Yerevan-to-Sevan road turnoff to Seagull Island is about 10 minutes.

The North and West Shores

Sevanavank, the monastery on the Sevan Peninsula, is a great place to start your exploration of the Lake Sevan region. This peninsula had actually been an island until the 1930s, when the lake's waters began to be used over-intensively [see box,

"Protecting Lake Sevan," this chapter]. From the road near the town of Sevan you can see the two churches of the monastery, **Arakelots** and **Astvatsatsin**, both of which date back to the ninth century. They have both been extensively renovated during the past few years. The foundation ruins of a third ancient church are located just a few meters away on the hilltop, and there are several interesting *khatchkars*. These churches sit high on a hill, and from the churchyard you will have a wonderful view of the lake and the encircling mountains.

To get there, from Yerevan travel north on the Yerevan-to-Sevan highway for about 60 km. Travel roughly two km past the town of Sevan and turn right onto the paved access road to the peninsula.

Farther south along the road to Kamo, which has been renamed **Gavar**, the beautiful monastery of **Hairavank** is perched atop a cliff at the water's edge. This church is also from the ninth century, and the hall (gavit) dates from the twelfth century. There are several magnificent *khatchkars* in the churchyard and there is a Bronze Age fortress nearby.

To get there, take the south turnoff at the rotary near the town of Sevan. This turnoff is located well before you reach the Sevan Peninsula. Hairavank is located 23 km south of the main road turnoff, on a cliff that abuts the lake.

Noraduz, which is famous for its cemetery of nearly one thousand *khatchkars*, is nearby. The cemetery is located at the eastern edge of the town of Noraduz, and it dates back to the Middle Ages. The stone crosses here from the 1500s and 1600s represent the most recent style developments of the *khatchkars*, which by this era had become very simple. *Khatchkars* generally face east, which is to say that the side with the engraving faces west, and the crosses at Noraduz are oriented in this traditional manner. Late afternoon and early evening is therefore the best time to photograph khatchkars, since this is when the setting sun will be shining directly on the engraved side of the cross [for more on *khatchkars*, see box, "Ancient Stone Crosses," this chapter].

To get there, travel about eight and one half km south of Hairavank (i.e. roughly 31 km south of the main road turnoff). Turn left at the second of two turnoffs into the town of Noraduz. These turnoffs are located roughly one and one half km apart. The cemetery is located at the east end of town, about two km from the main road.

Travel time from Yerevan to Sevanavank (at the Sevan Peninsula) is about one hour. From Yerevan to Kamo (Gavar) is about eighty minutes. From Yerevan to Noraduz is about 100 minutes. Hire a driver for roughly $30-half day, $40-full day.

Hotels and Places to Stay

Blue Sevan has 10 cottages and a large building with 37 hotel rooms. Hot water, private baths, shared baths for cottages. Per person rates are roughly $12 to $18. This was once the best spot on the lake, but now there's plenty of better competition. Located just past the old Soviet hotel on the north shore. Make reservations by calling Delta Armenia Travel Agency in Yerevan (Tel. 56-60-99) or Elitar Agency (Tel. 54-33-11). Seasonal.

stone crosses are an original form of Armenian national art. In a land with a bounty of stones, it should not be surprising that artisans and craftsmen would have used this medium to express their talents.

This artistic expression found its voice, beginning early in the fourth century AD, in the Christian exaltation of the cross. Winged crosses, made from large stones, were erected to replace some of the earliest wooden crosses of the era. The earliest of these winged crosses have been discovered at the ancient Armenian capital of Dvin.

From these early prototypes, the Armenians developed the *khatchkar*—an art form of engraved stone crosses that is unique to their culture. The western face of the stone is engraved, and the reverse side is typically smooth. The height of the stone is usually about twice the length of its width. These *khatchkars* first became a national art form in the ninth and tenth centuries, and the oldest of them is believed to be one that was erected in AD 879 by the wife of an Armenian king. Ironically, or perhaps intentionally, the chosen site was in Garni, next to a pagan temple that had been built during Armenia's pre-Christian era.

These early stone crosses were probably commissioned in order to secure salvation of the soul. But by the twelfth and thirteenth centuries, they were also erected to commemorate historic events such as military battles or the construction of a monastery. Others, especially those that are set into the walls of churches, may honor individuals who made significant contributions to that church. *Khatchkars* were also used as tombstones. Three of these, dating back to AD 1211, are at the Haghpat Monastery in northern Armenia.

Sacred images were often carved on the stones, as well, showing images of Jesus and Mary. Some of the artisans who carved these stones were master architects who also constructed many fine churches. Today, experts acclaim their engravings from the medieval era as the finest the Armenians created. Some of these thirteenth century masterpieces are found at the monastery of Geghard, which is located about 30 km outside Yerevan, and at Goshavank, which is in the Dilijan region.

Foreign invasions disrupted the artistic development of *khatchkars* in the thirteenth and fourteenth centuries, but there was eventually a limited revival. From the sixteenth through eighteenth centuries, *khatchkars* were mostly used as tombstones. Thousands were created during this time, and there are hundreds of examples at the cemetery of Noraduz, on Lake Sevan's western shore.

The course of the artistic development of khatchkars from the ninth through the eighteenth centuries had until recently been demonstrated by the thousands of stone crosses in a huge cemetery in Jugha. This old Armenian trading post is located in Nakhijevan, a region that is today controlled by Azerbaijan.

There were about 5,000 of these ancient stone crosses standing in Jugha in 1903. They didn't fare well under Azeri custody. By 1973 half of them had been destroyed. In 2002 Armenia's Minister of Foreign Affairs complained to the UN about Azerbaijan's willful destruction of this legacy of Armenian culture. The Armenian Foreign Minister testified that witnesses had recently described and photographed the "individual destruction of each huge monolith" at the cemetery. Observers reported that the crosses were bulldozed to the ground and then hauled away on the state-owned railway. In 2003, said the Foreign Minister, "there are none left standing."

Fishermen at Lake Sevan just after sunrise

Edem Hotel, built in 2001, has a dozen deluxe domiks that it has converted into fairly comfortable cabins, each with kitchenette and private bath. Each domik can accommodate 5 people. There's direct access to clean beach, with rough gravelly sand. Good value at $40 ($25 off-season). Located roughly 13 km from the Sevan Peninsula, roughly seven km from the Dilijan turnoff (Tel. (0-61) + 2-72-50). Open year-round. Electric space heaters.

Hotel Harsnakar is the best of the hotels at the north shore. This large complex includes cottages, Western-style rooms, and an outdoor water park that children will love. There are 30 rooms in the main building, many with good views of the lake. This is the first hotel you'll see when driving to Sevan from Yerevan, and it is the best in the built-up tourist area on the north shore. Facilities include a restaurant and bar, casino, billiards, tennis courts and, of course, the water park and beach access. The water park is free for hotel guests, and 3,000 drams (about $5) for visitors. Economy single $70; Double suite $150; 2-3 BR Cottages $150-170. Located at the north shore in the town of Sevan, on the main Yerevan-to-Sevan highway (Tel. (0-61) + 2-04-50; (0-61) + 2-33-58). Open year-round. Winter rates available.

Sevan Two Motel has balconies overlooking the lake, and run-down rooms in two large buildings. Most of the 101 rooms in this huge complex have hot water, but some don't get any. Reservations advised in August. Cafeteria food for additional $5 daily. Single $15; Double $25. Located on the water just seven km from the Sevan Peninsula, or one kilometer from the Dilijan turnoff (Tel. (0-61) + 2-42-13) (E-mail: marat@arminco.com) Seasonal.

Prices *are listed in US dollars for those hotels that quote US dollars when advertising their rates. Otherwise, prices are listed in Armenian drams.*

Telephone: *The area code for Sevan is 61. When calling Sevan from Yerevan, enter (0) + (61) + (local phone number).*

A couple takes in the view of the lake at sunset

The South and East Shores

The south shore road between **Martuni** and **Vardenis** are the most heavily populated parts of the lakeshore, with several larger villages. The waterfront here is largely spoiled by grazing cows, and we don't advise swimming here. Midway between Martuni and Vardenis, at the village of Artsvanist, is the monastery of **Vanevan**. The main church there, St. Grigor, was completed in AD 903 and it sits beside a stream in town. To get there, drive roughly three km to the center of the town of Artsvanist from the main Sevan roadway. Then, roughly one-half kilometer from the center of town, turn left at the post office.

Artsvanist is also the location of the 48 kilometer-long Arpa-Sevan aqueduct, which feeds water from the Arpa River into Lake Sevan. This aqueduct was built during the 1970s and 1980s in an effort to stem the declining level of the lake.

East of Vardenis, the road continues to the small gold-mining village of **Zod (Sodk)** and then through Kelbajar to Dadi Vank monastery and northern Karabagh. The Kelbajar region, which is now called Karvachar, is part of the internationally recognized territory of Azerbaijan. For more than a decade it has been held by Karabagh Armenians as a buffer zone to protect them from hostilities, however. Enemy forces had used Kelbajar to lay siege to Karabagh during Karabagh's war of independence. You'll have to pass through a military checkpoint near Zod (Sodk) in order to get into this region. We have done this—bearing Karabagh visas—without great difficulty. Although it is safe to travel through Kelbajar, this is probably a journey for the more adventurous souls. It's easy to get lost, so the drive should not be attempted at night [for more on Kelbajar, see Chapter 10, Karabagh].

A stone cross at the Hairavank Monastery at Lake Sevan

NATURE AND CONSERVATION

The Lake Sevan National Park comprises the lake and surrounding area and is beautiful and ecologically unique. The Lake Gilli Watershed, which is just a few km northwest of Vardenis, is a favorite area for bird watchers. Lake Sevan's east shore is also a great birding destination. Unlike the area surrounding Lake Gilli, this area is unspoiled, with almost no commercial development, and just a scattering of villages. Most of the open land is used for agriculture, and you'll see fields of poppies and alfalfa during the late spring and early summer. There are no historic sites along this long east shore road, however, and very little sightseeing. The natural beauty of the area makes the region worth the trip, nonetheless. The Artanish Peninsula, located at the midpoint of the east shore, has unique ecological features that may be of interest to conservationists. The remote location of this peninsula has allowed it to remain virtually unmolested by development. There are about 1,000 plant species, including 94 trees and shrubs, in this area. The peninsula is also host to many rare animal species [for more information see Chapter 3, Ecology].

Hotels and Places to Stay

Avan Marak Tsapatagh Hotel, which is part of the Tufenkian Heritage Hotels chain, opened a 14-room hotel near the east shore town of Tsapatagh in 2003. This environmentally friendly facility is on a hill overlooking the lake, on a remote part of the eastern shore. Swimming pool, restaurant, and bar. Some rooms offer balconies and terraces with direct views of the lake. Breakfast included. Single $47-$71; Double $83; Suite $120. Located roughly 65 km beyond the Sevan Peninsula (driving clockwise around the lake), which is roughly 125 km from Yerevan (Tel. 52-08-81; 54-78-88; Fax 52-09-13) (E-mail: hotels@tufenkian.am; lilit@tufenkian.am) (Internet: www.tufenkian.am). They also have a booking office in Yerevan at 21/1 Tumanian Street. Open year-round. Group rates available.

Camping is available throughout much of the park, and campers with their own tents and gear may find that the secluded areas on the east shore, particularly those near Tsapatagh, are desirable. There are no commercial campgrounds with rest facilities. A campground did exist on the south shore during Soviet days, but it has been closed for several years.

Lake Sevan

Northeast Armenia

seven

188

To Tbilisi
63 km

Haghtanak
Berdavan
EYEROOM
Chochkan
Koghb
Dom
Shamloogh
Lchkadzor
Noyemberian
Lalvar 2543m
Akhtala
AKHTALA
Archees
Shnogh
Joojevan
Alaverdi
Debet River
Teghoot
Voskevan
ee
Haghpat
Baghanis
dzoon
vee
Voskepar
Joghaz Res.
Aghstafa Res.
Kober
Toomanian
Chateen 2243m
Keerants
Berkaber
Karahan River
Acharkoot
Sareegyugh
oortan
Keerants
Samson Gorge
Sevkar
Achajoor
Azatamoot
Dsegh
Kareenj
Eyegeh
gyugh
Marts
Makaravank
Ditavan
Aghstev R.
Loroot
Shamoot
Shkhmoorad
Debet
Atan
Yenokavan
Khashtarak
Marts River
Karagyugh Lodge
Yeghegnoot
Ahnidzor
Getahoveet
Lori Bridge
Hamza
Vahagnadzor
Ijevan
Saroomsakhloo 2023m
Pombak
Ijevan Res.
Gandzakar
ogark
Hovk
Hakhoom R.
t R.
Haghartsin
Lermontov
Dilijan
Gosh
Khachardzan
Margahovit
Fioletovo
Aghavnavank
Mets Mymekh 2642m
Moor
Tezh 101m
Chermakavan
Dprabak
2993
n 3052m
Composers' House
Sevan Pass 2114m
Dzoravank
Lake Eyegoot
m
Gomasar 2843m
Eyegoot
Getik R.
Getik
Arkhashan Gorge
Meghradzor 2433m
Semyonovka
Martuni
Ttoojoor
Meghradzor Gorge
Tsovagyugh
eek
Meghradzor River
Chamba
Meghradzor
Marmarik R.
AKHTAMAR
saghkoonyats 2821m
Tsaghkoonk
Geghamavan
Sevan
Drakhtik
Drakhtik River
Dallyar 2616m
Hrazdan Res.
Tsaghkadzor
Gagareen
Sevan Peninsula
Lchashen
Sevan Bay
Gull Island
Shor

Northeast Armenia

N
W E
S

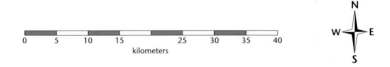

0   5   10   15   25   30   35   40
kilometers

INTRODUCTION

The most lushly vegetated and verdant part of Armenia is in the northeast, in the regions of **Tavush** and **Lori**. This is the section of the country that extends north from Sevan National Park all the way to the Georgian border. Unlike elsewhere in Armenia, trees are a significant natural resource here. You're much more likely to see homes here that have been built from wood than anywhere else in the country.

The northeast is home to Dilijan, and Armenians call the forested resort their Little Switzerland. The moist and cool climate makes this a great retreat from the summer heat of Yerevan, and the region is as popular with local vacationers as it is with those who have traveled here from afar. Fewer travelers make it to the far northeastern town of Noyemberian, however, because it is so difficult to go there and return to Yerevan on the same day. A new hotel that opened in this region in 2004 may help draw more visitors. The northeast is also home to Alaverdi and its wealth of historic sites, in the region of Lori.

DILIJAN

The forested Dilijan area, which is located in the region of **Tavush**, is famous not only for its forests, but also for its mineral water, which is bottled and sold as a health tonic. The bottling plant is located about three km outside town on the road that leads to Vanadzor. Hiking and mountain biking are also popular in Dilijan, especially at the **Dilijan National Park**. You'll have to bring your own bicycle, however. Rentals are not available. Outside the town, the greatest regional tourist attractions are the monasteries of Haghardzin, Goshavank, and Jukhtakvank, which were all built in the Middle Ages.

The historic Dilijan town center is located roughly one half kilometer from the major traffic rotary on the main highway. The town features an ethnographic museum with some interesting prehistoric tomb stones in the front yard. There's also a row of century-old wood framed houses that are now occupied by quaint boutiques, and which are protected as historic sites. Elsewhere in the town center in an old stone building facing the pedestrian walkway on Sharambeyan Street, an old wood carver named Revik still plies his trade from his small shop, and sells gift items to tourists. Visit his shop and he'll carve something to your specifications, or sell you a wooden jug or spoon or other knick knack that he has already made.

Northeast Armenia

Note About Traveling in the Northeast

Winter arrives early in this wooded mountain region, and roads may have icy spots as early as November, especially in the morning. Many roads lack guardrails and other safety features, and there is no lighting. Avoid driving on these roads after sundown.

In the far northeastern corner, a very small area along the road that runs close to the Azerbaijan border, just south of Noyemberian, may be hazardous. In 2003 there were reports of sporadic small arms gunfire originating from Azerbaijan, aimed at civilian targets in Armenia. The affected area is very small, but travelers who are going to Noyemberian may need to travel by way of Alaverdi, and not by way of Ijevan. Check with the Consular section of the US Embassy in Yerevan before you go (Tel. 52-16-11; 52-46-61).

Photograph, previous page, Parz Lake

There's an old Soviet-era sanatorium on the ridge overlooking the town, in a beautiful wooded setting. This spa, and the entire area, was one of the leading summer resort areas before 1990. We recommend that you plan an overnight stay here so that you may explore the beauty of the nature reserve in addition to seeing the town and the historic sites.

Traveling east to Dilijan from Vanadzor, you'll see several villages along the scenic and pastoral road. Two of them, **Lermontovo** and **Fioletovo** are unusual because of their heritage. These villages are populated only by Russians who had been exiled from their homes. We've never encountered anyone there who understands the Armenian language, which suggests how insular these communities are.

The ethnic Russians of Fioletovo are descendants of a group of Russians that had been forced from their central Russia homes in the nineteenth century because of religious persecution. These Russians were Molokans—a Christian sect that broke from the Russian Orthodox Church in the seventeenth century. The Molokan faith preaches pacifism and communal values. These Molokan Russians were scattered throughout the Russian Empire, including to the village of Fioletovo in Armenia. Their population throughout Armenia is about 5,000, of whom 1,500 live in Fioletovo.

To get there, from Yerevan, travel to the north shore of Lake Sevan and then head north through the Sevan Pass. There's a new 2.4 kilometer tunnel that opened in 2003 that dramatically reduces the travel time through this pass. The tunnel also makes winter travel safer. To get there from Vanadzor, travel east on the Vanadzor-to-Dilijan road. Traveling from Vanadzor is now quite easy, thanks to a newly re-engineered and resurfaced roadway.

Travel time by car from the north shore of Lake Sevan to Dilijan is about 30 minutes. Travel time from Yerevan to Dilijan is less than two hours. Travel time from Vanadzor is about 30 minutes.

Historic Monasteries

Haghardzin draws more visitors than any other site in Dilijan. The monastery is located several km east of the center of town in a remote mountain setting. There are six surviving buildings at the complex today. The oldest of the churches, St. Gregory, was built in the tenth century. The other churches, St. Stepanos and St. Astvatsatsin, as well as the refectory, date back to the thirteenth century.

It is not unusual to find inscriptions on the walls of church buildings in Armenia. The inscriptions tell about restorations, donors, and of political and cultural life. On the walls of the church of St. Astvatsatsin, an inscription tells of Haghardzin's destruction by Seljuk hordes during the mid-eleventh century and how, during the following century, the monastery was reconstructed.

To get there, travel east from Dilijan on the main road toward the town of Ijevan. After about eight km there's a left turnoff, marked by an Armenian-language sign. Drive up this winding and forested mountain road until it ends. The road is paved, and the drive on this road should take only about 15 minutes.

The nearby monastic complex of **Goshavank** consists of three churches, as well as a large reading hall. The smallest of the churches, St. Gevorg, also served as a court-

Harvesting carrots in the village of Fioletovo

room and it housed Armenia's first collection of law books. Mkhitar Gosh, for whom Goshavank is named, had compiled an Armenian law digest in order to help resist the influence of Muslim shariah (religious) law.

The mid-sized chapel of St. Gregory the Illuminator features four alcoves that are built in the style of Jewish, Muslim, Persian and Armenian architecture, supposedly as part of an effort to discourage foreign invaders from destroying the church. There's a sundial on the south side of this chapel. The buildings here were all constructed in the late twelfth and early thirteenth centuries. The monastery itself was founded in 1188 and it formed a significant cultural center during the Middle Ages. There's a modest museum located next to the monastery with a few interesting artifacts.

To get there, travel east from Dilijan on the main road toward the town of Ijevan. Travel several km past the turnoff to Haghardzin and then take the right turnoff that crosses the river. Then take a second right turnoff onto a poor road that leads to the monastery.

Travel time from the main road turnoff up to Haghardzin is about 15 minutes. Travel time from the main road turnoff to Goshavank is also about 15 minutes.

Jukhtakvank is the least-visited of Dilijan's monasteries. The architecture and setting just cannot compare with the beautiful offerings of Haghardzin and Goshavank. Still, Jukhtakvank is historically significant and is worth a visit if you still have time after you have first seen Haghardzin and Goshavank. The buildings are about 800 years old, and are nestled in a wooded setting that would be great for a picnic.

To get there, travel west from Dilijan on the main road that leads to Vanadzor. Travel roughly one kilometer until reaching the right turnoff that goes uphill toward the monastery. Drive to the end of the paved road, which should take about 10 minutes, and then get out and hike up the rest of the way on the gravel and stone path. The hike is not too difficult, and will take about 10 to 15 minutes.

NATURE AND CONSERVATION

Dilijan National Park

Dilijan Reserve was elevated to National Park status in 2002 and it occupies an area of approximately 28,000 hectares—an area roughly one-sixth as large as the area of Lake Sevan National Park. The park is almost entirely forested. The territory of the Dilijan parklands range in elevation from 1,200 to 2,900 m and is host to a wide variety of flora and fauna. Within the reserve there are unique coniferous forests of yew and pine, and also sub alpine meadows. There is also a population of brown bear, wild boar, wolf and porcupine. There have been occasional sightings of bobcats.

The ecosystem of Dilijan is at risk from uncontrolled (and unauthorized) development, and from the large-scale and illegal harvesting of trees. The park's Beech and Oak forests are typical to the Caucasus Region [for more about Armenia's specially protected areas, see Chapter 3, Ecology].

Parz Lake

For a restful picnic spot, try the small lake known as **Parz** (clear) **Lake** . The English translation of the name is Clear Lake, which seems to be a misnomer for the greenish-hued water. The surface of the lake does look like glass, however. There's no swimming at this lake, but the forested environs make it a pleasant stop and in summer you may be able to rent a rowboat.

In the Spring and early Summer you'll find some beautiful fields of daisies along the way, and some great views, too. The lake is located within the Dilijan National Park.

The Alaverdi Mining District

Mining and the processing of sulfide ores have taken place in the Alaverdi region for centuries. The rate of extraction, however, was greatly expanded during seventy years of Soviet dominion. At its height of operations, roughly 50,000 tons of copper were produced here each year. The mines were shut down in 1989 for economic, environmental and political reasons.

Following the dissolution of the Soviet Union, the copper mines and smelter were abandoned for nearly a decade, and were reopened only in the late 1990s. New production at the mines has not reached the pre-independence levels of the 1980s, but fresh tailings in addition to the existing tailing piles and open pits on the banks of the Debed River's tributaries, are exposed. As a result, the Debed River— a fast-moving body of water that passes through the mining district and which has cut a deep gorge in the region—continues to be contaminated with leached metals.

To get there, travel seven km east from Dilijan on the main road toward the town of Ijevan. Just before reaching the Haghardzin turnoff there is a right turnoff that crosses the river. An Armenian-language sign marks the turnoff to the road. Drive up this winding and poorly paved road until you get to the top.

Travel time from the main road turnoff and then up to Parz Lake (10 km) is about 20 minutes.

Hotels and Places to Stay

Bed and Breakfast operated out of the home of Nunufar Ghazoumyan, in Dilijan at 17 Shahoumyan Street. Roughly $10 per person. This B&B is part of fledgling network of B&B's in Armenia (Internet: www.bedandbreakfast.am) (Tel. (0-680) + 54-35).

Cinematographers' Union House, cottages and private rooms with hot water. Double $20; Cottage $50. Located in vicinity of Hotel Dilijan. Restaurant open during the Summer (Tel. (2720) + 61-39) (E-mail: dina@arminco.com).

Hotel Dilijan, Soviet era accommodations. Singles from $2-$10. Prominently located near the town center.

Geytap Hotel and Restaurant, built in 1999, is a campus-like facility with four modern cottages and three dreary singles, which are located in the restaurant building. Choose the cottage, which is clean, and has two bedrooms, a private bath and fireplace. Cottage $50 (sleeps four); Single $10. Located on the Dilijan-to-Ijevan road, roughly four km past the center of Dilijan on the east (right) side of the road (Tel. (0-680) + 56-14; (0-680) + 43-41).

Soonk Motel, clean and modern, with friendly proprietors and 24-hour hot water. Single 8,000 drams (roughly $13). Located on the road that leads to Parz Lake, just one kilometer from the turnoff from the main highway (travel time from the main highway is about two minutes). This is certainly the best of the Dilijan-area motels.

Zorapor Motel, austere. Their overpriced rates beg to be negotiated. Single 8,000 to 10,000 drams (roughly $13 to $17). Located on the Dilijan-to-Ijevan road, roughly five km past the center of Dilijan. Look for their restaurant, which sometimes has a large bilingual "Welcome" sign on the front, and which is located on the west (left) side of the road. The motel is on a hilltop at the end of a gravel road, 100 m behind the restaurant.

Prices *are listed in US dollars for those hotels that quote US dollars when advertising their rates. Otherwise, prices are listed in Armenian drams.*

Telephone: *The area code for Dilijan is 680. When calling Dilijan from Yerevan, enter (0) + (680) + (local phone number).*

IJEVAN

Ijevan is located just 35 km (30 minutes) northeast of Dilijan, and is easy to get to from the main Dilijan-to-Ijevan road. The town *shuka*, or market, is located directly on this main road, and there's a large high-rise hotel from the Soviet era here, as well. You will not confuse Ijevan with the nearby town of Dilijan, however. Ijevan is not a resort and it doesn't normally attract tourists. There are a couple of sites just beyond Ijevan, however, that make this region an interesting day-long diversion for tourists who have had their fill of Dilijan or for travelers who are interested in exploring some of the country's less-known treasures.

Ten km beyond Ijevan, tucked away in the tiny village of **Lusahovit**, is the equally tiny monastery of **Tsrviz**. The highlight is the one-room Astvatsatsin Church, which dates from the fifth century. Villagers have told us that the site is *voch inch*, which in this context is roughly equivalent to saying "it's OK." We think it is better than that, and

A family rides to market on a remote country road near the village of Ardvi in Lori Region

certainly worth the 15 minute detour from the main road. To get there, from Ijevan drive north 10 km until reaching the clearly marked right turnoff to Khashtarak. Drive two km, all of it uphill and most of it paved, until reaching a sharp right turnoff to Lusahovit. Drive three km on this road until reaching a right turnoff onto a gravel road. The church is at the end of this 100-meter-long gravel road.

A bit farther north, where the main road forks left to Noyemberian, there's an easy-to-miss turnoff for Achajoor (located 18 km north of Ijevan). Just beyond this village is the monastery of Makaravank, which is nestled into a hillside and surrounded by trees and several picnic areas. The oldest of Makaravank's four chapels is accessible only from inside the church hall (gavit), and it dates back to the tenth century. The facade of the hall features engravings of a sphinx and lion, and the entrance to the main chapel is ornamented with turquoise-colored stones. From the mountain road that leads to Makaravank you'll have a clear view of the Aghstev Reservoir in Azerbaijan.

To get there, from the Ijevan-to-Noyemberian road take the left turnoff to Achajoor, and travel roughly eight km through town and uphill on roads that are at times rough.

Travel time from the main road to Makaravank is about 30 minutes. Part of this road is unpaved and rough.

NOYEMBERIAN

Most tourists don't make it any farther north than Dilijan and fewer still will venture past Ijevan. But there are a handful of sites, in addition to the beautiful countryside, that make it worthwhile to journey to the northeastern town of Noyemberian, assuming, of course, that you've already been everywhere else and are adventurous. Noyemberian made the news briefly in 2002 when a man who was working in his garden uncovered a Bronze Age burial pit, as well as clay mugs, bronze arrowheads, and other relics characteristic of the Bronze Age.

To reach this remote part of Armenia will require several hours of driving from Yerevan. To make the most of your trip, start at sunrise on a long summer day, or plan to combine this trek with an overnight stay in Dilijan or in the Lori Region. To get there, from Yerevan you can travel to Noyemberian as part of a journey to either Alaverdi or Dilijan. There's no fast route. Either (1) travel north to Sevan and Dilijan, and then northeast past Ijevan or (2) travel north through Spitak and Vanadzor, and then northeast past Alaverdi.

Advisory: it may be hazardous to travel to Noyemberian from the direction of Ijevan because of the road's proximity to the border with Azerbaijan [See box, Note About Traveling in the Northeast, this chapter].

Kirants Monastery

From the main road southeast of Noyemberian, take the west turnoff at the village of Kirants to reach the unusual **Kirants Monastery**. The maps show this as a fairly straight shoot west from the main road, but road conditions are poor, making this a tough-to-get-to site. The main chapel has brick and glazed-tile elements that make it unusual for an Armenian church. The remains of frescoes are still visible. Located about 12 km west of the village of Kirants.

Note About Traveling to the Lori Region

There are two main roadways in Lori and two distinct geographic areas: (1) from the east side of Vanadzor there's a road that goes north through Alaverdi to the Georgian border; and (2) from the west side of Vanadzor there's a road that goes north through Stepanavan to the Georgian border.

To visit the monasteries, travel the first route. The section below describes the sights you will see along this route. Drive eastward past Vanadzor on the road that lies north of the river, and then head northeast toward Alaverdi. You can make it to Alaverdi and back to Yerevan in one tiring day if you start early.

The second route described above takes you to Stepanavan and Lori Berd. This region is included in chapter 9, Northwest Armenia. This road also serves as an alternate route to Noyemberian and you could actually drive one huge loop from Vanadzor, through Noyemberian, then Dilijan, and finally finish back where you started in Vanadzor. This would take two full days and would be an interesting itinerary for only the heartiest of travelers.

LORI REGION

The region of **Lori** is home to several significant historic sites. Because of the geography, the vast size of the region, and the layout of the roadways, it would be impossible to see everything in a day or two. This section covers the historic sites of Lori that are located in northeastern Armenia. For Lori Berd and Stepanavan, which are located within Lori but are nevertheless accessible by a different roadway in northwestern Armenia, please refer to Chapter 8, Northwest Armenia.

Monasteries of Sanahin, Haghpat and Odzun

The lush and remote region of Lori in the northeast is home to three of the most magical and beautiful monasteries of Armenia: Sanahin, Haghpat and Odzun. Any one of them alone would be worth the trip. Because of their proximity to each other near the town of Alaverdi, however, it is an easy matter to visit all three during one outing. The Sanahin and Haghpat Monasteries are located on wooded mountainsides in the towns of Alaverdi and Haghpat. UNESCO (the UN Educational, Scientific and Cultural Organization) recognizes both Sanahin and Haghpat on its list of World Heritage sites. Odzun, which isn't on the World Heritage list but probably should be, is nearby and is perched on a large table of flatland atop a gorge.

Before reaching any of these monasteries, however, you will pass the mountainside marvel of **Kober**. This site dates back to 1171 and is located immediately past the town of Tumanian, hidden amid the trees on the west (left) side of the road. The main church of this monastery, which dates to the twelfth century, is in ruins, and there are spectacular frescoes exposed to the open sky. The hike up the mountain to the site will take approximately 15 minutes along a trail that is often muddy. Wear hiking shoes. The best time of day to photograph Kober is in mid-afternoon. The high ridge blocks the late day sun, and the morning sun does not shine on the exposed frescoes.

Northeast Armenia

The sixth-century monastery of Odzun, Lori Region

Northeast Armenia

Sanahin was founded in AD 966 and its surviving complex today consists of a bell tower, library, cemetery and a pair of churches. The bell tower dates back to 1211 and is said to be the oldest of its kind in Armenia. Many more buildings, including libraries and dwellings, had formed part of the monastery campus in the past.

To get there, from Vanadzor travel north to the town of Alaverdi. Immediately before reaching Alaverdi, take the right turnoff across the Debed River and drive up to the end of the paved mountain road.

Haghpat was built at roughly the same time and it shares many architectural elements with Sanahin. This fortified monastery is only another three km farther away, and is built at the top of the Debed River Gorge. Haghpat served as a major literary and cultural center during the Middle Ages. Sanahin and Haghpat are both exceptionally rich in *khatchkars*, with more than 80 that still exist at the two sites. To get there, travel 300 m past the town center of Alaverdi. Immediately after passing through the center, take the right turnoff and go over the Debed River Bridge. The monastery is located roughly eight km from the bridge.

The oldest of the trio of monasteries is **Odzun**, which was built in the early sixth century. This complex also sits atop the Debed River Gorge, where it could be defended against invaders. Just a few meters from the main church is a sixth century funeral monument on which is engraved scenes that depict the early spread of Christianity.

To get there, turn left off the main highway at a point just a few km before reaching the town of Alaverdi and nine km before the Haghpat turnoff. Take this road, which is full of switchbacks and is poorly paved, to the top of the gorge. Turn right at the center of the town of Odzun.

Travel time from the main road is about 15 minutes.

There's an ancient bridge, built in 1192, that spans the Debed River and that you will see on your way to Sanahin. It had been open to motor vehicles as recently as the 1970s, but it is now closed and cars are directed over a modern bridge. There are also copper and lead mines along the Debed River in Alaverdi, which both spurred the town's growth and also spoiled some of its appearance. The mines are operating at very low capacity today and scientists are monitoring their effects upon local water resources [see box, Alaverdi Mining District, this chapter].

In the town of Alaverdi there's a cable car that spans the gorge from one mountain to the next. The cable car was operating at time of research. The historic sites worth seeing, however, are all located on the side roads high above the gorge. Approximately 15 km north of Alaverdi, in the town of Akhtala, there's a thirteenth century monastery that warrants a visit. The **Akhtala monastery** is also located at the top of the Debed River Gorge. The monastery is located within the walls of a tenth century fortress. The site's well-preserved frescoes, coupled with the dramatic location of the complex at the top of the gorge, make this a worthwhile extension of any trip to the Alaverdi region.

To get there (Akhtala), from Alaverdi travel north toward the town of Akhtala until reaching a bridge on the left side of the road that spans the Debed River. Cross the bridge and turn right at the other side.

Travel time from Yerevan to Alaverdi is about four hours. Travel time from Alaverdi to Akhtala monastery is about 30 minutes.

Ardvi and Hnevank

Ardvi Monastery is a seldom-visited site that is located, literally, just down the road from Odzun. Don't travel to Odzun without also taking time for Ardvi, which features an oddly shaped bell tower, complete with a working bell. To get there, from Odzun travel south on the main road until you reach the village of Aygehat and then take the right turnoff for the village of Ardvi. The monastery sits in a bucolic setting at the end of the unpaved road.

If you are adventurous you may want to continue driving southeast from Ardvi and toward the towns of Kurtan and Vardablur. The rough road is filled with potholes and in parts it is just a gravel and stone trail. But the reward is **Hnevank**, a seventh century monastery that sits in the gorge not far from where the Dzoraget and Gargar rivers meet. The surviving church there dates back to 1144. Continuing east on this road will take you to the village of Gyulagarak, from which you can easily travel south to Vanadzor or north to Stepanavan.

Caution: The roads are in poor condition. We recommend visiting Hnevank only if you have a good Jeep and plenty of time. You'll need to do some easy hiking through tall grass and wildflowers, so wear good shoes and long pants.

The Monastery of Hnevank, Lori Region

Hotels and Places to Stay

Anoush Motel, clean, affordable and fairly new (built in 2000), with 24-hour hot water (convenient to Alaverdi). This micro-motel has a restaurant and just four loft-style suites, each with a porch that overlooks the river. Not handicapped-accessible. Single 12,000 drams (roughly $20). Located just north of the village of Pambak, and several km south of the regional center of Tumanian, on the main roadway that links Vanadzor to Alaverdi. One hour drive to Alaverdi (Tel. (8-257) + 4-08-08).

Avan Spa Dzoraget, a modern (opened in 2004) 34-room hotel in the town of Dzoraget (convenient to Alaverdi), with Western accommodations. Swimming pool, restaurant and conference center. Located just south of Tumanian and 16 km north of the **Anoush Motel** (see above) on the main roadway that links Vanadzor to Alaverdi. Thirty-minute drive north to Alaverdi (Yerevan Tel. 54-31-22; Yerevan Fax 54-78-77) (E-mail: hotels@tufenkian.am) (Internet: www.tufenkian.am).

Northwest Armenia

eight

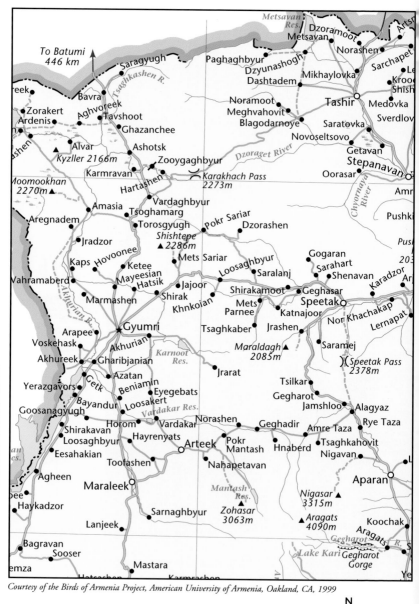

Courtesy of the Birds of Armenia Project, American University of Armenia, Oakland, CA, 1999

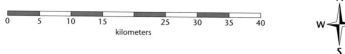

N
W ✦ E
S

0   5   10   15   25   30   35   40
kilometers

INTRODUCTION

The road to Gyumri is a desolate stretch of highway, and to the casual traveler it might look like there is little reason to stop and look around. Mile after mile, it seems that there's nothing more alluring here than the boulders and rock shards that fill the fields.

Cloistered-away among those rocks, and within some of the many villages that subsist among them, however, there's a bevy of historic sites that beckon. The apparent desolation is a false façade that falls away when you pause to look around. It's possible to plan a trip to Gyumri, with a couple of stops along the way, as a daytrip. But there's enough to see here to justify an overnight stay in Gyumri, at one of the comfortable new hotels that have opened in the past couple of years.

ON THE ROAD TO GYUMRI

Tegherivank and Kosh

Tegherivank, a thirteenth century monastery located in the village of Tegher, has a menacing look thanks to the black stones of its façade. The placement of two chapels on the roof of its main hall (gavit) is unusual, and adds to its forbidding look. There are several interesting *khatchkar*s nearby, and their location is a great vantage point from which to photograph this unusual monastery.

To get there, from Yerevan drive beyond Ashtarak, over the new four-lane bridge, and toward Gyumri. The divided four-lane highway narrows to an undivided two-lane road immediately after you have passed through Ashtarak. At this point, after you have passed through Ashtarak and the road has narrowed to two lanes, turn right (north) at the village of Agarak and continue northward up to the top of this windy mountain road.

The village of **Kosh**, which is roughly 17 km west of that big four-lane bridge over the Kasakh River, is a worthy stop for a seventh century church that is precariously perched at the edge of the gorge. The church, **St. Stepanos**, is almost impossible to

Note About Traveling on the Road to Gyumri

There are very few services along the road to Gyumri from the Ashtarak-Yerevan region. Start with a full tank of gasoline, and bring bottled drinking water and food.

The road was well paved at time of research, but there are barely any other improvements. The absence of lighting and other safety features, along with the lack of services, are good reasons to avoid driving on this road after dark.

This section describes the sights in the sequence they would be encountered by a traveler who is driving northbound from Yerevan to Gyumri. To get onto the Gyumri highway, drive northeast from Yerevan, on the Ashtarak highway. Cross the new four-lane bridge that spans the Kasakh River and take the turnoff that is signposted for Gyumri.

Photograph, previous page: Foothills of Mt. Aragats

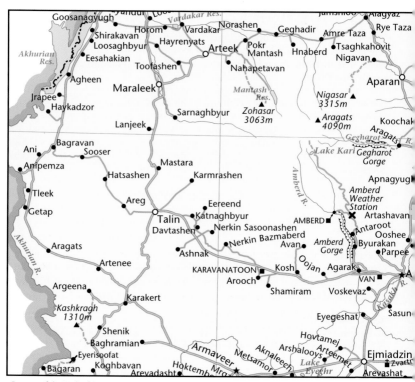

Courtesy of the Birds of Armenia Project, American University of Armenia, Oakland, CA, 1999

see from the road. The grounds include the ruins of the monastery of Koshavank as well as many khatchkars and other monuments. Faint remnants of frescoes are still visible on the interior walls of the church. This is a hidden treasure that one never hears about. Immediately before the first turnoff to Kosh, a strong candidate for the **World's Largest Khatchkar** is located on the north side of the main road, just 50 meters from the pavement. The *khatchkar*, which is as tall as a house and was carved in 1195, has survived here for more than 800 years.

To get there, take the first turnoff for Kosh, which is marked by a winged eagle on a 12-foot tall pile of rocks on the right side of the road. Drive north roughly three km and then take a right turn to go off-road onto a dirt and stone trail. The trail is short. If you don't have a Niva or other 4-wheel drive vehicle, you can hike the 200-meter-distance in about ten minutes. This beautiful site is literally off the beaten path!

When Armenia was a station along the **Great Silk Road**, there were many active rest stops for the caravans that passed through. These rest stops were known as caravansaries, and the ruins of many of them can be seen along the modern roads. A partly restored— and partly ruined— caravansaray from the thirteenth century is located roughly eight km past the Kosh turnoff on the south (left) side of the main road to Gyumri.

This caravansaray is right next to a left turnoff that leads to the village of **Aruch.** As you drive toward the village you approach the massive Cathedral of **Saint Gregory,** which was built in AD 666.

Talin is just a little beyond the halfway point to Gyumri for travelers driving from Yerevan. It's the biggest settlement in the area, and is worth the stop for the seventh century church of **St. Astvatsatsin** and for the Talin Cathedral that is just about 50 m away. The turnoff to Talin, on the left side of the main road to Gyumri, is about 75 km from Yerevan and is marked with a sign. Talin is also one of three routes available to travelers who are seeking a distant glimpse of the Medieval Armenian Capital of Ani. The alternate routes are (1) from Yerevan by way of the Echmiadzin-Armavir road and (2) from Gyumri by driving past the Akhurian Reservoir.

Ani Promontory

The **Ani promontory** is a lookout from which viewers can see the medieval Armenian capital of Ani. This stunning view is available from the Armenian side of the international border with Turkey by simply looking across the deep gorge formed by the Akhurian River. Ani is a dreamed-of pilgrimage for many travelers. This is partly because Ani is stranded in Turkey, and (for political reasons) it is so difficult for anyone to get there from Armenia. Turkey closed and militarized its border with Armenia in 1993, shortly after Armenia became independent. Before this, it had been possible to cross the frontier at a major customs station located west of the Armenian city of Gyumri. For now, the best that many can hope for is to go to this promontory and view it from afar, with binoculars.

It's probably not surprising that it is just as difficult—again for political reasons— for anyone to even reach the promontory on the Armenian side. On the Armenian side, the lookout is located near the village of Kharkov, roughly 30 km west-north-west of Talin and roughly 40 km south of Gyumri.

Kharkov is so close to the border with Turkey that it is in a military zone where Russian soldiers restrict access. Russia, which is obligated by treaty to protect Armenia's western frontier, allows access only by special permission. Permission might be granted by the Armenian Foreign Ministry in Yerevan, or might be arranged by a travel agent (presumably for a fee paid to the local Russian commander or to the Russian base in Gyumri). You would be well advised to get your permission "documents" before traveling there.

The ugly reality is that for Armenians to visit their own ancient Armenian capital of **Ani** they have to somehow travel to Turkey (the border is closed) and get permission from Turkish soldiers. Then they must buy an admission ticket in the nearby town of Kars from a sales agent who is, judging from the population statistics for Kars, very likely to be Kurdish or Azeri.

And for Armenians to simply view the ancient Armenian churches of Ani from within the modern borders of Armenia, they have to get permission from Russian soldiers. The result is that this mythic site of extraordinary historical significance, located directly on the present-day border of Armenia and Turkey, is least accessible to the people for whom it means the most. It's a site that few Armenians get to see.

Northwest Armenia

To get there (to the Ani lookout), from Talin take the back road that passes through the villages of Areg, Sooser and Bagravan. Cross the railroad tracks at the village in Armenia that is also called Ani (in honor of the original Ani across the border). You will see the Russian army checkpoint at roughly six km from the main road. If you can get across the checkpoint, you will be escorted to a lookout, not far from a noisy quarry that was recently opened.

Travel time from Yerevan is about two hours. Travel time from Talin is about one hour. Travel time from Gyumri (40 km) is about 45 minutes.

Travel Note: *The road on each of the routes to the lookout is in poor condition. A Jeep, Niva or other 4-wheel drive vehicle would be helpful, but is not essential. Traveling south from Gyumri along the Akhurian Reservoir is the preferred route because it is the shortest and because this route allows you to drive close to the frontier, where you can see across the river to historic Armenia.*

Anipemza

This remote village is home to the basilica-style **Yereruyk** church, which historians cite as an architecturally significant example of fifth century design. Roman architectural elements are evident in its construction. Anipemza is located south of the Ani Promontory, and its location directly on the Turkish border—as is the promontory village of Kharkov—raises questions about the reasons for all the restrictions on access to Kharkov.

If military security is the reason for restricting access to Ani (in modern Turkey) and to Kharkov (the Armenian village that overlooks Ani) then one would expect similar concerns for places such as Anipemza and all the villages along the frontier. The Yereruyk church in Anipemza, for example, is only a couple of hundred meters from the Turkish border.

Akhurian Reservoir

The **Akhurian Reservoir** is a dominant sight along the roadway between the Ani lookout (see above) and Gyumri. This beautiful body of water may help keep your mind off the horrible road that you are traveling on while viewing it.

The reservoir was formed by a dam on the Akhurian River, part of which serves as the border between Armenia and Turkey. (Just south of Gyumri, the Akhurian River meanders inside the Armenian frontier.) By treaty, Armenia and Turkey share the water resources. [For more about Armenia's water resources, see Chapter 3, Ecology].

Harichavank

Harichavank is a magnificently sited complex that's just 20 minutes from the main Yerevan-to-Gyumri road in the village of Harich, close to the town of Artik. A seventh century chapel, **St. Gregory**, juts out at an angle from the main hall. Another tiny chapel, which dates back to the twelfth century, is perched on a 100-meter tall rock ledge, completely inaccessible to anyone. The ledge had been sheared away during the 1926 earthquake and now the chapel just teeters at its top. The main church dates from 1201 and there are several beautiful carvings on its façade. The

Photograph: Poppies in bloom atop a gorge, northern Armenia

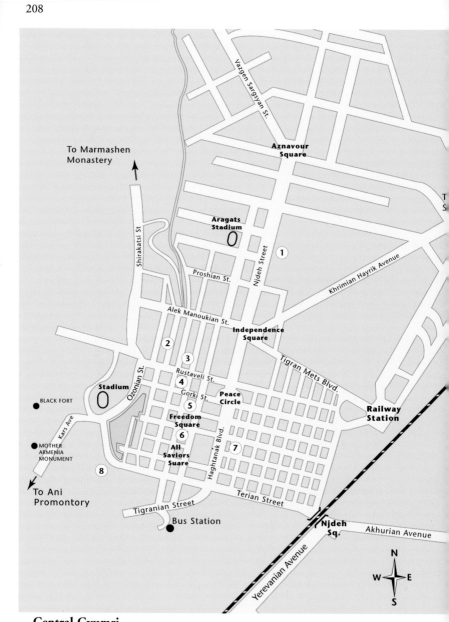

Central Gyumri

1 Hotel Isuz; 2 St. Astvatsatsin Catholic Church; 3 Hotel Araks; 4 St. Nishan Church;
5 St. Astvatsatsin Armenian Church, also known as Yot Verk; 6 All Savior's Church;
7 Hotel Berlin; 8 Russian Chapel

Map Research Courtesy of the Shirak Development Center

many engravings include an elaborately decorated sundial, a pair of lions, and the image of the two wealthy brothers who donated the building to the monastery some eight hundred years ago. A pair of modern monastery buildings is nearby.

The founding date of Harichivank is believed to have been in the seventh century coinciding with the construction of the seventh century chapel of St. Gregory identified above. Along the road to Harichavank, near the village of Pemzashen and roughly three km from the main Yerevan-to-Gyumri road, is the ruined eleventh century church of the Arakelots Vank. Also nearby, on a hill just southwest of Artik, are the seventh century church of **St. Stepanos** and the monastery of **Lmbatavank**. As you drive through this region, you will see many tuff mines. Tuff is used as a building material throughout Armenia, and it is popular for its varied palette of colors.

To get there, from the main Yerevan-to-Gyumri highway, take the right turnoff at Maralik, just opposite a big old factory building. Follow this road, which is parallel to the railroad tracks, as far as Artik and then take the bridge that overpasses the train tracks. Turn left at the rotary and go up the hill to Harich.

Travel time from the turnoff at the main roadway to Harichavank (15 km) is about 25 minutes.

Beniamin, located seven km south of Gyumri, is the site of an archaeological excavation that has revealed a settlement from at least 500 BC. The excavations were started in 1989, and they are ongoing. Visitors today will see the foundations of pillars and walls, and be able to imagine how significant this settlement must have been.

To get there, from the main Yerevan-to-Gyumri highway, turn left opposite the bus stop at the main entrance to town. There is a dirt path that leads to the site, about 30 m from the road, but obstructed from view by a small hill.

GYUMRI

Gyumri, located in the region (*marz*) of Shirak, is Armenia's second-largest city and has a population of somewhere between 180,000 (the government figure) to roughly 140,000 (the word on the street). Regardless of which figure is closer to the actual number of people in the city today, everyone agrees that there has been significant emigration during the past 15 years as a result of the economic downfall that followed the earthquake of December 7, 1988. Before the earthquake the population had been roughly 240,000.

Today, Gyumri remains notorious as the biggest city in the earthquake zone, so-called for that huge earthquake. The notoriety deserves to fade a bit. The city has made great strides in the past couple of years. The horrible shipping containers (domiks) that people actually lived in for more than a decade still exist in some pockets of the city, but most of them have now been replaced with permanent—and attractive—apartment buildings.

Earthquake Relief

International donors and foreign governments have helped with the reconstruction of Gyumri, and Diaspora Armenians have also made sizable contributions. The United States Agency for International Development (USAID) supports an ongoing **Earthquake Zone Recovery Program** for the region.

Northwest Armenia

Statue of Mother Armenia, Gyumri

The Shirak Development Center (SDC) in Gyumri is a cheerleader for economic development in the area, and it acts as a sort of chamber of commerce. Their website is a good source for additional maps and further travel information (www.shirakinfo.am).

Forgive the people here if they seem to have an identity crisis about their hometown. Gyumri has been named and re-named many times over the years. The city had been **Leninakan** during much of the Soviet era, and many older folk—and many road signs—persist in using that name. **Alexandropol** had been the city's pre-Soviet name, but earlier still, it went by the Armenian name Kumayri. The city briefly called itself **Kumayri** again after independence in 1991, but the period was so brief that few people even remember. There's been some talk lately about changing the name back to that centuries-old moniker Kumayri, but there's also been some talk that enough is enough.

The current name Gyumri is a derivation of the Russian word for a customs place—which is not a surprising name for a frontier city with a strong Russian presence. The area had been incorporated into the Russian Empire in 1804 and this was once the frontline between NATO and the USSR. Soldiers on each side of the line still spy on each other through binoculars, and the Soviet Army base at the edge of the city is still there, except that now it's a Russian Army base. Russia recently opened a Consulate in the center of town and relations between the Russians and the Armenians are good. The city's long ties with Russia are evident in the numerous historic buildings that date back to the nineteenth century period of the Russian Empire.

Armenians were here, of course, long before there were Russians anywhere. The earliest recorded reference to Kumayri is from AD 773, and describes a rebellion against Arab domination by an Armenian freedom fighter named Artavazd Mamikonyan. The rebellion succeeded. Local people may tell you that Greek historian Xenophon mentions "Ghiumri" as having been a locality even earlier, in the seventh through sixth centuries BC. This is far from settled, however. Some scholars question whether Xenophon was referring to Gyumri, or instead referring to another location on the Armenian plateau, as reported by historian Robert Hewsen in the book "Armenia: A Historical Atlas."

Travel time from Yerevan to Gyumri (125 km) is a bit more than 90 minutes. Hire a driver for about $40 for a full-day excursion. A bus departs daily each morning from Yerevan's Kilikia Central Bus Station, but it's very slow.

Attractions And Sightseeing

Every important city deserves a monument to Mother Armenia. Yerevan has one. And Gyumri does, too. Gyumri's monument is perched on a hilltop next to the dark Russian garrison known as the **Sev Ghul** (Black Sentry). Both sites are accessible from the road that runs parallel to the Akhurian Reservoir, southwest of the city. Beyond Mother Armenia lies the Turkish border and lands that had been part of Armenia until Turkey seized them in 1920.

Central Park offers a great vantage point from which to photograph Mother Armenia. "Central Park" is a bit of a misnomer: the park is located at the southwestern edge of the city. There are carnival rides for children, cafes for adults, and a bandstand where everyone can enjoy musical performances on summer evenings. There's a famous opera house here, too. The Russian Orthodox **Piplan Zham** (Shimmering Chapel) is located just outside the park's southern edge.

The historic **Kumayri District** in the heart of town has roughly 1,600 monuments and buildings of historical significance, and which date from the eighteenth and nineteenth centuries. In two strokes of fortune, the district survived major earthquakes in both 1926 and 1988. The architecture, which is similar to the style seen in the old sections of Kars, is a reminder of the city's past as a major outpost of the Russian Empire. Kars is a nearby historic Armenian town that is now part of Turkey. [For more about Kars, see Appendix 1].

Freedom Square is located within this District, and there are several Armenian churches nearby. While standing in the Square, you can see the peaks of three of them. **St. Astvatsatsin** is impossible to miss. This grand church is a solid anchor for the northeast corner of the square. Local residents prefer to call it Yot Verk—a reference to the seven wounds of Christ. **All Savior's Church** had dominated the southern flank of the square until the earthquake ruined it in 1988. The design of the church building was influenced by the architecture at the ancient Armenian capital of Ani. The building was under reconstruction at time of research, however, and was expected to dominate the square once again. When it does, it will also preside over the park and popular meeting place adjacent to the south side of the church, All Savior's Square.

St. Nishan is two blocks north, but you can still see its peak from Freedom Square. This church was originally built in 1870 and was re-consecrated in late 2003. The fourth church is hidden from view. In 1926, some families who had lost their homes during that year's earthquake occupied a building that had been, before the Soviet era, the **St. Astvatsatsin Armenian Catholic Church**. The dome of the church had fallen during the earthquake, but the building was otherwise in habitable condition, so these homeless families just moved in. They've installed windows and made so many other modifications for residential use that it is easy to walk past and never notice its history. Descendants of the displaced families are still living there, but it is nevertheless possible to view the exterior. The church is located a couple of blocks west of the square.

Museums

The **Gyumri Museum**, also known as the Museum of National Architecture and Urban Life of Gyumri, 47 Haghtanaki Street, shouldn't be missed. On display you will see urban artifacts; paintings by Minas Avedisian; and a gallery of 23 original Yosef (Hovsep) Karsh photographs that includes his world-famous images of Churchill, Reagan, Einstein, Kennedy, and others (Closed Mondays) (Tel. 0-41 + 2-36-00).

Isahakyan House Museum, 91 Shahumyan (Varpetats) Street. A shrine to Gyumri poet Avetik Isahakyan (Closed Mondays).

Shiraz House Museum, 101 Shahumyan (Varpetats) Street. Artifacts honoring the life of Gyumri poet Hovhannes Shiraz (Closed Mondays).

USEFUL INFORMATION

Safety

Gyumri's proximity to the border of Turkey, which is closed and militarized, demands that visitors exercise prudence near the Akhurian Reservoir border region, and elsewhere near the border. Don't make provocative gestures or engage in acts that might be misinterpreted as hostile. Do not photograph the guard towers or the Russian soldiers who, pursuant to a Russian treaty with Armenia, patrol the region. Serious incidents along the border were not common at time of research and the area has been quiet and peaceful, albeit not quite neighborly.

Health

Gyumri is a major city and health care is readily available from: Shirak Marz Regional Hospital, 51 Sevyan Street (Tel. 0-41 + 2-46-44); Polyclinic No. 1, 201 Shirakatsi Street (Tel. 0-41 + 2-26-08); and the ICRC (Red Cross) Polyclinic, Ani District No. 5 (Tel. 0-41 + 3-97-60). An Ambulance station is located at 3 Kuybishev (Tel. 0-41 + 2-12-50).

Climate

Gyumri is colder and snowier than Yerevan, and its winters are longer. Its summer weather isn't much different from Yerevan's—hot and sunny. Weather reports for all of Armenia are available from www.wunderground.com and from www.weather.com.

Transportation

Local taxi service is available from Milenari Taxi (Tel. 0-41 + 3-93-33); Samba Taxi (Tel. 0-41 + 3-00-93); and Jazz Taxi (Tel. 0-41 + 3-04-07). Flights to Moscow and other cities in Russia depart from Shirak International Airport, near the entrance to the city. Intercity transportation is available from the bus station on Tigranyan Street, at the southern edge of the city.

Tour Operators

Local guides can be arranged through the following agencies: Shirak Tours/Berlin Guesthouse Tours (Tel. 0-41 + 3-75-59); Isuz Hotel Tours (Tel. 0-41 + 3-33-99); Kumayri Historic District (Tel. 0-41 + 2-34-34); and Shirak Development Center (0-41 + 3-39-61).

Telephone

The area code for Gyumri is 41. When calling Gyumri from Yerevan enter (0) + (41) + (local phone number). When dialing Gyumri from outside Armenia, dial (374) + (41) + (local phone number).

Hotels and Places to Stay

Araks Hotel opened in January 2004 and is the city's newest. Conveniently located near the city center, across from St. Nishan church. No handicapped access. 27 Gorki Street (Tel. 0-41 + 3-58-15).

Hotel Guesthouse Berlin offers 11 clean and modern rooms with private baths and satellite television. This boutique hotel was built in 1996, and it is Gyumri's best value. Single $40-$50. Handicapped-accessible. Breakfast included. Accepts MasterCard and Visa. 25 Haghtanak Street (near the Gyumri Museum). Look for the sign that discreetly says only "Berlin" (Tel. 0-41 + 3-76-59) (E-mail: info@berlinhotel-gyumri.am) (Internet: www.berlinhotel-gyumri.am).

Isuz Hotel offers eight large rooms and four suites, each with private bath, kitchenette, and satellite television. Single $60; Deluxe Suite $100. No handicapped access. Accepts MasterCard and Visa. 1/5 Garegin Njdeh Avenue (Tel. 0-41 + 3-33-99; Fax 0-41 + 3-99-93) (E-mail: isuz@shirak.am) (Internet: www.isuz.am).

Places to Eat

Gyumri Brewery, historic pub that brews its own beer. Traditional Armenian and Georgian cuisine. 30 Gorki Street (Tel. 041 + 2-37-69); **Kumayri Restaurant**, historic site of a Soviet-era prison. Access from an old courtyard. Armenian and international cuisine. 246 Abovian Street (Tel. 0-41 + 2-11-62); **Phaeton Alek**, historic restaurant attached to the Gyumri Museum. Traditional Armenian and Georgian cuisine. 47 Haghtanak Street (Tel. 0-41 + 3-29-88).

If you are preparing your own food, try the **Gyumri Market**, which is the largest outdoor food market in Gyumri. Located on Haghtanaki Avenue, near Terian Street and the Gyumri Museum.

MARMASHEN AND NORTH OF GYUMRI

Marmashen Monastery rests on a beautiful site beside the Akhurian River, surrounded by an apple orchard. This magnificent monastery is more than one thousand years old, and among the buildings that have survived is a church that dates back to AD 988. Archaeologists have also uncovered the remnants of other buildings, and they have unearthed the foundation of a church that had an unusual circular base. Visitors have full access to all the ruins. You will see that one of the ruined churches has been preserved with concrete patches to prevent further damage and water seepage, but is not otherwise restored or rebuilt. There's an ancient burial ground on an adjacent hill, and a nearby waterfall.

To get there, from Alek Manoukian Street in Gyumri, turn north onto Shirakatsi Street and drive 2.3 km. Turn left at the major intersection there, and drive for seven and one half km on this paved but very rough road. There's a signpost for a left turn onto a stretch of dirt and gravel road that winds down to the monastery.

Travel time from Gyumri to Marmashen (10 km) is about 20 minutes because of the bad road. Travel time from Yerevan to Marmashen (135 km) is about two hours.

SPITAK, VANADZOR AND STEPANAVAN

Spitak was completely leveled in the earthquake of 1988 because of its proximity to the earthquake's epicenter. Much of the town has been rebuilt during the past couple of years, following more than a decade of inaction. At the approach to Spitak there's a whimsical church on the left side of the road that looks every bit like a traditional Armenian church, except that it is made from sheet metal. This non-traditional material was used so that the church could be erected quickly to accommodate the many funerals that were held after the quake, and the sprawling cemetery below speaks to the church's initial purpose. You really should stop and take a closer look at this one.

This is also the vicinity of the so-called Nor (New) Spitak. Nor Spitak was built with foreign assistance to replace some of the housing that was destroyed in the quake. Many of the people in this cohesive community felt isolated by this new suburban development. The reconstruction of the past few years has accommodated this concern, and has instead been concentrated in the core of the town.

To get there, from Gyumri travel east on Khrimian Hayrik Avenue; From Yerevan, travel north on the Yerevan-to-Spitak highway.

Small village at sunset, northern Armenia

Travel time from Gyumri to Spitak is about 30 minutes. Travel time from Yerevan is about 90 minutes.

Vanadzor is Armenia's third largest city but it still doesn't have much to offer tourists. There isn't much to see, and the huge chemical plant at its center (Vanadzor is also the second largest industrial city in Armenia) took away the town's natural beauty. Local chemical products included paint thinner, glue, and varnish, but today only ammonia is produced. Vanadzor's location east of Spitak makes it a major hub for travelers nonetheless. Many Armenians continue to refer to the city by its Soviet-era name Kirovakan.

Despite the paucity of historic tourist attractions, Vanadzor is historically significant. This is the site of a significant battle in May 1918 during which outnumbered Armenian soldiers successfully defended against an invasion by Turkey. The Turkish army was pushed back to Sardarapat [see chapter 5, Central Armenia], where Armenia was again the unlikely victor in a battle that was to prove crucial to Armenia's existence. But for these victories in 1918, the Republic of Armenia would probably not exist today.

From Vanadzor one can choose to continue one's journey to Stepanavan (see below), to Alaverdi, or to Dilijan. Both the Alaverdi and Dilijan regions are covered in Chapter 7, Northeast Armenia.

Travel time from Spitak to Vanadzor is about 20 minutes. Travel time from Yerevan to Vanadzor is a bit less than 2 hours.

Telephone

The area code for Spitak is 550. When calling Spitak from Yerevan, enter (0) + (550) + (local phone number. The area code for Vanadzor is 51. When calling Vanadzor from Yerevan, enter (0) + (51) + (local phone number).

Place to Stay

Hotel Argishti opened in 2002 and is Vanadzor's premiere hotel, with 23 modern but poorly furnished rooms. Single $50; Double $80. No handicapped access. No credit cards. 1 Batumi Street (Tel. 0-51 + 4-25-56) (Internet: www.spyur.am.argistihot.htm).

Stepanavan and Lori Berd

Driving eastward from Spitak, there's a left turnoff just before reaching the city-limits of Vanadzor. This turnoff isn't signposted, but you'll see several new apartment buildings on the corner.

Traveling northward toward Stepanavan from Vanadzor on this road will take you through the Pushkin Pass. Thanks to a long (and dark, and damp) tunnel, you can drive under most of the pass and save a lot of time. Gargar is the first "big" village after the tunnel. Driving through Gargar's main thoroughfare, you will see as many as a dozen loaves of homemade bread sunning themselves on chairs that are all lined up along the road. Stop near one and someone will come running out of his home to sell you a freshly baked loaf. There's an interesting church in this village, too. The neighboring village of Pushkino may catch your eye for its onion dome church. Ethnic Russians, as you might guess, settled this village.

Lori Berd (Fortress) is Stepanavan's claim to fame. This grand fortress is surrounded on three sides by the gorges of the Dzoraget and Urut Rivers. On the fourth side, which is exposed, there is a huge stone wall with guard towers. Within the fortress walls, two baths and a church have been preserved. Lori Berd was the heart of an Armenian kingdom in AD 989. Like so many other ancient communities in Armenia, the history of this one includes periods of devastation by Mongol and Turkic invaders. One of the churches, and a small section of the fortress wall, have survived the centuries.

Although this area is within the geographic region of Lori, the roadways make it more convenient to visit Stepanavan as part of a trip north past Vanadzor. If you are traveling through Hnevank, you can also make the trip to Lori Berd by taking the Vardablur-Kurtan road.

To get there, from Stepanavan cross the bridge that spans the Dzoraget River. After the bridge, turn right at the rotary and drive east to the village of Lori Berd.

Travel time from Yerevan to Stepanavan is a bit more than three hours. Travel time from Vanadzor to Stepanavan is roughly 90 minutes.

Telephone

The area code for Stepanavan is 56. When calling Stepanavan from Yerevan, enter (0) + (56) + (local phone number).

Place to Stay

Motel Lori (convenient to Stepanavan) is a modern facility (built in 2002) that features six suites with 24-hour hot water. No handicapped access. Single/Double 7,000 drams (roughly $12). This motel and restaurant complex offers horseback riding, billiards and a sauna. Located just south of Stepanavan, in the town of Amaragits, along the main road that links Vanadzor to Stepanavan. Views of Lori Berd on the other side of the gorge. Twenty minute drive to Lori Berd (Tel. 0-56 + 2-20-05; E-mail: stepcenter@infocom.am).

NATURE AND CONSERVATION

Arpi Lake is tucked away in the far northwest corner of Armenia and it doesn't get many visitors. Conservationists and bird-watchers will find it enticing, however. Arpi's watershed has been identified as a wetland of "international significance" under the Ramsar Convention, a multi-national treaty to which Armenia is a party. One reason for this significance is the reservoir's role as a major stopping point for migratory birds. Many species of migratory birds fly over Armenia each year, and bodies of water such as this play a role in attracting them and encouraging them to stop. The reservoir is the result of a dam at the source of the Akhurian River. [For more about bird watching, water resources, and Armenia's rich biological diversity, see Chapter 3, Ecology].

The village church of Gargar, located just south of Stepanavan

Armenia's first arboretum, the **Stepanavan Dendropark**, was established in 1933 just south of Stepanavan in the village of Gyulagarak. This serene 35-ha site is divided into roughly equal areas of natural forest and ornamental trees. Although arboretums such as this one attract visitors and are valued for their aesthetics, they are also important because they can help protect species that are threatened by human activities or by natural disasters.

In addition to protecting native plants, these gardens also permit the evaluation of introduced plant species, particularly species with potential use in soil conservation, and environmental restoration. At Dendropark, more than 500 flora species have been introduced for these purposes from Europe, North America, and Eurasia. Nursery activities at these gardens are currently providing plant material for reforestation and agriculture, and are potential sources of revenue as Armenia's economy continues to improve.

SouthernArmenia

nine

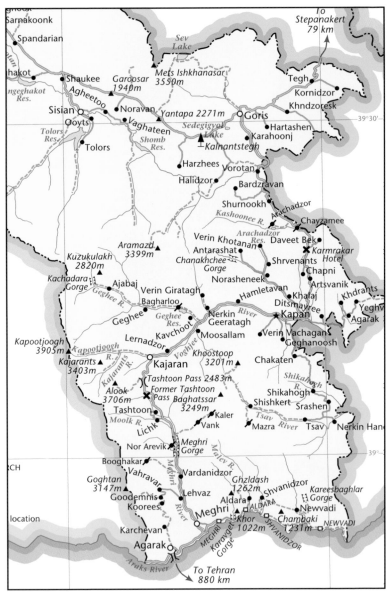

Southern Armenia

To Stepanakert
79 km

Sarnakoonk

Spandarian

hakot

Shaukee *Garoosar 1940m*
Agheetoo

Sev Lake

Mets Ishkhanasar 3550m

Tegh

Kornidzor

Khndzoresk

Sisian
Ooyts

Noravan *Yantapa 2271m*

Vaghateen

Goris

Hartashen

Tolors Res.

Tolors *Shomb Res.*

Sedegigyol Lake

Karahoonj

Kalnantstegh

Harzhees

Halidzor

Vorotan

Bardzravan

Shurnookh

Kashoonee R.

Arachadzor

Chayzamee

Verin Khotanan *Arachadzor Res.* Daveet Bek

Antarashat

Chanakhchee Gorge

Shrvenants

Karmrakar Hotel

Aramazd 3399m

Kuzukulakh 2820m

Norasheneek

Chapni

Artsvanik

Kachadara Gorge

Ajabaj

Verin Giratagh

Hamletavan

Khalaj

Khdrants

Geghee R. Bagharloo

Geghee *Geghee Res.*

Nerkin *River*

Geeratagh

Ditsmayree

Kapan

Yeghv

Agarak

Kapootjoogh 3905m

Lernadzor

Kavchoot

Moosallam

Verin Vachagan

Geghanoosh

Kapootjoogh R.

Kajarants 3403m

Kajaran

Voghjee R.

Khoostoop 3201m

Chakaten

Shikahogh R.

Tashtoon Pass 2483m

Former Tashtoon Pass

Alook 3706m

Baghatssar 3249m

Shikahogh

Shishkert

Srashen

Tashtoon

Moolk R.

Kaler

Vank

Mazra *Tsav River* Tsav

Nerkin Han

Lichk

Nor Arevik

Meghri Gorge

Matev R.

Booghakar

Vahravar

Goghtan 3147m

Goodemnis

Koorees

Vardanidzor

Lehvaz

Aldara

ALDARA

Ghzldash 1262m Shvanidzor

Kareesbaghlar Gorge

Newvadi

location

Karchevan

Agarak

Meghri

Meghri River

Khor *Karavgel Gorge* *1022m*

Chambaki *1231m*

SHVANIDZOR

NEWVADI

To Tehran
880 km

Araks River

Courtesy of the Birds of Armenia Project, American University of Armenia, Oakland, CA, 1999

0   5   10   15   25   30   35   40
kilometers

N
W   E
S

Vayots Dzor was a ring without a stone. So I cut and set that stone in the ring.

—*Princess Sophia, referring to the monastery she built near Jermuk in AD 936*

INTRODUCTION

The Zangezur panhandle region in southern Armenia is strategically important for its role as the country's only overland link to Iran as well as for its status as the only currently viable route to Karabagh. Armenia's neighbors—Turkey, Azerbaijan and Nakhijevan—have all closed their borders to Armenia, making Zangezur a critically important transit point.

The panhandle is also interesting to travelers for its starkly beautiful landscapes. The terrain is mountainous and so are its roads, which are full of switchbacks, and which are sometimes blocked by snow and ice as early as November and as late as March. As if for consolation, only one major road forms the backbone of the panhandle, so it's tough to get lost.

Zangezur is the historic name of the entire panhandle area, and this name may be missing from many modern road maps. Most maps today identify Zangezur by the names of its two *marzes* (administrative regions). The administrative region of Vayots Dzor sits in the northern third of Zangezur. The regional *marz* of Syunik lies in Zangezur's southern portion.

Note About Traveling to Zangezur

Zangezur is a region that many tourists ignore because there's just too much driving involved. If you are sightseeing in Armenia for at least one week, however, a journey through the northern panhandle *marz* of Vayots Dzor is a journey that you should definitely add to your itinerary.

Descending south of Goris and farther into the southern panhandle *marz* of Syunik will probably be of interest only to the heartiest travel enthusiast. This is because there are just not enough interesting historic sites to warrant the heavy investment of time. The driving time from Yerevan to Meghri, on the southern border, is about twelve hours. Because of this, traveling south of Goris is usually the lowest priority on anyone's itinerary during their journeys through Armenia and Karabagh.

There's a customs checkpoint near Sisian, but private cars are usually waved through. Many stretches of this road have been re-engineered and are freshly paved, but there are still enough potholes and rough spots to warrant continued caution.

Note: Do not attempt to reach the panhandle by the alternate route from Lake Sevan and through the Sulema Pass (sometimes called the Vayots Dzor Pass). This road is very rough and driving on it is unpleasant. This is not one of Armenia's "scenic" roadways. If you wish to go to the Sulema Pass (there is an ancient caravansary there) drive north from Yeghegnadzor, instead.

Photograph, previous page: Wheat field near Spandarian Reservoir

Southern Armenia

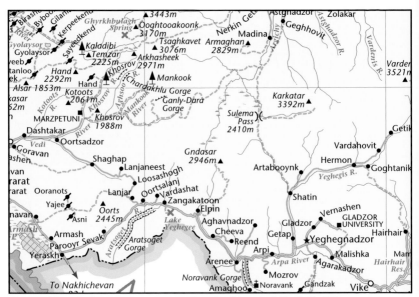

Courtesy of the Birds of Armenia Project, American University of Armenia, Oakland, CA, 1999

THE TOP OF THE ZANGEZUR PANHANDLE

Vayots Dzor Region

After driving through the fertile Ararat Valley, which is home to the Khor Virap monastery and which boasts some of Armenia's most spectacular views of Mt. Ararat, the road will take you quite close to the frontier with Nakhijevan, an enclave over which Azerbaijan has sovereignty. You cannot cross into Nakhijevan from Armenia. The border is closed. This wasn't always true, and the fastest route south to Meghri had at one time been the straight shot through the fertile flatlands along the Nakhijevan-Turkey border.

Nakhijevan's population once had a plurality of Armenians, but today it is a non-contiguous administrative unit of Azerbaijan, and the Armenians have all disappeared. Azeri authorities are feverishly removing all evidence of Armenian cultural history there, too. In 2003, the United Nations took notice when an ancient Armenian cemetery in Jugha and all its priceless *khatchkars* were bulldozed and hauled off [for more on cultural preservation, see Chapter 1, Land and People]. Nakhijevan is located along the entire length of Zangezur's western frontier.

On the right (west) side of the road in the Ararat Valley, a couple of km before you reach the Nakhijevan border, there are several fish farms where trout are produced. You'll see fish for sale at the roadside here, too. The marshes around these fish farms are great birding locations and you will probably be able to see cranes nesting atop utility poles here, too. Just beyond the fish farms is the village of Yeraskh, the last Armenian village before the border.

To get there (the Zangezur panhandle), from Yerevan travel south through the Ararat Valley and then make an abrupt left turn (east) at the village of Yeraskh, just before you approach the Nakhijevan-Armenia border. This left turnoff is roughly 70 km from Yerevan.

Travel time from Yerevan to the Yeraskh circle is about one hour.

The first significant town you reach in the panhandle is **Areni**, which gives its name to the famous Armenian red wine. Grapes are grown throughout this region, and if you visit in October, you may be able to see the winemaking process here or in the nearby towns of Getap and Arpi. Some of the wineries, apparently having heard about how the wineries in California's wine country stimulate consumer interest, will allow you to watch their operations and to taste some of their wines.

The history of winemaking here may be longer than we have previously appreciated. A scientist from the University of Pennsylvania has traced the prehistory of winemaking to this part of the world. The claim is made in the 2003 book "Ancient Wine: The Search for the Origins of Viniculture." The report says that the domestication of the Eurasian grapevine—which spurred the foundation of the world's first wine industry—occurred in the south Caucasus, eastern Anatolia or northwestern Iran. Areni is located at roughly the geographic center of these three areas.

Areni is also the site of the **St. Astvatsatsin** church, which was built in 1321. There are several unusual tombstones and *khatchkars* in the churchyard. **To get there**, take the right turnoff onto a paved road at Areni, then cross a low bridge that spans the Arpa River, and take a rough gravel road a few hundred meters to the top of the hill.

Travel time from the Yeraskh circle to Areni (42 km) is about 45 minutes.

Sulema Caravansary is located north of Getap and just south of the Sulema Pass. This mountain pass, which is sometimes called the Vayats Dzor Pass, is the passage to Lake Sevan. Traveling through the pass is difficult, and the road is rough, so we don't recommend that you take this route as a means of reaching Sevan. This is not a shortcut. It is worthwhile, however, to make the trek from Getap as far as the caravansaray, thereby avoiding the top of the 2,410 meter high pass. The building dates back to 1332 and is in remarkably good condition for such an ancient structure.

The large town of **Yeghegnadzor** is not a tourist destination in its own right, but there are several fascinating sites in the immediate area, with a great deal of history. Just north of Yeghegnadzor, after passing through the village of Gladzor, there is a 17th century church that has been converted to a museum of **Gladzor University**. This university is hundreds of years old, and enjoyed its prime in the late thirteenth century. Its museum is located in the village of Vernashen, and it contains photographs and maps that explain the course of higher education in Armenia, dating back hundreds of years. Back when this museum was a church, it was known as St. Hagop. There's usually an admission fee of about 1,000 dram.

Immediately after the museum, there's a "T" in the road. The left turn leads up an unpaved Jeep track, to the spectacular monastery of **Spitakavor**. This monastery is situated on a mountainside in a stunning location. The church here was built in

1321. There's also an unusual bell tower, different in architectural design from others that we have seen in Armenia, that was built in 1330. To get to Spitakavor you will need a four-wheel drive jeep or Niva. The road is not passable in winter, or when it is muddy. The monastery is approximately eight km from the museum.

Travel time from Yeghegnadzor to the Gladzor Museum is about 15 minutes. Travel time from the Gladzor Museum to the Spitakavor Monastery (8 km) is about 40 minutes.

To see the actual site of the Gladzor University, take a right at the "T" in the road near the museum. This road, unlike the road to Spitakavor, is paved all the way to the university site. Foundations from some university buildings remain. Today, however, the main attraction of the site is **Tanahati Vank**, which also dates from the thirteenth century.

SPELUNKING AND CONSERVATION

There are many opportunities in Armenia for serious spelunkers—those adventurous people who are also known as cavers. There are several caverns in the Vayots Dzor region, near the towns of Areni and Arpi, with dramatic stalactite and stalagmite formations. Most of these areas are dangerous, however, even for experienced cavers. At the entrance to the **Noravank** canyon there is a cluster of shallow caves called **Trchunneri Karayr** (Cave of Birds). Farther down the road, the Magili Cave is quite deep and is home to a colony of rare fruit bats. Some of these areas, including the bat habitat, are environmentally sensitive. We have omitted directions to the caves to discourage casual amateur visitors.

Two of the more notorious caves in the region are the Mozrovi Caves, which are located near Arpi, on the south side of the Arpa River, and the Arjeri Caverns, also nearby. These caves are deep and unmapped, and exploration is risky even for experienced cavers. There are said to be vibrantly colored stalagmites here. Cavers who explore these areas with experienced guides are urged to tread lightly and not damage the ecosystem. Locked gates have been installed at the entrances to the caves to deter visitors who might otherwise cause damage, whether intentionally or not.

Jerovank, the English translation of which is water church, is the name given to a cave that is located just beyond Arpi. The so-called church is a cave with a pool of spring water just outside the entrance. There are many stalactites in the cave.

Spelunkers estimate that there are approximately 10,000 caves throughout Armenia, and it is clear that with proper training, spelunking and conservation can co-exist. Cavers must use care not to disturb bat colonies, and to tread lightly.

Historic Sites

Immediately after passing Areni, there's a turnoff on the right side of the main road that leads to a stunning bedrock canyon and the **Noravank Monastery**. The complex blends in with its natural surrounding. Here, as at most monasteries, there is no competition between man-made architecture and natural architecture. Instead, the architecture and the building materials complement each other. Most of the buildings here date from the 1200s and 1300s. This ancient monastery's name has renewed meaning now that the complex has been completely rebuilt. The English translation of Noravank is "new monastery."

Two flights of extremely narrow steps form a cantilever on the west side and lead to the main hall of St. Astvatsatsin Church. Above the second-floor doorway of the church there is a carved relief of Christ, flanked by St. Peter and St. Paul. Above the ground-floor doorway, directly below the cantilevered stairs, there is a carved relief of the Holy Virgin with the baby Jesus seated on her lap and a pair of angels at their side. There are several *khatchkars* in the churchyard of great significance. The most important of them, a 1308 *khatchkar* by Momik, is historically significant for its design, which features fine carving on the entire slab. From the church you'll have a panoramic view of the rocky setting.

Along the access road to Noravank, at a distance of four km from the main highway (when you are halfway to the monastery), you'll see a roadside cave that has been converted to a cafe. The owner, Vartkes, is a friendly man with many stories to tell about the caves and other natural attractions of the area. He has a small display of old artifacts, too. The menu at his cave-cafe is usually limited to Armenian coffee, tea, and a small assortment of candies. For a meal, there's a full restaurant (since 2001) right next to Noravank.

To get there, take the signposted (in the Armenian language) right turnoff through the canyon, which is one kilometer after the town of Areni. Travel eight km to the end of this cul-de-sac road.

King Trdat Church was newly constructed in 2001, just north of Vayk. The church is located along the main north-south road that links Yerevan to Yeghegnadzor. There's no reason for a tourist to venture off into the town, however. Neighboring Malishka is another large village that boasts a brand new church, but if you travel beyond the church and ascend the fields behind the village along a windy but paved road, you can get a great view of Mt. Ararat.

Jermuk

Just after passing the town of Vayk, there's a left turnoff for Jermuk. Actually, there are two left turnoffs—one on each side of the Arpa River. The old road on the west side of the river leads to **Gndevank Monastery**, which was founded in AD 936 by Princess Sophia of Syunik. The road here is known as the Old Jermuk Road and it is not marked. The entire monastery is surrounded by fortress walls, which contain chambers that descend as much as three stories deep. The new road on the east side of the river is modern, and this is the one that's marked with a sign for Jermuk.

Jermuk is also the site of he famous mineral springs that produce the bottled water of the same name that is popular throughout the country. There's a pavilion in town where you are offered a selection of water that comes out of spigots directly from their underground pools, at temperatures of 35°C, 45°C, 50°C and 53°C. The hot springs here are supposedly a cure for absolutely everything. All that is required is for you to soak in a tub full of the magic liquid.

Jermuk Resort is a great break on a longer journey. It is also a fine destination for hiking or for recreation near the waterfall along the Arpa River. Don't expect paradise, though. This could be a great spa get-away. But it isn't. Jermuk was a popular resort at one time, but it is run down today, and the vintage Soviet-era health spas in the area (called sanatoriums) are really unappealing. The Ararat Sanatorium is one example of such. There are several unfinished building projects that have been spoiling views since they were abandoned more than a dozen years ago.

This could also be a fine spot for a winter vacation. But again, it isn't. Most of the shops and places to stay are closed in winter. We don't advise spending the night here in any season, although there are a couple of hotels that are scheduled to open in 2005—including one that looks like a castle—which could change our recommendation. Despite all of this, the natural environment is breathtaking and it makes Jermuk worth a visit. Traveling farther south from Jermuk, you reach the **Spandarian Reservoir** (180 km from Yerevan), a man-made lake that serves the region's hydropower needs. This is a beautiful sight, but there are no camping or picnic facilities here.

Travel time from Yerevan to the Jermuk turnoff is about three hours, and then the drive eastward on the access road to the resort (24 km) is another twenty-five minutes. Travel time from Yerevan to Spandarian Reservoir is about three and one half hours.

Syunik Region

Sisian (210 km from Yerevan) is a good stop-off point for travelers headed to Karabagh, since it is roughly the halfway point from Yerevan. Sisian is also a worthwhile final destination because of the many interesting sites either in the town, or nearby. The town itself, however, is rather gritty. At the top of a hill near the center of Sisian, the seventh century church of **Sisavan** is tough to miss. It's just a two-minute drive from the town's main square, and from the churchyard you'll get a view of the entire region. Construction of Sisavan was completed in AD 689. **To get there**, travel to the town center and follow the sign to the top of the hill. The town center can be reached by taking the right turnoff from the main Yerevan-to-Goris road immediately following the military-customs checkpoint.

Shaki Waterfall and Zorakar

Sandwiched between the town of Sisian and the village of Shaki, the famous **Shaki Waterfall** is an refreshing diversion. In recent years the access road to the fall has been locked, but there's usually someone around to open the gate. There's a hydro-electric power station nearby that uses some of the water, but we haven't noticed any reduction in the flow of water during the past several years.

To get there from Yerevan, take the right turnoff from the main Yerevan-to-Goris road immediately following the military-customs checkpoint. This is the first of two paved roads that lead to Sisian. Then take the second right turn onto a dirt and gravel road (located after the turnoff for the village of Shaki, and before reaching the entrance to Sisian itself). Drive until you reach the locked gate. From here, it is a ten-minute walk to the waterfall.

At the far (southern) end of Sisian, within sight of the main highway, you'll find **Zorakar**, a circular arrangement of 204 stones that is believed to be a celestial observatory. The site is similar to England's Stonehenge, but Armenia's is from the

Photograph: Noravank Monastery

Bronze Age, and is believed to date back to roughly 5,000 BC, making it much older. The site is also sometimes referred to as Zorats Karer or Karahunje.

To get there directly from the main Yerevan-to-Goris road, travel four km past the first (main) turnoff to Sisian, which is also the location of the region's military-customs checkpoint. Turn right onto the paved road and then travel one kilometer to a signposted dirt Jeep trail. The site is located in a desolate field on the right, at the end of the jeep trail. This worthwhile detour is just five minutes from the main road.

Vorotnavank, a thousand-year-old monastery that sits on a fortified hill overlooking the Vorotan River, is worth the short trek on the back roads just 10 km (30 minutes) east of Sisian. **To get there**, travel to the eastern edge of town and past the village of Aghitu (also known as Aghudi) and through Vaghatin. There are several other historic sites in the region, but none of them is as accessible as Vorotnavank and all are likely to be of interest primarily to specialists.

In Aghitu you will pass a seventh century funeral monument on the right side of the road. The village of Shamb is located just beyond Vorotnavank. Shamb is well known for its warm but unappealing (it's green!) natural spring water. The Shamb Reservoir, which is not suitable for swimming and is not recommended, is also nearby and of interest to ecologists.

Travel time from Yerevan to Sisian is roughly four hours if you drive without stopping at Jermuk or any of the other interesting sights. If you are continuing your journey south, or to Karabagh, then Sisian is a good place to spend the night.

Hotels and Places to Stay

Basen Hotel in Sisian is a surprisingly large complex for such a remote area. There are accommodations for as many as 72 people in five buildings. The design is a bit odd. Each building contains two duplex-style apartments with private suites. But everything is clean and new (built in 1998) and there's 24-hour hot water with fairly modern bathrooms. They'll even demonstrate how to make lavash (Armenian flat bread) for tourists who are interested. The flat rate of $20 per person is a bit pricey, especially for travelers in groups. The owner might be willing to accept less for larger groups, especially off-season. Located on Ara Manukian Street, near the Post Office (Tel. 0-830 + 53-70).

Dina Hotel in Sisian was built in 1936, but the new management has made this a comfortable and clean place to stay. Comfort level is a notch below neighboring Basen Hotel (see above). Each of the 31 rooms has 24-hour hot water, telephone, television, and a pair of twin beds in each room. Prices are local. Single 3,000 drams (about $5); Double 5,000 drams (about $9); Deluxe 8,000 drams (about $14). Located at 35 Sisakan Street (Tel. 0-830 + 33-33).

Noy Hotel near Yeghegnadzor is new and comfortable. There are only eight rooms, but they each have 24-hour hot water and modern bathrooms. The deluxe rooms on the top floor are 10,000 dram (roughly $18). Standard rooms are only 7,000 drams ($12). All rooms face the Arpa River, and not the street. The deluxe rooms have porches and are worth the extra few dollars. Located at the rest stop just nine km north of the town of Yeghegnadzor and immediately south of Noravank. Convenient to the wineries of Areni and Getap.

Antoine Terjanian's B&B in Yeghegnadzor is the best spot in town, especially for families. The three-room suite sleeps six, is equipped with a kitchen, and has a lovely view. The price varies according to the number of occupants. Located at 11 N. Khachatryan Avenue (Tel. 0-81 + 2-48-37).

Yeghegnadzor has an un-named Soviet-era hotel at the north end of town, near the park. The facilities are exactly what you would expect in this kind of hotel. Better choices are the Noy Hotel, which is located near Noravank just nine km away, and the Antoine Terjanian B&B, which is located in Yeghegnadzor (see above).

Zorats Qarer B&B in Sisian will appeal to travelers who prefer a Bed and Breakfast-style accommodation in a beautiful hilltop setting. Three of their four bedrooms have a private bath and 24-hour hot water. Rates are a bit pricey, especially for a family with children, but they include "organic" food from the village. Single $30; Double $50; Children $10. Located at Third Street #30, roughly 100 m from the Sisian Church on the hill. Follow the signs to the church, and you cannot miss it (Local Tel. 0-830 + 36-11). Reservations also available through Aries Tours in Yerevan (Tel. 22-01-38) (E-mail: info@bedandbreakfast.am; aries@arminco.com) (Internet: www.bedandbreakfast.am); booking agent located at 43 Gulbenkian Street, Yerevan.

Prices *are listed in US dollars for those hotels that quote US dollars when advertising their rates. Otherwise, prices are listed in Armenian drams.*

Telephone: *The area code for Sisian is 830. When calling Sisian from Yerevan, enter (0) + (830) + (local phone number).*

Places to Eat

Traveling south from Yerevan, just nine km before reaching Yeghegnadzor you'll see Armenia's version of a rest stop. There are a dozen or so vendors selling farm produce, sandwiches, coffee and drinks. If you didn't pack a lunch from home, you may be able to find something here. The comfortable **Noy Hotel** (see listings above) is here, and there are a couple of gasoline stations. For eating and sleeping, this rest stop is better than anything you'll find within the nearby town of Yeghegnadzor. Located 120 km (two hours) from Yerevan.

Along the main highway between Yeghegnadzor and Jermuk, there are dozens of *khorovats* (barbecue) restaurants, some of which are open year-round. In the town of Vayk, next to the new King Trdat Church, there's a modest place called the **Armenian Kitchen Restaurant**, where you can order pork barbecue.

THE MIDDLE OF THE PANHANDLE

Tatev

Tatev Monastery looms high above the town of the same name. You'll see the complex long before you reach it along winding dirt roads. The monastery was originally built in the ninth century, and it served for many years as a regional center and as a fortress against foreign invasion.

St. Gregory of Tatev (AD 1346-1409), one of the staunchest defenders of the Armenian Church, is buried here, and his grave is a pilgrimage destination for

Armenians. An earthquake ruined the monastery in 1932, and a major renovation has been underway for the past several years. It appears to be nearing completion, but at the time of research there was still a large crane towering over the church and spoiling its appearance.

One of the many interesting monuments at Tatev is a 25-foot tall octagonal pillar with an engraved *khatchkar* at the top. This uncommon structure, named Gavazan, which is the Armenian word for a walking stick, was built in AD 904. The structure is considered to be a unique work of Armenian architectural and engineering art, according to the historian O. Khalpakhchian, author of "Architectural Ensembles of Armenia." In AD 930, shortly after Gavazan was erected, the interior walls of the main church of Poghos and Petros were decorated with frescoes, but the imagery is now almost totally lost. On the eastern façade of the exterior, there are two deep triangular niches that are crowned with thin ornamented edges which have survived the ages with greater success. This façade also features four human faces, with snake heads attached.

The church of St. Gregory adjoins the main church of Poghos and Petros on its southern side. This church dates to 1295, and it is believed to have replaced an earlier structure from AD 836. To the west of St. Gregory, there is a vaulted gallery with arched openings on its southern side. There are many other ancient monuments and examples of unique or uncommon buildings at Tatev, making this one of the most admired and cherished architectural sites in Armenia. At its zenith, more than 600 monks studied and prayed at Tatev, making this one of the most significant religious sites, as well.

As you approach Tatev, just off the dirt access road and spanning the Vorotan River, there's a natural rock formation known as Devil's Bridge, and a hot spring. Either of these attractions would make a good stop-off point on your way to the monastery.

To get there, traveling south from Yerevan, there's a right turnoff several km before reaching Goris. You'll see an old Soviet-era sign, written in Russian, marking the road. Located 257 km from Yerevan. This is not a quick detour. Once you make the turnoff, Tatev is still another 23 km away.

Travel time from the main road turnoff to Tatev is almost one hour on poor roads. There is no lodging at Tatev, so allow enough time to return to Goris or Sisian before dark. Be sure to have enough gasoline to make the round trip.

Goris

Goris is a quaint town surrounded by mountains, and located along the main north-south highway. The narrow tree-lined streets and private single-family homes that comprise much of the town give it the feel of a small town where one needn't worry about getting lost. The older part of town, with homes that pre-date the Soviet era, is quaint. At the far end of town, near the government buildings, there's a seventeenth century church which bears the scar of an Azeri artillery shell. The House Museum of Armenian poet Axel Bakunts is located about one kilometer west of the church.

Shaki Waterfall, Sisian

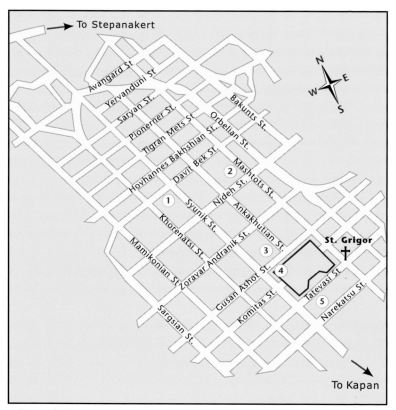

To Stepanakert

To Kapan

Central Goris

1 Bed and Breakfast; 2 House Museum of Bakounts; 3 Post Office;
4 Government Building, Parks; 5 Bank

Probably more interesting than the town, however, are the caves and exotic rock formations at nearby **Khundzoresk**. Many of the caves are today used as barns for farm animals. Several centuries ago people occupied them. Khundzoresk is a fabulous place to stop and spend a couple of hours hiking or picnicking.

To get there, traveling south from Yerevan, go about two km past Goris, in the direction of Karabagh. This is the Goris-to-Stepanakert road, which has been completely rebuilt during the past several years. From this road, on the right side, there is a paved turnoff to the village of Khundzoresk. Travel down this road for less than two km and turn right again.

Travel time from Goris to Khundzoresk is about fifteen minutes. From Sisian, the drive is about one hour. Travel time from Yerevan to Goris without stopping is about five hours.

Southern Armenia

Hotels and Places to Stay

Khachik Bed and Breakfast has three rooms and one full bath, with beds for as many as six people. This is probably the best you'll find in Goris, and we recommend it. The friendly owner, Khachik Mirakyan, plans a modest expansion in coming years. 24-hour hot water. Breakfast included. Expect to pay about $15 per person. Located two km from the main highway at 12 Davit Bek Street (one of Goris's major arteries) near the intersection with Syunik Street. There's a bright yellow sign on the utility pole (Tel. 0-84+ 2-10-98) (E-mail: mirakyanbb@rambler.ru). Reservations also available through Aries Tours in Yerevan (Tel. 22-01-38) (E-mail: info@bedandbreakfast.am) (Internet: www.bedandbreakfast.am).

Goris Hotel is a filthy and rundown Soviet era hotel located at the far end of Goris. Foreigners pay about $20 for a bed in a room, which is roughly ten times what travelers with Armenian passports pay. You should avoid this hotel.

THE BOTTOM OF THE PANHANDLE

After reaching Goris, you will have two travel options. You can either travel east to Karabagh, by way of the Goris-to-Stepanakert highway, or you can continue south to the Iranian border. Either destination will add two full days to your journey from Goris, or three days from Yerevan [For more on Karabagh, see Chapter 10]. If you are a tourist with limited time, we do not recommend that you travel south of Goris to the Armenian towns of Kapan and Meghri. There simply aren't enough interesting sites to warrant such a lengthy and tiring trip.

Travel time from Goris to the Iran border, on winding mountain roads, is likely to be at least six hours.

The Town of Kapan

If you do opt to travel along the mountainous and winding southern route from Goris to the Iranian border, you will first pass through the Armenian town of Kapan. The most significant historic site in this area is probably the **Vahanavank** monastery, located just 15 minutes outside the center of town. The buildings are in ruins and the site is overgrown. Vahanavank is historically interesting, but for the average tourist it is not really worth a special trip all the way to Kapan. **To get there**, travel six km from Kapan center, heading uphill south of town. Take the left turnoff from the main road, cross a narrow bridge, and then wind your way up the mountain for about five minutes.

This was a strategic military location during the Soviet era, and it was also the site of many mining operations. Today, acid mine drainage is the unfortunate legacy in many areas. An orange-brown reservoir, polluted from heavy metals and closed to the public, is one of the first sights you will see when driving into town. Today many of the mines are closed or are operating at limited capacities, and there are no big attractions for tourists. The heart of Kapan is lined with mature trees and is fairly pleasant. The trees, together with the Voghji River, which flows through the center of town, help to make the summer climate more temperate.

The one-hundred square-kilometer **Shikahogh Reserve**, which is located south of Kapan along the northern slopes of the Meghri Ridge, is noted for its forests of oak and hornbeam, and holds the only beech grove in the southern region. It is also Armenia's only nature reservation with primeval forests. The reserve was established in 1958, and it covers an area of approximately 10,000 hectares, which makes it about one-third as large as the Dilijan National Park in northeast Armenia [for more on this reserve and Armenia's other specially protected areas, see Chapter 4, Ecology].

Travel time from Goris to Kapan is about two and one half hours. The mountainous roads make the 65 km journey from Goris seem much longer, however. From Yerevan to Kapan, figure roughly eight and one-half hours.

Hotels and Places to Stay

Caravan Hotel and Restaurant Complex just ten minutes outside Kapan, has four modern rooms, each with a private modern bath and hot water. The campus-like setting, on a hilltop beside the Voghji River, is pleasant and convenient for travelers. There's a restaurant here, too, with outdoor booths. This is the best you'll find in Kapan, and we recommend it. Expect to pay about $20 per room. Located on the main Kapan-to-Meghri road, eight km south of the center of Kapan (Tel. 0-85+ 5-49-00).

Darist Hotel in the heart of Kapan was built in 2001 but it still looks like a contemporary version of a Soviet building. It's clean, and it's new, but it isn't anything special and its location is fairly mundane. Expect to pay about $30 per room. Located along the main Kapan-to-Meghri road, known locally as Aram Manukian Street (Tel. 0-85+ 6-26-62).

Hotel Lernagorts in Kapan is a genuine Soviet era hotel. The Spartan rooms are clean, and there's running water, although it's usually ice-cold. Foreigners can expect to pay $20 each, whether they sleep one to a room or three to a room. The rate for Armenian citizens is about 1,000 drams (less than $2). Located in the center of Kapan in the relentlessly sunny main square.

The Town of Meghri

Meghri is the final Armenian town before reaching Iran. The climate here is subtropical, and it is common to see pomegranates and figs growing on trees along the roads. There are several old sites here, including a fortress, but for most travelers, Meghri is merely the Armenian outpost on the way to Iran.

Still, there are three churches of minor interest, each of which dates from the fifteenth through seventeenth centuries. The fortress dates back to the tenth century, but its greatest significance is for the role it played in the early eighteenth century. Armenian leader **Davit Bek**, fighting from within the fort, held off a Turkish invasion and saved Meghri from destruction.

The Armenia-Iran border is open, and relations between the two countries are friendly, making this an open crossing for access to Iran. Visas are required for transit into Iran, and you can apply for one at the Iranian

Embassy in Yerevan. [For embassy information, see Chapter 2, Essentials]. Teheran is quite far from the Armenian border, however. For most tourists who are interested in seeing Iran, it would be preferable to fly directly to Teheran from Yerevan on one of the regularly scheduled flights between the two cities.

Travel time from Yerevan to Meghri without stopping is about twelve hours. Travel time from Goris to Meghri is about six hours. Travel time from Kapan to Meghri is about two and one half hours. Snow and ice obstructed some of the mountain passes south of Kapan as early as October during our visits. We recommend that you stay overnight in Kapan, and that you avoid traveling south to Meghri after dark because of the poor road conditions.

Hotels and Places to Stay

At time of research we had not yet visited either of these new bed-and-breakfast style hotels in Meghri. These independently owned and operated B&Bs are affiliated with a nationwide chain of such mom-and-pop lodges. There are no major hotels that we can recommend in Meghri. Good lodging alternatives are located in Kapan.

Haer Bed and Breakfast in Meghri has two bedrooms with a shared bath for $10 per person. Reservations available through Aries Tours in Yerevan (Tel. 22-01-38) (E-mail: info@bedandbreakfast.am) (Internet: www.bedandbreakfast.am)

Grigor Margaryan Bed and Breakfast in Meghri has two bedrooms with a shared bath, TV, air conditioning for $15 per person. Reservations available through Aries Tours in Yerevan (Tel. 22-01-38) (E-mail: info@bedandbreakfast.am) (Internet: www.bedandbreakfast.am).

NagornoKarabagh

ten

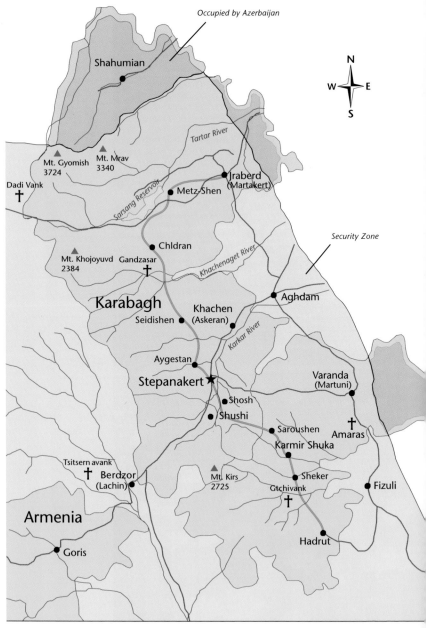

North - South Highway (by 2004, about half of the road had been complete

Map of Karabagh © 2004 Stone Garden Productions

INTRODUCTION

The Nagorno Karabagh Republic (NKR) was proclaimed on September 2, 1991. A popular referendum followed in December and overwhelmingly supported independence. This tiny independent Armenian state (1,853 sq mi) is situated within the borders of the ancient Armenian province of Artsakh—an ancient name that you will still hear used. Throughout ancient times, this lushly vegetated and mountainous region had been Armenia's easternmost principality.

As with many parts of historic Armenia, Karabagh's borders have been mangled over the centuries. It has been bounced back and forth between the competing imperial powers of the region, which viewed it as a prize. Karabagh was controlled by Arabs in the eighth century, by Turks in the eleventh century, and more recently by Persians and Russians. Today it enjoys self-rule and the region has enjoyed a cease-fire since 1994.

There's a lot of history here. Visitors will discover friendly people, a wealth of ancient sites, and of course the beautiful mountains for which Karabagh has such fame. You'll need at least three full days in order to add Karabagh to your itinerary because of the long drive (there are no flights) from Yerevan. It's absolutely worth spending the time to visit. Karabagh deserves to be a destination in its own right, and not just a side trip from Armenia.

LAND AND PEOPLE

Climate

Temperatures are cooler here than they are in central Armenia, and there's a great deal more rain and fog, too. Travelers should bring a sweater or sweatshirt even in the summer, and rain gear, too. The mountainous elevations frequently result in bitterly cold winters.

Note About Traveling to Karabagh

Karabagh is not a part of the Republic of Armenia. It is an independent country, notwithstanding the international community's reluctance to grant it formal diplomatic recognition. Karabagh restricts immigration, controls its borders, and requires visas for foreign visitors. For the purpose of tourism, travelers must therefore treat Karabagh as a separate and independent country.

Karabagh's borders with Azerbaijan are closed and militarized, and the only point of access to Karabagh is through Armenia. So, to get there you must first travel to the capital of Armenia. There are no scheduled commercial flights to Karabagh, but there is reliable ground transportation from points throughout Armenia. The roads are in good condition, but expect patches of ice and early-morning fog from November to April. Driving at night can be hazardous on these unlighted mountainous roads and should be avoided.

You need a separate visa in order to visit Karabagh. An Armenia visa is not acceptable. Information about visas appears later in this chapter.

The year-round average temperature is 11°C (51°F). The warmest months are July and August, when the average temperatures is about 22°C (72°F). The coldest months are January and February, when the temperature averages 0°C (32°F). The highest annual temperatures are 40°C (104°F) in the lowlands, and 37°C (99°F) in the highlands.

Severe thunderstorms are common in the spring and summer. The average annual precipitation ranges between roughly 48 to 71 cm (19 to 28 inches) depending on the elevation. The valleys are generally the driest, and the highlands the wettest. Torrential rains and hail are common in May and June. It is foggy 100-125 days per year.

Geography

Karabagh is located in the southeastern part of the Caucasus region, and the landscape features are rugged and mountainous. Most of Karabagh's rivers flow from the western and southwestern mountains to the east and southeast into the Artsakh valley. Over centuries, these fast-flowing mountainous rivers formed deep canyons and picturesque valleys. The biggest is the valley of the Tartar River in Martakert. Sarsang Reservoir, a man-made lake in the north, is the largest body of water.

The Karabagh Mountain Range includes the lofty peaks of Mt. Mrav (3,340 m) and Mt. Kirs (2,725 m). The Artsakh Highland, like the entire Armenian Highland is seismically active. Volcanic formations, such as limestone and other sedimentary rocks, originated in the Jurassic and Cretaceous periods and are common here.

Natural Resources

Karabagh has a rich biological diversity. It is estimated that there are about 2,000 species of plants, which is a considerable number for such a small country. Forestland comprises more than 36 percent of the surface area, and it is represented by large stands of oak, hornbeam, linden, ash, and birch.

These forests are a habitat to brown bears, wolves, bobcats, foxes, hares, and boars. Karabagh's bird population includes the wild goose, as well as the partridge, magpie, kite, cuckoo, turtledove, woodpecker, lark, and owl. Turtles, hedgehogs and several species of snakes are abundant in the lowlands and on rocky foothills. Locusts and butterflies are also present in abundance.

Inorganic resources include large deposits of marble and marbleized limestone in the region of Shushi and Stepanakert. Other significant resources include granite, basalt, tufa, limestone, as well as raw materials for cement, graphite, gypsum, sand and clay.

There is no heavy industry here and as a result Karabagh's natural environment is mostly unpolluted and unspoiled. The environment is protected not at the ministerial level—there is no Ministry of Nature Protection—but there exists a State Committee with oversight authority.

Language

The Indo-European language of Armenian is the primary language in Karabagh. Russian is also spoken. The people of Karabagh speak a unique dialect of Armenian, which can be difficult to understand, even if you are fluent in

Karabagh at a Glance

Area	5,500 sq km (Roughly the size of the Delaware)
Population	144,300 (2002 census)
Language	Armenian
Ethnic Composition	Armenian (95 percent)
Capital	Stepanakert
Government	democratic republic
Religion	Armenian Apostolic Christian
Life Expectancy	74 years
Literacy	More than 90 percent
Tourism	Issued more than 4,000 tourist visas in 2003

Armenian. According to the official estimates, the population is roughly 145,000, of whom roughly 95 percent is Armenian. The remaining five percent of the population is mostly Russian, Greek or Assyrian.

Economy

Agriculture, animal husbandry and light industry dominate the small and fragile economy of Karabagh. The economy was ravaged by an Azeri blockade and by rising military operations that began in 1988, with an estimated $90 million in infrastructure damage to buildings and roads. Roughly 2,000 hectares of farmland and orchards have also been lost to the economy because of land mines.

Construction of a transport link to Armenia has helped. This route, the Goris-Stepanakert Highway, has permitted greater trade with Armenia. A north-south highway within Karabagh is also serving as an impetus for commercial traffic.

Government

The Nagorno Karabagh Republic is a democratic republic that elects a President and a parliament. The President appoints his cabinet, including ministers. The current president, Arkady Ghoukasian, is the third person to have been elected to this office. Previous presidents were Arthur Mkrtchian and Robert Kocharian. Two unelected Presidents then served in quick succession until December 1994, when Robert Kocharian was elected. Kocharian resigned in 1997 and moved to Armenia to accept a position as Prime Minister. Today he is that country's President.

The nation's legislature is the National Assembly, a unicameral body of representatives from throughout Karabagh. Administration of the republic is managed through eight regions, or *marzes*. Stepanakert, the capital city, forms one of these eight regions. Karabagh defense forces are in control of some lands outside the borders of Karabagh proper, which it holds as a security buffer zone.

A BRIEF HISTORY

By Ronald Grigor Suny

Karabagh is at the same time one of the most beautiful parts of the South Caucasus and the source of some of its most bloody conflicts. Its recent history has been bitterly contested by Armenians and Azerbaijanis, and both peoples have laid claim to the land as part of their respective national heritages. Turkic invasions began in the eleventh century.

Like Armenia, Karabagh was on the frontier of the Christian and Muslim worlds, and the region has been a highly contested prize for the past thousand years. Turks, Mongols, and Persians vied with Armenians, Georgians, and Russians for control of the legendary "Black Garden," which is supposedly the English language translation of Karabagh. Even after the Bagratuni kingdoms of Greater Armenia fell before the Byzantines and the Seljuks, Armenian princes and nobles managed to control tiny principalities in Karabagh and Siunik.

A Catholicos, the heir to the Caucasian Albanian Church, continued to preach at the Armenian Church at Gandzasar in Karabagh, and this position soon became hereditary in the prominent Hasan-Jalalian family of nobles. The local *nakharars* eventually evolved into the semi-independent meliks, who ruled parts of Karabagh until the coming of the Russians in the early nineteenth century. These noble rulers made the earliest gestures, along with enlightened clerics, to interest European leaders in the liberation of Armenia from Muslim domination. Early in the eighteenth century the Patriarch of Gandzasar, Esai Hasan-Jalalian, traveled with the patriot Israel Ori to seek Russian aid for the Armenians.

In the eighteenth century the South Caucasus became the object of a military-political struggle between three empires: Ottoman Turkey, Tsarist Russia, and Safavid Persia. As Persian rule weakened over eastern Armenia, various Georgian, Armenian, and Muslim local lords vied for a degree of independence. From the north the energetic Russian emperor, Peter the Great, launched a campaign against the Persians along the Caspian coast in 1722. His action stimulated the Turks to set out on their own campaign in the South Caucasus against the failing Persians. Armenians in Karabagh rose up to fight the Turks, led by Davit Bek Siunetsi and Avan Yuzbashi.

The Turks took most of the southern Caucasus, including most of Georgia and Armenia, and Peter decided to withdraw his battered, disease-ridden troops. The Armenians of Karabagh were divided between those who hoped for future aid from Russia, those who wished for a return of the Persians, and those who were ready to make peace with the Ottomans. Avan Yuzhbashi was committed to the Russian orientation and wrote to the tsar, "We will fight until the time when we will enter the service of the tsar, and all will perish to the last one but we will not leave Christianity; we will fight for our faith."

Davit Bek, who later became the legendary hero celebrated in novels and an opera, also continued the struggle, fighting primarily against the Persians and pro-Persian Armenians. Resistance continued for many years, but eventually a stronger Persia under Nadir Shah reasserted its power over Karabagh. The Shah granted autonomy to many of the meliks. Finally, in 1813, the Russians under Alexander I defeated the Persians and took Karabagh and much of what is today Azerbaijan.

Nagorno Karabagh: The Land of the Bagh?

The ongoing political misfortunes of this region are well illustrated by the etymology of Karabagh's name. The name is either a mixture of Persian and Russian meaning Black Garden, as is widely accepted, or it's an Armenian compound meaning land of the Bagh. The Bagh, or Balayi, are a tribe of Armenians who lived in this area in ancient times. The Russians added the adjective Nagorno, which means mountainous, and dubbed the region Nagorno Karabagh. The historic Armenian name is Artsakh, although the state is officially known as the "Nagorno Karabagh Republic, Artsakh."

Armenians preferred the Russians as their overlords to the Persians or Turks. In 1822 the Catholicos at Echmiadzin, which as part of Yerevan province was still under the Persians, moved to Karabagh to be under Russian rule. Six years later, the Russians conquered the fortress at Yerevan and annexed eastern Armenia. Karabagh became one of the six dioceses under the Holy See of Echmiadzin, but for much of the century of tsarist Russian rule Karabagh was part of the predominantly Muslim province of Elizavetpol (Ganja).

When the revolutions of 1917 brought down the tsar and raised the Communists to power, a new round of fighting broke out over Karabagh. Both the newly independent Armenian and Azerbaijani republics claimed the region. The British intervened, prevented the Armenian commander Andranik from taking Karabagh, and appointed an Azerbaijani as governor of Karabagh. Fighting broke out again in March 1920, and the Azerbaijanis burned Shushi (Shusha), the largest town in Karabagh, and massacred more than 20,000 of its Armenian inhabitants. A month later independent Azerbaijan fell to the Soviets.

Soviet Influence

Soviet Azerbaijan grandly gestured its fraternal relations with its neighbor (once it became Soviet at the end of the year) and granted Karabagh to Soviet Armenia. The next year, however, the Communists decided that, for pragmatic political and economic reasons, Karabagh should be part of Soviet Azerbaijan. The Azerbaijani Communists were insistent on the transfer, while the Armenian Communists protested; but Stalin, then in the Caucasus, agreed to the transfer. In 1923 Mountainous Karabagh (Nagorno Karabagh) was declared an autonomous region within Azerbaijan, but in fact the autonomy was largely fictitious and real control lay with the Azerbaijani authorities in Baku. Armenian culture and language were restricted in the region.

Gradually the percentage of Armenians in the region declined. At the time of Sovietization, 94.4 percent (124,000) of the 131,500 people in the district were Armenian and only 5.6 percent (7,400) were Azerbaijani. By 1979 Armenians made up less than 76 percent (123,000), a net decline of 1,000 people, and Azerbaijanis had increased five times to nearly 24 percent (37,000).

Armenians were fearful that their demographic decline would replicate the fate of another historically Armenian region, Nakhijevan, which had also been placed under Azerbaijani administration as an autonomous republic. There Armenians, a significant minority in the 1920s, had declined from 15 percent (15,600) in 1926 to 1.4 percent (3,400) in 1979, while Azerbaijanis, with in-migration and a higher birth rate, had increased from 85 percent (85,400) to nearly 96 percent (230,000).

Although they lived better than Azerbaijanis in neighboring districts, the Armenians of Karabagh saw that their standard of living was not as high as that of the Armenians in the Armenian republic. Hostile to the Azerbaijanis on whom they blamed their social and cultural discontent, the Karabagh Armenians preferred to learn Russian rather than Azeri in a ratio of eight to one. Throughout the Soviet period, the Karabagh Armenians continually petitioned the central authorities in Moscow to reunite the region with Armenia.

Demands for Independence

Periodically, local Armenians protested against Azerbaijani control and petitioned to be joined to Armenia, which lay only six miles away. The era of glasnost and perestroika helped the Karabagh Armenians to renew their demands for reunification with Armenia. On February 13, 1988, Karabagh Armenians began demonstrating in their capital, Stepanakert, in favor of unification with the Armenian republic. Six days later they were joined by mass marches in Yerevan. On February 20, the Soviet of People's Deputies in Karabagh voted 110-17 to request the transfer of the region to Armenia.

This unprecedented action by a regional soviet brought out tens of thousands of demonstrators both in Stepanakert and Yerevan, but Moscow rejected the demands of the Armenians. In response to Armenian demands, Azerbaijanis in Sumgait, an industrial town on the Caspian, went on a rampage for two days, and at least 31 Armenians were killed before Soviet troops ended the pogrom. With Sumgait the peaceful transfer of Karabagh to Armenia became impossible. Through the next year, while Moscow hesitated to take decisive action, Armenians increasingly grew disillusioned with Gorbachev and the program of perestroika, and Azerbaijanis organized into a powerful anti-Armenian nationalist movement. The popular movement, led by the Karabagh Committee in Yerevan and the Krunk (Crane) Committee in Stepanakert, continued to grow until its leaders were effectively the most popular and influential political forces among the Armenians.

On December 7, 1988, a massive earthquake devastated northern Armenia, killing at least 25,000 people and rendering hundreds of thousands homeless. World attention focused for several weeks on Armenia, and aid poured in from many countries. Gorbachev flew to Armenia to survey the damage, but he was received with hostility because of his Karabagh policies. Even as the country lay crippled by the earthquake, the Communist Party decided to arrest the Karabagh Committee members and place the region under the direct administration of Moscow.

The attempt by the Communist Party to rule Armenia without the popular representatives of the national movement only worsened the political crisis. In March 1989 many voters boycotted the general elections. Massive demonstrations started up again in early May, demanding the release of the members of the Karabagh Committee, and in the elections to the Congress of People's Deputies in May Armenians chose people identified with the Karabagh cause. Finally, on the last day of May, the Karabagh Committee members were released to the cheers of demonstrators who greeted their arrival in Yerevan. On December 1, 1989, the Armenian Supreme Soviet defied Moscow and declared Karabagh a part of Armenia.

When Armenia became an independent state two years later, Karabagh declared itself an independent republic (December 1991). Meanwhile, Azerbaijan formally dissolved Karabagh's autonomy, claiming it was an integral part of the republic. With the breakup of the Soviet Union, Azerbaijan launched an all-out war against Nagorno Karabagh and laid siege to Stepanakert.

By the time the Russians brokered an armistice in May 1994, the Armenians had won the war. A hero of the Karabagh war, Robert Kocharian, became, first, president of Karabagh, then prime minister of Armenia and, later, its president. But the costs of victory were enormous. Besides the tens of thousands of dead and hundreds of thousands of refugees on both sides, Armenia continued to suffer from the economic burdens of the war. Karabagh was a showpiece of Armenian national revival, but politically it experienced serious infighting between civilian and military leaders.

Armenia and Karabagh became ever more closely allied to Russia, while Azerbaijan drew closer to Turkey. Iran, although Muslim, tended to be closer to Armenia because of its fear that Azerbaijan might try to stir up nationalist or separatist sentiments among the Azeri-speaking people of northern Iran. The United States has tried to broker agreements between Armenia and Azerbaijan but with little success.

The American government, which had hobbled its oilmen in Iran and Iraq, was reluctant to do it to them once again in the Caucasus. Baku now found new friends in Washington and Texas. Most analysts believe that the conflict over Karabagh hinders the future of both Armenia and Azerbaijan. A settlement of the conflict would spur economic development, trade, and cooperation throughout the South Caucasus. But deep resentments prevent easy solutions, even though both sides would benefit from peace.

The authors thank scholar Ronald Grigor Suny, Ph.D. for writing this history for *The Stone Garden Guides.*

ESSENTIALS

Planning Your Trip

The tourism infrastructure in Karabagh is in its formative stage. This means that you are not likely to encounter crowds of tourists here. It also means that your journey here will probably be better characterized as an adventure than as a routine vacation. Still, there are comfortable hotels in Karabagh now, and if you are wary about traveling independently in such a remote area, you can easily find a travel agent who will arrange a private or group tour.

When to Go

For good weather, the best months to visit are May through September when conditions are temperate. Winters can get very cold. Weather in March and April is usually rainy, and this will hamper tourism in remote areas that are served by dirt roads.

Significant national holidays, which are unique to Karabagh and which might add unique cultural flavor to your visit, are Artsakh Revival Day (February 20), Shushi Liberation Day (May 9) and two independence days honoring the establishment of the republic (September 2) and its national referendum on independence (December 10).

GETTING THERE

Visa and Red Tape

To travel to Karabagh you will need to carry your passport, and you will need a visa from the office of the **Nagorno Karabagh Republic Permanent Representation in Armenia**, which has its office in Yerevan. You can usually fill out the application, pay the fee, and get a visa all within 30 minutes while you wait. With this kind of service, this has got to be the most efficient office in all Armenia.

You may also be able to apply for a visa at the office of one of the Karabagh Representatives that operate in the US, France, Russia, Lebanon and Australia. Karabagh doesn't have official diplomatic relations with foreign countries, but its office operate as de facto embassies. At time of research, these offices were not actually issuing visas, but were instead forwarding the applications to the Karabagh Representative in Yerevan. The Karabagh office in Yerevan is the only location where a traveler can take physical possession of a visa. You cannot obtain a visa at the Karabagh border.

Getting the visa is quite simple. Apply in-person at their office at 17/a Zarian Street, which is located north of the center of Yerevan, several blocks east of the Barekamutyun subway station (Tel. 52-64-28) (E-mail: ankr@arminco.am). (Note that this is a new address. In early 2004 they closed their office at 11 Moskovian Street). There's a short application form that you can fill out in English, Russian or Armenian. You also need two passport-sized photographs. If you didn't bring spare passport photos with you from home, you can get some made while-you-wait at many of the photo labs throughout Yerevan.

The fee is $25 for a one-week visa, which you must pay in US dollars, and an additional processing fee of 1,000 drams (less than $2), which you must pay in Armenian currency. You can also get a 21-day visa on the day of application for $45 plus the 1,000-dram fee.

Visa exemptions apply in limited circumstances. Armenian citizens who hold Armenian passports do not need visas. If you are not an Armenian citizen, but you nevertheless hold an Armenian residency card, you are also exempt from the visa requirement. Citizens of countries other than Armenia who hold a "Special Residency Passport" from Armenia are exempt, as well [see chapter two, "Essentials," for information about these special passports]. Children under age 16 are also exempt. For general information or to request a visa application form you can call the Office of the Nagorno Karabagh Republic in Washington, DC at 202-547-3166 or visit online at www.nkrusa.org.

Safety

In dozens of visits over the past nine years we have always found Karabagh peaceful and friendly. Foreigners, and especially Westerners, are well liked in Karabagh, and are not the targets of violent crime. In Stepanakert there are no areas that one must avoid at night, and the streets are peaceful.

World events have not had any apparent effect upon the ability to travel to Karabagh. Officials have reported no new restrictions on travel throughout

Travel Note: A Karabagh visa in your passport will bar you from any subsequent travel to Azerbaijan. In Azerbaijan, it is a crime for a person to have traveled to Karabagh. Keep this in mind when making your travel plans. If you want to avoid having a Karabagh visa in your passport, tell the clerk before you apply. You may be able to have it attached with a paper clip instead. Trying to cross into Karabagh with an Azeri visa in your passport is probably not wise, either, although officials tell us that it's not a crime. Since you must first travel through Armenia in order to get to Karabagh, this means you will need a visa for the Republic of Armenia, too. [For details on getting an Armenia visa, see Chapter 2, Essentials].

Karabagh, but there are still many in place because of the unresolved conflict with Azerbaijan. Martial law remains in effect. Visitors must be mindful of this when traveling in the region, and should remember that travel near the border is dangerous and prohibited. Azerbaijan has been known to harbor terrorist cells, which gives one an added reason for staying away from the border.

Land mines are a problem in Karabagh, although many areas have been cleared. A bucolic-looking pasture could easily prove to be deadly if you walk through it. Signs posted by HALO Trust (a British non-profit organization) will remind you of this on some roadways.

Travel Advisories

The US Dept. of State posts travel advisories on its website at **www.state.gov**. They advise that travelers exercise "caution" near the Armenian and Azerbaijan border. The UK Foreign Office also offers travel advisories, at **www.fco.gov.uk** and it

Goats grazing in the mountains of Shushi

Nagorno Karabagh

reports that most visits to Armenia are "trouble free." Canada's Consular Affairs Bureau offers country-specific travel reports at **www.voyage.gc.ca** (Tel. 1-800-267-6788). All three countries currently advise against travel to Karabagh, and note that they do not have embassies or consular services there to assist their citizens. We have been traveling there regularly since 1995 without incident, however.

Official Travel Information

The latest information about conditions in Karabagh is available on the Internet from www.nkrusa.org. This is website, provided by the NKR government, is operated by the NKR office in Washington, DC. Other sites with solid information are www.artsakhworld.com; www.artsakh.org, and www.nkr.am. Karabagh maintains a representation in the US where you can talk to a real person, instead of surfing the web. Contact: Vardan Barseghian, Representative; Office of the NKR in the USA; 122 C Street, NW; Suite 360; Washington, DC 20001 (Tel. 202-347-5166; Fax 202-347-5168) (E-mail: info@nkrusa.org).

Getting There By Air

There are no commercial flights into Karabagh but it might still be possible to fly in. Many tour agencies in Armenia, including **Sati Tours** in central Yerevan, can help you charter a private helicopter. A recently quoted fare was $2,500 for a round trip, but the 20-seat government-owned helicopter has to return to Yerevan the same day—the operator won't leave it in Karabagh overnight. These flights can be hazardous. Besides the risk of mechanical failure, there's always the chance that you will be shot down by enemy forces. Flying time is about one hour. Karabagh-based **Asbar Travel Agency** can also charter a helicopter for your group as part of a three, four, or five-day tour. Details are available on their Website www.asbar.nk.am. Contact them at 25 Vazgen Sargsian (Yerevanian) Street, 3rd floor; Stepanakert. You can call them from the US using their Yerevan number (Tel. / Fax 374-1-28-65-10) (E-mail: travel@asbar.nk.am). **Pan-Folk Ararat** also offers helicopter tours to Karabagh, with departures from Yerevan (Tel. 64-04-40) (E-mail: panfolk@web.am) (Internet: www.magistros.am/ararat).

Getting There By Land

The safest and easiest roadway into Karabagh passes through the Armenian town of Goris, and then through the area that was once called the **Lachin Corridor**. Thanks to a new highway that links Karabagh and Armenia, this journey has been dramatically shortened. One can expect to travel by private car from Yerevan to Stepanakert, the capital city of Karabagh, in only about six or seven hours. This is roughly half of the travel time of just a few years ago. And today the journey no longer requires a four-wheel drive automobile or long delays while bulldozers clear you a path through the rocks and soil, as was the case during the highway's construction.

The land corridor through which the new road passes got its name during Karabagh's war of independence. International observers had dubbed it a humanitarian corridor, and they attached the name Lachin to the corridor because this is the main town along the route. Today, Lachin is known by its original Armenian name, **Berdzor**. The mountainous region that it sits astride, and which had once been a mere corridor, has now been integrated into Karabagh. But habits die hard, and some foreign travelers still refer to the area as the Lachin Corridor.

The new roadway between Goris and Stepanakert is 90 km, and it has been re-engineered, widened, and re-paved all the way to Stepanakert, thanks to the massive financial support of Diaspora Armenians through the Hayastan All Armenian Fund. The road is still unavoidably full of switchbacks and hairpin turns because of the mountainous terrain, and travel time is about two and one-half hours.

There is also a passage to Karabagh through the **Karvachar (Kelbajar)** region, which is north of the Goris to Stepanakert roadway. This is a winding and mostly unpaved road with no facilities for fuel or food. The road is also in a military zone and land mines are thought to still be present, so we do not recommend this road to tourists [for more on Kelbajar, see "Driving to Armenia," later in this chapter].

You can rent a car from **Lemon Rent-a-Car** in Yerevan (4 Abovian Street; Tel. 54-55-47) or from one of the other car rental agencies on Abovian Street, and drive to Karabagh on your own for about $30 per day plus gasoline. You may have greater peace of mind if you just hire a private driver who knows his way around. You should be able to hire a driver for about $100 to $150 for a round-trip journey of two or three days. Your hotel can help you find a driver, or you can call one of the cab companies and make special arrangements, if you are unable to locate a reliable driver on your own. Negotiate the fare, as well as compensation for food and lodging, before departure.

For a less expensive alternative, travel by bus or minivan. Vans operate every day from Yerevan's **Kilikia Central Bus Station**. Departures are at 8 am and at 9 am. Travel time is roughly six hours, and the fare is 5,000 dram (about $10). From Hotel Shirak, a van departs daily at 7:30 am. Arrival in Stepanakert, Karabagh's capital city, is roughly six hours later, and the fare is only 4,000 dram (about $8). Private drivers offer one-way transportation for $50.

There are daily busses, as well, and they cost even less than the vans. These are the big red Intourist busses from the Soviet era. Travel times are dreadfully slow, sometimes 12 hours or more. They're uncomfortable, too, and we cannot recommend them. The one-way fare, however, is only 3,000 dram (about $6), so it's popular with the locals.

Travelers should arrive at the bus station or the hotel one hour before the scheduled departure of a van, in order to claim a good seat next to a window, and also to make sure that you'll get any seat at all—the seats get filled quickly. Sit on the right side of the van, where you'll have unobstructed views of Mt. Ararat. Bring a bottle of water and some food, since you may be in the van for four or more hours before stopping. If you are susceptible to carsickness, brace yourself for the winding mountain roads that connect Goris to Stepanakert.

Vans and busses arrive in (and also depart from) Stepanakert at the **Stepanakert Central Bus Station** at 31 Azatamartikner Street, which is south of Republic Square. In mid 2004 it was rumored that the bus station might relocate (Tel. 4-06-61).

Returning to Yerevan

Vans depart for Yerevan from the same location, the Stepanakert Central Bus Station, each day at 8 am, 9 am and at 10 am. As is the custom in Armenia, these vans do not depart until every seat is filled, so the actual departure times may vary. One-way fare to Yerevan is 5,000 drams. Private drivers offer one-way transportation for $50.

AFTER YOU ARRIVE

An immigration officer will check your visa and record your passage in a hand-written ledger. This stop is made near Berdzor (Lachin), the first town along the roadway into Karabagh. The driver will also be required to present his automobile and driving documents. This is the same routine that is followed in Armenia and Georgia, with one big difference. There are rarely any hassles or unnecessary delays at the Karabagh frontier. Car trunks are sometimes checked for contraband. But if your papers are all in order, you'll be sent on your way within a few minutes. If you don't have a visa, you will be turned back. Visas are not available at the border checkpoint.

There is no formal customs procedure here. Once you reach the capital, Stepanakert, however, you are required to register with the Karabagh Foreign Ministry. They'll give you travel papers that will list the towns or regions that you are allowed to visit, and you'll be warned to stay away from risky areas. Expect entry to be forbidden to regions near the Azeri frontier, or to any towns that formerly had Azeri populations, and which may be polluted with land mines. The Foreign Ministry is centrally located at 28 Azatamartikner Street.

This registration requirement does not appear to be strictly enforced. Still, we advise you to comply with this requirement as soon as you arrive.

Getting Around

Public transportation into and out of Karabagh is convenient and easy, as explained above. Public transportation inside Karabagh is not reliable, however, and the delays would be unbearable for a tourist with limited time.

School girl in Stepanakert

The best way to tour Karabagh is with a private driver. As an alternative, there are several private group tours that you can join which have departures from Yerevan. These tours will typically travel by mini van through Goris in southeastern Armenia, and then into Karabagh through the Kashatagh Region (Lachin Corridor), past the town that is now known as Berdzor. Visa arrangements are sometimes left to the guests, so check this beforehand to be sure.

Asbar Travel Agency in Stepanakert, Karabagh, can arrange tours for individuals or for groups of two or more people by mini van. Because they are based in Karabagh, they are probably a bit more familiar with Karabagh than agencies located in Armenia or the US. Asbar can also assist with hotel and visa arrangements, if you prefer to travel independently. Asbar Travel Agency, 25 Vazgen Sargsian (Yerevanian) Street, 3rd floor, Stepanakert. You can call them from the US using their Yerevan number (Tel / Fax 374-1 + 28-56-10) (E-mail: travel@asbar.nk.am) (Internet: www.asbar.nk.am). **Shirak Hotel Tours** offers excursions to Karabagh, with a Yerevan point of origin (Tel. 52-39-88). **Sidon Travel and Tourism** is also a reputable agent, located at 50 Nalbandyan Street, Yerevan (Tel. 52-29-67) (E-mail: sidon@arminco.com) (Internet: sidontravel.com). Sidon Travel also has offices in Los Angeles (Tel. 818-553-0777) and in Beirut (Tel. 961-1-261-887).

Helicopter tours of Karabagh can be arranged through Asbar Travel Agency [see listing in preceding paragraph] and by **Pan-Folk Ararat Tours**, 6 Malyan Street, Yerevan (Tel. 64-04-40) (E-mail: panfolk@web.am) (Internet: www.magistros.am/ararat).

Independent Touring

Upon arrival in Karabagh, it is a simple matter to hire a private driver to take you around. Many taxi drivers will agree to work for about 100 dram (20 cents) for each kilometer traveled. A flat rate of $20 for the day is also reasonable for traveling within Stepanakert or Shushi. There are no meters in the taxis, and all fares should be negotiated in advance. Either agree on a flat rate, or pay by the kilometer. On longer journeys of several hours you should offer a few dollars extra, and buy the driver's lunch. Keep in mind that many drivers are unemployed professionals, and that your driver may be a physicist or an engineer who has been forced to drive a cab in order to feed his family.

To arrange for a taxi in Stepanakert, call Taxi Service (Tel. 4-02-43). This taxi dispatch service can also be called by using a two-digit telephone number (Tel. 1-6). Yura Gasparian of Stepanakert is a driver we know who operates a mini van that can seat about ten people, and a sedan that can carry three passengers (Tel. 4-71-80; 4-49-10). He is a good driver and he knows Karabagh's roads and historic sites well.

HEALTH

Health precautions for travelers in Karabagh are the same as in Armenia. Bring any special medications you believe you may need, including prescription medicines and fever reducers such as aspirin and ibuprofen. Bring anti-diarrheal medicine and check with your doctor about bringing antibiotics. Karabagh does not require proof of any immunizations in order to gain entry, but travelers should consult a traveler's clinic to learn about recommended vaccinations. The Centers for Disease Control can provide the most current medical information for travelers to Karabagh, and to the rest of the Caucasus (Tel. 1-888-232-3299) (Internet: www.cdc.gov/travel).

ELECTRICITY AND WATER SUPPLY

Electricity and natural gas are available 24 hours per day to most parts of Stepanakert. Outside Stepanakert, however, service may not be as reliable or consistent. Water is supplied to homes and businesses in Stepanakert on a varied schedule, with some locations receiving a 24-hour-per-day supply.

MONEY

The local currency is the Armenian dram. Some merchants may accept US dollars, but it will be tough to get change for denominations of $5 or higher. Visitors should change their dollars to Armenian dram before arriving in Karabagh, or use one of the half dozen officially licensed exchange offices that are located throughout Stepanakert.

Banking services are rudimentary. There is only one **ATM machine** in all of Karabagh, and it is located at the Artsakh Bank on Sasuntsi Davit Street, near Republic Square in Stepanakert. Wire transfers can also be arranged at this bank.

TELEPHONE

Placing International Calls from Karabagh

Karabakh Telecom (Internet: www.karabakhtelecom.com) provides local, long-distance, and wireless telephone services in Karabagh. From most locations in Karabagh, if you wish to place a call to someone located anywhere else in the world you must go to the Telecom office and request an international line. In Stepanakert, the Karabakh Telecom office is located at 16 Vazgen Sargsian (Yerevanian) Street. They also operate an Internet café there. When logging onto their website, note that they do not use the letter "g" in their name.

Calls to the US are roughly $4 for each minute. Calls to Armenia are much less expensive. Payment must be made in Armenian currency. There's a bank located two doors away if you need to exchange money.

Placing Calls to Yerevan from Stepanakert

To reach Yerevan from Stepanakert it is not always necessary to use the Karabakh Telecom office, however. From many Stepanakert phones you can call Yerevan direct. Enter (1) + (0) + (local telephone number).

Placing Calls to Stepanakert from Abroad

To reach Stepanakert from any international location other than Armenia, enter (011) and then Armenia's country code (374) followed by the Karabagh country code (7) followed by the Stepanakert city code (1) and finally the local five-digit phone number. For example, to call Stepanakert from the United States, you would enter: 011 + (374) + (7) + (1) + (local phone number). Codes for many other locations in Karabagh are listed below.

Placing Calls to Stepanakert from Armenia

To reach Stepanakert from any location within Armenia, enter (0) followed by the Karabagh country code (7) followed by the Stepanakert city code (1) and then the local five-digit phone number. For example, to call Stepanakert from Armenia, you would enter: (0-7) + (1) + (local telephone number).

Stepanakert Emergency Codes

Fire (101); Police (102); Ambulance (103) and Information (109)

Karabagh Area Codes

Askeran (6); Hadrut (5); Kashatagh (7); Martakert (4); and Martuni (8); Shushi (7); and Stepanakert (1).

Cell Phones

Cellular telephone service in Stepanakert is provided by Karabakh Telecom. When calling a cell phone in Stepanakert, enter (7) and then the mobile phone number.

INTERNET

The fastest Internet service in Karabagh is available from Karabakh Telecom. They operate an Internet café in Stepanakert called **KT Surf** which is open 10 am until midnight. Their 400-dram per hour charge for Internet time is embarrassingly inexpensive for a tourist, but is affordable for local residents. Their offices and also their café are located at 16 Vazgen Sargsian (Yerevanian) Street.

Other internet cafes in Stepanakert are **Gayane Internet Café**, 18 Vazgen Sargsian (Yerevanian) Street (open 10 am to 10 pm, 300 dram per hour) and Arminco Ltd., 25 Vazgen Sargsian (Yerevanian) Street (one dollar per hour).

Internet-café 24 Hours is the name of an internet cafe that is, illogically, not open 24 hours per day. They charge 300 dram per hour for internet access and are located at 26 Mamikonian Street (Tel. 5-04-54) (E-mail: internet24@yandex.ru).

MAIL

Letters and postcards sent to the US directly from Stepanakert's main post office generally arrive in about two or three weeks. Mail that is posted here will be routed first to Yerevan, where it is combined with Armenian mail and then sent to its final destination in Karabagh. The post is located on Hakopian Street, between Vardan Mamikonian Street and Vazgen Sargsian (Yerevanian) Street, and it sells its own Karabagh postage stamps for all mail and for collectors. The rate for letters to the US is 250 dram (about 45 cents), and the rate for a post card is 170 dram (about 30 cents).

To send a letter to Karabagh, address it to the recipient, at the recipient's street and town address, in care of **Artsakh State Post Office**, Stepanakert. Then on the next three lines write: State Post Office; Moskovian #11; Yerevan, Armenia 375000. All mail destined for Karabagh must be routed through Yerevan.

Nagorno Karabagh

Sergei Galandarian is a private dealer who sells stamps for collectors, and reports significant interest among foreigners. He is located at 21 Vazgen Sargsian (Yerevanian) Street, Apt. #3, Stepanakert (Tel. 4-36-77).

MAPS

Other than the ones in this book, there are no commercially available street maps currently in print for Stepanakert and Shushi. Maps of Karabagh are widely available in print, but it will probably be easier to find one in Yerevan than in Stepanakert. In Yerevan, you can find a good selection of maps for less than $10 each at the Artbridge Bookstore Café, 20 Abovian Street (Tel. 52-12-39) (E-mail: artbridge@netsys.am). Also try the Noyan Tapan Bookstore on Republic Square in Yerevan.

BOOKS AND TELEVISION

There are no English-language periodicals, and English-language books are a rarity. Stepanakert's largest public library is the Mesrop Mashtots Republican Library, at 3 Azatamartikner Street. There's also a public library located at 9 Vardan Mamikonian Street, but their 53,000 volumes are all in Armenian or Russian. Broadcast television is from Armenia and Russia, and there is also a local station that broadcasts in Armenian for a brief time each day.

FOREIGN OFFICES AND NGOS

There are no foreign embassies in Karabagh. There are many international non-governmental organizations (NGOs), however. All of the offices listed below are located in Stepanakert and the phone numbers are all local Stepanakert phone numbers. To make a call from Yerevan, dial (0) + (7) + (1) + (local phone number).

Armenian Assembly of America, 28 Azatamartikner Street (Tel.4-37-74) (E-mail: office@aaa.nk.am); **Armenian Relief Society** (ARS), 25 Vazgen Sargsian (Yerevanian) Street (Tel. 5-27-93); **Armenian Technology Group** (ATG), 61 Tumanian Street (Tel. 5-11-58) (E-mail: zakiyan@arminco.nk.am); **Catholic Relief Services** (CRS), 10 Saroyan Street (Tel. 5-17-86) (E-mail: crs@arminco.nk.am); **Family Care** (FC), 35a Baghramian Street (Tel. 4-21-97) (E-mail: family@arminco.nk.am); **HALO Trust**, (Tel.4- 34- 96) (E-mail: simon_porter@halo.nk.am); **International Committee of the Red Cross** (ICRC), 50a Sasuntsi Davit Street (Tel. 4-37-40, 28-07-26) (E-mail: icrcstenk@icrc.nk.am); **Karabagh Committee of the Helsinki Initiative**, 26 Azatamartikner Street (Tel. 4-27-55) (E-mail: karandje@hca.nk.am); **MSF-Belgium** (Doctors Without Borders), 18 Baghramian Street (Tel. 4-06-79) (E-mail: watsan@msfb.nk.am or mhealth@msfb.nk.am); **Organization for Security and Cooperation in Europe** (OSCE), 2 Vazgen Sargsian (Yerevanian) Street (Tel. 4-57-78) (E-mail: office@osce.nk.am); **Save the Children Federation** (SCF), 24 Sasuntsi Davit Street (Tel. 4-07-01, 5-17-21) (E-mail: bob@sAvenuenk.am); **United Methodist Committee on Relief** (UMCOR), 5a Mashtots Street (Tel. 4-11-04) (E-mail: umcor@arminco.nk.am).

ON THE ROAD TO KARABAGH

Heading east-northeast past Goris, the road winds past the village of **Khundzoresk**, which is famous for its caves and exotic rock formations. Many of the caves are today used as barns for farm animals. The turnoff for Khundzoresk is located just a

The newly-restored fifth century monastery of Tsitsernavank, in Karabagh

couple of km past Goris, on the south (right) side. There's a large metal archway over the road to serve as a convenient landmark. There is also a new road sign.

The village of **Tegh** follows quickly. Tegh is noteworthy not only for the caves which you can see on the north (left) side of the road as you drive toward Karabagh, but also because of its geo-political location. Tegh is the last Armenian town that you pass before crossing over into the Kashatagh region of Karabagh, the principal town of which is Berdzor. This location made Tegh a frontier town with Azerbaijan beginning in 1920 and continuing until Karabagh regained its independence. Now, the political border is insignificant and it's difficult to tell exactly where Armenia officially ends—except to know that it's sometime after passing through Tegh. If you stop in Tegh, check out the fifth century church of St. Gevorg and the Iron Age tombs.

Note*: The names of many places and streets have been changed since independence. This text identifies streets and towns by their new names, followed (in parentheses) by the previous name, whenever confusion might otherwise result.*

The Pan Armenian Highway

The roadway that links Armenia and Karabagh, stretching west to east from Goris to Stepanakert, has been dubbed the **Pan Armenian Highway**. The name is appropriate not only because the road links two Armenian states, but also because the road was funded by Armenians from all over the world. Armenians from Armenia, Karabagh, and the Diaspora contributed millions of dollars in order to pay for the construction. The project was organized by a charitable group called the Hayastan All Armenian Fund.

The willingness of so many individuals to give so generously to fund such a seemingly impossible-to-pay-for road demonstrates the resolve—and the resurgence—of a once-battered nation.

The Pan Armenian Highway project was begun in 1995, one year after a cease-fire had put an end to the worst of the fighting in the Karabagh-Azerbaijan war. The road was built along the corridor between Armenia and Karabagh that had been liberated in 1992. This is the area that was known as the Lachin Corridor, and to this day this remains the only improved and viable land link between the two countries. The corridor was kept open during construction of the road, and we can recall trying to pass through on many occasions in 1995, 1996 and 1997 when we needed to wait for bulldozers to clear a path for our jeep. The highway was completed in November 1999, and it today plays a major role in preserving Karabagh's independence.

Berdzor

Berdzor is the new name for Lachin. It is Karabagh's frontier post and the location of its immigration and customs control. The region is still called the Lachin Corridor by many foreign visitors because of its past status, but officially it is now simply the Kashatagh Region. This area had been a humanitarian aid corridor during the Azeri siege of Karabagh in the early 1990s.

Today, almost every traveler will pass through Berdzor before going anywhere else in Karabagh. It is here in this areas surrounding Berdzor (if you venture off the main road) that you will find the fifth century monastery of **Tsitsernavank** (Swallow Monastery). This 1,600-year-old monastery is located in the Aghavni (Aghavnaget) River valley. Some scholars believe the building may have existed, although as a pagan temple, even earlier than the fifth century. The complex has been fully restored during the past couple of years, thanks to the generosity of an Armenian-American doctor.

To get there, Take the north turnoff from the main road near the customs checkpoint. The road is located at the bridge near the town of Berdzor (Lachin). Drive along the narrow road for 14 km. The road is rough, but you can travel it without a jeep. (The authors had no difficulty making the journey in a mini van.)

Travel time from Goris to Berdzor is about one hour. Travel time from the main road turnoff to Tsitsernavank is about 45 minutes.

KARABAGH

Visitors to Karabagh should use either Stepanakert or Shushi as a base from which to visit the surrounding regions. Stepanakert and Shushi have the best lodging, and you can get to everything and still return the same day. Stepanakert is the capital of Karabagh, and all travel times listed here are by private car from Stepanakert unless stated otherwise. For travel times from Shushi add roughly 20 minutes for northern destinations.

SHUSHI

Shushi is the first major town in Karabagh that you drive past when you travel to Karabagh from Armenia. The topography is stunning, and the sheer cliffs that limit the potential sprawl of the town have also served to insulate and protect it from outsiders. This small town is just 15 km outside of Stepanakert, and it deserves to be on every visitor's itinerary. There's a magnificent **Persian fortress**, which was built in 1724, and two working Armenian churches. There are a couple of

Children gathering flowers, Ghazanchetsots Cathedral, Shushi

mosques, too. The mosques are damaged from the war and closed, but they are otherwise untouched and their four minarets are still there.

Shushi's history has been tragic. As many as 35,000 Armenians had lived in Shushi until 1920, when they were either killed or expelled by invading forces from Turkey and Azerbaijan. Seven thousand Armenian homes were destroyed. Shushi's status as one of the region's leading cultural centers was also snuffed out.

The Armenians recovered Shushi in 1992, and it is still in ruins from the war. One of the large tanks involved in the battle to recover Shushi now forms part of a monument located on the roadside between Shushi and Stepanakert.

Don't photograph military sites here. There's no express law prohibiting other photography, but police or security agents might stop you if you are walking around with a camera. Carry your passport, or at least a photocopy of it, so that you can identify yourself as a tourist if you are stopped and questioned. You'll get a good view of Stepanakert from Shushi's high perch. It was from this same perch that Azerbaijan bombed Stepanakert during the war.

The **Ghazanchetsots Cathedral** in Shushi is a massive structure with a façade of white stone that dominates its surroundings. It's also known as the Cathedral of Christ the Savior. The freestanding belfry that stands near the front entrance was built in 1858, a decade before construction was begun on the main church. The church has seen many uses over the years, not all of which have been religious.

During the period of Azeri control of the town, beginning in 1920, the church was used a granary, as a garage, and finally as a munitions storehouse until May 9, 1992, when the Azeris retreated. The building was heavily damaged and its artwork was defaced. The Armenians have made extensive repairs during the past few years, however, and reconstruction was completed in 2000. This cathedral is one of at least 19 churches and monasteries throughout Karabagh that have been restored

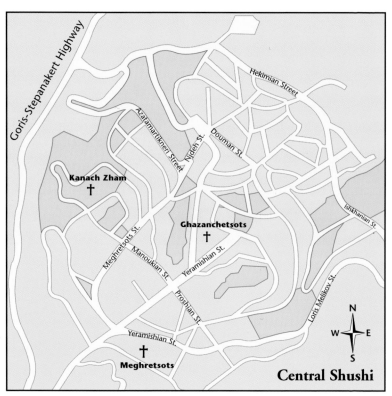

Map of Shushi © 2004 Stone Garden Productions

during the past decade or so. If you cannot pronounce its name, call it the Shushi Cathedral and you'll be understood.

Kanach Zham is another Armenian church located uphill from the Cathedral. This church is sometime called Karabaghtsots in honor of the farmers from Karabagh who built it in 1847. More frequently, however, the people of Shushi call it Kanach Zham, which translates to "green church." The origin of the name is logical, inasmuch as the church domes were at one time painted green. The ruins of **Meghretsots Church** are also nearby. Only the eastern wall and two apses remain.

Despite Shushi's poverty, it has been largely overlooked by the international community. Armenians from the Diaspora have made many contributions to help rebuild the town and to provide activities to its youth. A group from the US recently constructed a basketball court near the Shushi Music School, and NK Arts, another US-based organization, has sponsored performing arts events in town.

To get there, from Stepanakert there are eight daily vans that depart from the Stepanakert Central Bus Station. One-way fare is 170 drams (roughly 30 cents). Arrivals in Shushi are near the Ghazanchetsots Cathedral and the Hotel Shoushi.

Hotels and Places to Stay

Hotel Shoushi (which the owners spell with an "o") is Karabagh's best hotel. This clean and comfortable facility has new furnishings, hot water, and Western-style bathrooms. There's also a restaurant on site. The location, just across from the Ghanzenchetstots Cathedral, is ideal, and many of the rooms have balconies with great views. Singles are roughly $35, doubles a bit more. This place is great, and we recommend it highly. You can use Shushi as a home base for touring the rest of the country without any difficulty. Located at 3 Amirian Street (Tel. 374-1-40-29-18) (Mobile: 07-24-25-26) (Local: 0-7-7-3-13-57) (Internet: www.Shoushihotel.com) (E-mail: reservation@shoushihotel.com).

STEPANAKERT

Stepanakert is a small-town capital, with narrow, tree-lined streets, modest buildings, and hospitable people. There's a human scale to this town that invites visitors and makes them feel right at home. In the current vernacular, you might say that Stepanakert is a livable city. Beneath the pleasant facade, however, is the reality that there are few jobs and that residents confront the daily challenge of surviving in a still recovering economy.

If this wasn't Karabagh's capital, it might not be a tourist destination. There simply aren't many historic attractions here. The city saw most of its development during the Soviet era, and there isn't a single church here—an omission that civic leaders in 2004 were making plans to correct. If you didn't visit, that would be a pity, because of the recent historical significance of Stepanakert as a city that survived under siege. This is also one of the few places in Armenia and Karabagh where travelers can stroll down the street as if they were in an old east European neighborhood, instead of in a centrally planned city.

If you enjoy walking, then the best way to see this town is by foot. Start your tour from the Karabagh Hotel on **Republic Square**. This is the oldest lodge in all Karabagh, and in the unlikely event that renovations are finally completed sometime in 2005, as planned, it will also be the largest. Walk east, past the **Karabagh Parliament** building, and down a flight of steps to Stepan Shahumian Park. There are children's amusement rides and a café in this park.

There's also a Ferris wheel that offers superb views of the area, including a view of the famous monument of **Tatik and Papik**. The monument was erected in 1967, and an inscription on the back reveals its official name "We Are Our Mountains." This monument generated great controversy when it was first erected. Azerbaijan exercised sovereignty over Karabagh at that time, and the statue was condemned by the Azeris because it expressed the love of Armenians for this land. The sculpture shows an elderly couple—a grandmother and grandfather—which symbolizes their union with the mountains. Despite all the fuss, it was built. And today it is cherished as a national landmark.

Cross over to Azatamartikner Street, which is actually a continuation of Vazgen Sargsian (Yerevanian) Street, and you can either walk down to the monument in about fifteen minutes, or take a 500 dram (less than $1) cab ride. Before trekking down there, however, take a short walk to the **Artsakh State Museum**, which is

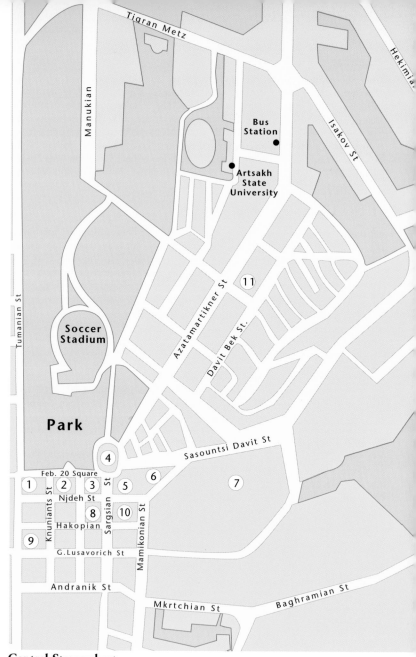

Central Stepanakert

1 Hotel Karabagh Building; 2 Parliament of Nagorno Karabagh; 3 Government Building;
4 Shahumian Park; 5 Artsakh Bank, ATM; 6 Artsakh Museum; 7 Shuka (Market);
8 Stepanakert City Hall; 9 Dramatic Arts Theater; 10 Post Office; 11 Foreign Affairs Minist...

Map of Stepanakert © 2004 Stone Garden Productions

located near Stepan Shahumian Park, just about 50 m from Republic Square, at 4 Sasuntsi Davit Street. The entrance to the museum is graced by a beautiful hand-carved wooden door. Here, an assortment of ancient archaeological artifacts, geological specimens, and Christian manuscripts are on display in an unpretentious manner in this two-story building. There are also modern relics from World War II and from the events of the past decade, which, in the local parlance, is simply "our war." The text placards that describe the displays are often in English, as well as in Armenian and Russian. English-speaking tour guides are generally not available, however. The building is open Monday through Saturday until 5 pm, or earlier if the handful of workers grows weary. Admission is free, but donations of a dollar or two are accepted.

There's a **carpet factory** called Hovani (formerly known as "Artsakh Rugs") at 31 Azatamartikner Street (a few blocks north of Republic Square, next to the Green Bar) that's worth a visit (Tel. 5-03-31). If you stop by on a weekday, you'll be able to see the craftsmanship in progress. The manager, Oleg Paghshian, says all tourists are welcome to stop by. You might even want to make a purchase, or place a custom order, which can be shipped home to you. There's a showroom where rugs are sold.

Travel time from Yerevan to Stepanakert (360 km) is about seven hours. Goris to Stepanakert (90 km) is about two and one-half hours. Travel time from the Berdzor Customs Station to Stepanakert (62 km) is about one and one-quarter hours.

Hotels and Places to Stay

Nora Babayan operates an informal **Bed and Breakfast** near the center of town. There are three rooms on the top floor of her private home, which can accommodate up to seven guests. Shared bathroom. Nora can help you make arrangements for a driver and translator, too. All prices, including the cost for laundry services and meals, are negotiable, but figure on paying roughly $10 to $15 per night for each person. Located at 11 Rubeni Street, near the residence of Karabagh President Arkady Ghukasian. Visitors should call from Yerevan before traveling to Karabagh to guarantee availability (Tel. 4-49-10).

Heghnar Hotel is Stepanakert's newest lodge. Each of the 12 rooms in this recommended micro-hotel is clean and modern, and has a private bath (with shower) and 24-hour water. Rooms also have balconies. Facilities include a restaurant and bar, and an Internet café. Single $30; Double $40; Deluxe Suite $70. Located at 11a General Barsegov Road, near the second traffic circle (Tel. 4-46-26; 26-66-66).

Karabagh Hotel has been a fixture of central Stepanakert since it opened in 1936. It was a dismal pit a few years back, and barely worth the nightly rate of only $3. Renovations are now underway and supposed to be finished by 2005. Until then, expect it to be closed. Located on Republic Square next to the Parliament Building (Tel. 1-37-93).

Lavanda Guest House has an outdoor swimming pool and mountain views from the balconies. The rooms are new and clean. Single $60 (Tel. 4-19-59). **Lousabats Guest House** also features extravagant accommodations, at least by local standards. Single $60; Double $120. These dachas operate near the Tatik and Papik monument at the northern edge of town, but are not recommended. They are remotely located, a bit pricey, and their managers do not specialize in catering to foreign tourists.

Nagorno Karabagh

Lotus Hotel in Stepanakert is only a few years old but it's already showing signs of fatigue. Each room has a private or shared modern bathroom with 24-hour hot water. This hotel is popular with tour groups because of its size: there are 26 rooms available with accommodations for 60 guests. Amenities: Twin beds, TV/VCR. Facilities include a low budget restaurant and an unappealing swimming pool. Single w/shared bath $25; Double $40. Walk to town in 15 minutes, or take a 500-dram (less than $1) cab ride. No handicapped access, stairs to all floors. Before entering the center of town, follow the signs to 81 Vargash Vagarsanyan Street (Tel. 4-38-82; or 4-16-20) (E-mail: lotus@nk.infostack.net).

Nairi Hotel is the most comfortable hotel in Stepanakert. The building is modern and is superior to the Lotus in comfort and cleanliness. Amenities include air conditioning, 24-hour hot water, and internet access. Great views of surrounding mountains. Single $40. The location near the Tatik and Papik monument at the southern edge of town is a 15-minute walk to Republic Square. Turn right at the gasoline station before reaching the monument and follow the signs to 14A Hekimian Street (Tel. 374-1- 7-15-03) (E-mail: nyree@arminco.nk.am).

Food

The food in Karabagh is similar to the food that is served in Armenia. *Khorovats* is popular. A local specialty is *jingalov hats*, which is a flat bread that is tilled with 15 types of greens and herbs.

Places to Eat

Express Bar, dark and has very slow service here. Coffee, beer, pizza and salads. Located on Grigor Lusavorich Street; **Green Bar**, favorite meeting place for expatriates since 1997. Pizza and beer. 31 Azatamartikner Street, below Republic Square (Tel. 4-56-71); **Haik Pizza**, Karabagh's first pizza joint. Basturma and other nontraditional pizza toppings. 1 Mkhitar Gosh Street, near Azatamartikner Street and below Republic Square; **Holsten Bar**, newest meeting place in town. Beer, coffee, *khorovats*, pizza. 20 Vazgen Sargsian (Yerevanian) Street (Tel. 4-56-09); **Niko Café**, sidewalk café. Beer and light food. Located just above Republic Square on Vazgen Sargsian (Yerevanian) Street; Pizza Delivery to your hotel or apartment is available for about 1500 drams (less than $3) from the creatively-named business **Pizza Delivery**. These are Armenian-style pizzas, and you can get them only by delivery (Tel. 5-26-92); **Victoria Bar**, kebob, *khorovats*, Armenian food. 31 Azatamartikner Street (Tel. 4-75-35).

Groceries

Magic City Supermarket, the most-Western grocery store in Stepanakert, is the most convenient place to shop for groceries. It is clean and well stocked and its shelves include Russian imports. Located on Azatamartikner Street, at the second circle; Outdoor Market (*Shuka*), largest outdoor food market in Stepanakert. Located on Baghramian Street, south of Republic Square.

Shopping

Artist's Studio, featuring local painter Samvel Gabrielian. Original artwork sold. 13 Vardan Mamikonian Street; **Konica Photo Express**, Polaroid® and 35mm film. Grigor Lusavorich Street, next to Express Bar; **Penta Electronics**, appliances, radios, batteries, 15 Vardan Mamikonian Street; **Photo Lab**, color print film, processing. 17 Vardan Mamikonian Street. Across the street, on Pavlova Street, there are a dozen or more sidewalk vendors selling food, clothing, and assorted goods; **Vernissage**, gift shop. Tourist trinkets. 11 Vardan Mamikonian Street.

SOUTH AND EAST OF STEPANAKERT

When traveling outside Stepanakert, pack a lunch and a bottle of water, because you're not likely to be able to purchase a meal in the countryside. Your chances of finding a restaurant inside Stepanakert is much better, but you will probably still want to purchase fruits, vegetables and bread from a market so that you can prepare your own meal.

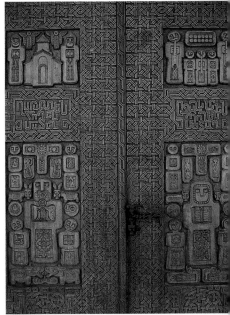

Door of the Artsakh State Museum

Do not stray off the roads and into fields when traveling outside of Stepanakert, unless you are certain that the area has been cleared of mines. The HALO Trust has placed warning signs near most of the dangerous areas, so be alert for these warnings.

East of Stepanakert, **clay pottery** is manufactured and sold at a small workshop in the microscopically small village of Nungi. The workshop was started in 2001 on the site of a historic pottery center. Because of the abundance of clay in this area, Nungi has been a pottery site since antiquity. Jeff Ryan, a ceramist from the US who serves as a volunteer, operates the workshop. He has enlisted the assistance of several local apprentices. The workshop is a project of NK Arts, Inc., a non-profit organization that promotes the arts in Karabagh (Internet: www.nungi.fly.to). Visitors are welcome.

To get there, from Stepanakert, take the east turnoff from Naberezhnaya Street, which is located near the Karkar River. Drive directly east from Stepanakert for about 17.5 km on the Stepanakert-to-Martuni road. From Nungi village there's a 15-minute hike up a hillside.

Shosh

On the midpoint along the roadway between Stepanakert and Shushi there's a south-bound turnoff for Karmir Shuka. This road first passes the tiny village of Shosh, from which you should be able to look across the gorge of the Karkar River to see the cliffs of Shushi. Americans who arrive is Shosh are prompted to declare "wow!" when they see the Russian language road signs that spell-out Shosh in Cyrillic letters.

At a distance of 26 km from Stepanakert you will reach the village of **Sarushen**. This is home to the ruins of the **Pirumashen Church**, which dates back to the twelfth and thirteenth centuries. The fieldstone church is only about 20 feet from the side of the road, but trees and shrubs partially screen it from view. This is another of Karabagh's off-the-beaten-path antiquities, and we recommend that you visit.

The small village of **Karmir Shuka**, which is located about eight km past the village of Sarushen, is a regional center. There isn't much economic activity here today, but at one time there was a large cognac factory just outside the village center. The building is still here, but it's been a while since any spirits have been distilled. The turnoff to the new North-South Highway is located about five km past the village (a distance of 41 km from Stepanakert). The nearby village of Azokh is home to the Azokh Caves. These are said to be the largest limestone caves in the Caucasus, and they cover an area of 8,000 square m with 600 m of maze-like passageways. The cave is believed to have been inhabited by Paleolithic humans as long as one million years ago.

The nearby village of **Skhtorashen** would be a tourist trap, except that it isn't. There are simply no capitalists to take advantage of you when you get here. There are picnic grounds here, and a huge 2,000-year-old tree that you can walk through. The anticipation of doing this is comparable to the "thrill" of driving a car through a Giant Redwood tree in California. Perhaps more interesting than the tree are the beautiful fields and pastures along the way, on the road that connects the villages of Shosh and Karmir Shuka. Foreign visitors don't normally journey down this road, which is a shame because this pastoral region may be one of Karabagh's most beautiful areas.

The North – South Highway

Traveling within Karabagh has gotten a lot easier during the past couple of years because of an ambitious road-building project that is being funded by Armenians from all over the world. After completing the east-west "Pan Armenian" highway that links Karabagh to Armenia, Diaspora Armenians and the people of Karabagh turned their sights to the road that they call the "North-South Highway." The **Hayastan All Armenian Fund** (Internet: www.himnadram.org) coordinated both projects.

When completed, this North-South highway will span 170 km from the southern town of Hadrut to the northern region of Martakert, at a cost of more than $25 million. By 2004, sections comprising less than half of the North-South Highway, not all of them contiguous, had been completed.

During the Soviet era, Azerbaijan had built a network of west-east roads integrating Karabagh into Azerbaijan. But they never permitted the construction of north-south roads within Karabagh—roads that would integrate Karabagh internally and permit it to have communications links independent of Azerbaijan. Thus, to travel from a town in the south of Karabagh to a town in the north, it was necessary to use a road that passed into, and then out of, Azerbaijan. The North-South Highway corrects this problem.

Amaras and G'Tichivank

From Karmir Shuka, you can reach the **Monastery of Amaras**. Amaras is located in the Varanda (Fizuli) Region, near the village of Machkalashen, which is to say that it's in the middle of nowhere. It's a bit puzzling to view Amaras for the first time. Farmland and endless fields of wheat surround the complex, and yet there's a fortress of tall stone walls surrounding the complex. The unlikely sight of the walls betrays the painful history of this monastery. The monastery has been repeatedly plundered and rebuilt for the past 1,500 years.

The oldest church at the complex was built by St. Gregory the Illuminator sometime around AD 310. The real claim to fame for Amaras comes from its connection with Mesrop Mashtots, the inventor of the Armenian alphabet. Mashtots taught here 1,600 years ago. Not surprisingly, his teachings included the alphabet that he had just created. The monastery is the oldest in Karabagh, but the main church and the current focal point of the complex is a more recent addition. It was built in the nineteenth century. This rectangular church is constructed from white stone, and is named St. Gregoris, in honor of the grandson of St. Gregory the Illuminator.

To get there, from Karmir Shuka, travel north (go left) to the village of Sos. From Sos, just drive south to the monastery. An alternate route is to travel east to Aghdam, then south to Martuni, and then take the west (right) turnoff to Sos.

Travel time from Stepanakert to Amaras is about two hours on poor roads.

If you take the route through Martuni, you may want to stop to take a look at the **Statue of Monte Melkonian**, an Armenian-American who became a hero of Karabagh's war of independence. The monument is located near the center of town, outside the city government building. There's a military hospital and a military base nearby, as well, and a new religious center, the Church of St. Nerses the Gracious (Nerses Shnorhali).

If you're looking for a challenge, try to locate **G'Tichivank**. And once you've located it, try to reach its mountaintop perch. Diligent and persevering explorers will find it near the village of **Togh**—a remote region south of Martuni and west of Varanda, in the Hadrut region. G'Tichivank dates to the thirteenth century and it stands today in disrepair.

G'Tichivank is not the kind of place that most travelers will ever see more than once (if that) so if you decide to make the trek, start early and with plenty of gasoline and water. The monastery was built from the tenth through thirteenth centuries, during an era when there was much destruction of the area from Mongol hordes. We were saddened

Monastery of Amaras, Karabagh

1,600th Anniversary of the Armenian Alphabet

Armenia observes the 1,600th anniversary of its alphabet throughout the year in 2005. The development of Armenia's unique alphabet is traced to the early days of Christianity.

When Armenia proclaimed Christianity to be its state religion in AD 301, the Church set about the task of translating the Bible and other religious texts into the Armenian language. The Greek alphabet had always been used, which was not unusual, considering that the Greek alphabet was the world's most advanced at the time. Ordinary people in Armenia, however, didn't understand Greek. The language barrier was impeding the spread of Christianity.

So, in the AD 390s, the Armenian King Vramshapuh asked the Armenian scholar and monk Mesrop Mashtots to find a solution. By AD 405 Mashtots had created an alphabet in which every sound of the Armenian language was represented by one of 36 distinct letters. His alphabetical creation had both upper and lower case letters—unlike all other alphabets in use in Eastern Anatolia and the Middle East.

The king and the leaders of the church accepted Mesrob's alphabet, and that same year they translated the Bible into Armenian, using the new alphabet. The new alphabet ushered in a golden age for Armenian literature. Mesrop Mashtots began the teaching the new alphabet at a school at the Karabagh monastery of Amaras. This is credited as one of the first Armenian schools. Mashtots is credited with helping to spread Christianity in Armenia.

This Armenian alphabet is still used today, in the same form. Advances and changes in the spoken language throughout the centuries made it necessary to add two letters, representing two new sounds, during the twelfth century.

to see the buildings horribly defaced by graffiti. For some reason, many people felt compelled to write their names—using both the Armenian and Cyrillic alphabets—on the inside and outside walls of the church.

If you make it to Togh but you cannot get up the mountain to see G'Tichivank, don't despair. There are three interesting churches here, St. Hovhaness, St. Stepanos, and Anapat, all from the thirteenth through eighteenth centuries. These are worth seeing, and the views of the surrounding countryside are great. We found a fourth church nearby, as well, but it was being used as an animal barn. Still, we have found G'Tichivank to be a real treasure, and the search for it to have been a worthy adventure.

To get there, drive south from Martuni, and then west at Varanda. The village of Togh is the last stop before the climb to the top of the mountain and to G'Tichivank. A standard jeep won't make it on the unpaved road that stretches for 10 km to the top, even during the dry months. You will instead need a Willys, which is a Russian-made army vehicle. Ask someone from the village to give you a ride. We asked an old-timer from the village whose name was Armen Gregoryan (Cellular Tel. 31-15-97). He was happy to receive 5,000 dram ($9) for his time and for the gasoline.

Travel time from Stepanakert to G'Tichivank is about four hours. Yet, the distance is only about 56 km. Note that the road from Togh to G'Tichivank will be muddy and impassable during the rainy months, and probably through June.

Hotel and Place to Stay

The government-owned **Artsakh Hotel** in Varanda (Fizuli) offers one deluxe and nine regular rooms in the center of town. There's no hot water, and the baths (such that they are) are shared by all in this depressing facility. All accommodations: 1,000 dram (about $2). Located on the main square.

NORTH AND WEST OF STEPANAKERT

The **Gandzasar Monastery** is located northwest of Stepanakert in the Jraberd (Martakert) Region near the village of Vank. If this is the only site you visit in Karabagh, your trip will still have been worthwhile. Many experts agree with the leading French historian who identified Gandzasar as the third most important artifact of Armenian monastic architecture.

Construction of the main church here, which honors St. John the Baptist (in Armenian, Hovhannes Mkrtich) was begun in AD 1216. According to legend, the church was built at the location of a shrine that contained the skull of this saint, which had been brought here from Palestine. A high wall, in addition to its natural fortification on a mountain top, protects the entire complex. The exquisite bas-reliefs on the exterior walls are unique, and have been compared to the elaborate inscriptions of Aghtamar, a church located in the distant region of Van in historic Armenia. The monasteries of Harichivank, which is located near Gyumri in Armenia, and the monastery of Hovanavank, which is located near Ashtarak in Armenia, are also said to replicate Gandzasar architecturally.

Gandzasar's **bas-reliefs** depict the Crucifixion, Adam and Eve, and two ministers holding models of the church above their heads, as an offering to God. There are about 150 separate inscriptions, engraved in stone using the Armenian alphabet, throughout the complex.

Gandzasar was the center of an Armenian independence movement in the eighteenth century. More recently, the monastery was damaged when Azeri bombers targeted it for destruction in 1991, and one building—the house of the Father Superior—was lost. The damage is being repaired, and extensive renovations and reconstruction were completed in 2004.

The English language translation of the name Gandzasar is "treasure mountain," and to view the splendor of its architecture is to understand why. Some scholars and historians consider the monastery to represent one of the top masterpieces of Armenian architecture. Gandzasar is actively functioning today, and is the seat of the Archbishop of Artsakh of the Diocese of the Armenian Apostolic Church.

To get there, travel to the northern edge of Stepanakert, and take the left turnoff onto a modern, paved road four km past the Tatik and Papik monument. Travel roughly 35 km on this new roadway until the signposted turnoff onto a dirt road. After 13 km on this dirt road you'll see the monastery at the top of the mountain. Just two more km on a steep dirt road and you'll be at the top (this road is planned to be reconstructed by 2005).

Travel time from Stepanakert to Gandzasar (50 km) is about ninety minutes, half of which is on that 15-kilometer-long dirt road. A jeep is advisable but not absolutely essential for the last stretch of road.

The town of **Askeran** is located about 12 km north of Stepanakert, in the region of Khachen (Askeran), and is the site of a fortress that spans the shallow Karkar River and the major roadway that runs along side the river, as well. The Persian leader Panakh Khan built this fortress in the eighteenth century during Persian hegemony over the region. It is known locally as Zoraberd (Strong Fortress). Just north of town there's a war memorial on the left side of the road which features a large tank that was used to defend the region.

Travel farther up this road to the **Vankasar Monastery**, which stands a lonely vigil outside Jraberd (Martakert). This building is located on a sparsely vegetated hilltop just off the main road that links the Jraberd Region to Aghdam, and it is visible from several km away as one approaches by car. The tiny church is built of a cream colored stone, and it sits on a peak that is about 100 m from a military radar and observation post. Because of this military post, government officials say that tourists are not welcome unless they have permission from the base commander, and that groups of more than three people are not likely to be admitted.

If you decide to visit, your first stop should be at the military post there, where you should identify yourself as a tourist, and get permission to walk around. We're told there's no risk of landmines, but use extreme caution anyway and walk only in designated areas. Hire a local guide or driver who can help you get permission. The military observation post occupies a house that had been the dacha (summer home) of a high-ranking Azeri official before the war. You are apt to see many wild rabbits, owls and other rare birds on the hilltop while you are there.

To get there, from Stepanakert travel north as far as the destroyed town of Aghdam, and then bear left (north, again) in the direction of Martakert.

Aghdam is notorious as the town from which enemy forces launched military operations against Karabagh during the recent war. The absence of any natural geographic barrier between Aghdam and Karabagh created a situation in which the force that held Aghdam was the force that would dictate conditions as far away as Stepanakert. Today, Aghdam is deserted and destroyed, except for a mosque, which, as a religious site, was intentionally spared from harm. Karabagh forces captured the city during the war and its population fled with the military to locations farther east in Azerbaijan.

Aghdam has been stripped clean of anything of value, and there has been no attempt made by Karabagh—or an interest expressed by them—to settle this area. Instead, this is now simply a military zone, and it is **off-limits to foreign visitors**. Some travel agents have advertised in recent years that their tour includes a stop in Aghdam. There doesn't seem to be much point in this, and we advise visitors to stay away.

Visitors who are interested in learning about the people of Karabagh may also choose to continue up the road for about 20 km (travel time from the church is about 20 minutes) and visit the town of **Martakert**, which was the site of fierce fighting during the war. Upon the approach to town there's a neat and orderly village of modern homes that was built with funding from Germany. On the horizon ahead of the main road a large Ferris wheel marks the location of the old town.

Photograph: Interior of St. John the Baptist Church, Gandzasar

Nagorno Karabagh

There are only two major roads within Martakert. On Azatamartikner Street (Lenin Prospekt), the people of the town built a tiny Local History Museum in 1997, to replace the one that had been destroyed by enemy forces during the war. One large room in the museum is a portrait gallery featuring the images of local men and boys who were killed during the war. This type of portrait gallery is not unique to this museum. We have encountered such memorials in towns all over Karabagh. The museum is open weekdays from 8 am to 6 pm.

Travel time from Stepanakert to Vankasar (40 km) is about one hour. (From the turnoff at the main road, the drive to the top and to the church is about 15 minutes.) Travel time from Stepanakert to Martakert is about one hour.

We recommend that you do not travel north of Martakert. The roads north of town will lead you dangerously close to the front line with Azerbaijan, which is militarized, and one risks being subject to hostile fire. If peace comes to the region, visitors will be able to travel to the **Yeghishe Arakyal Monastery**, which dates to the fifth century, and to the **Yeritsmankants Monastery**, which was built in the modern era in 1691. Yeghishe Arakyal is located on the bank of the Yeghsharakel River, which is a tributary of the Tartar River. Yerits Mankants, also known as the **Monastery of Three Youths**, is closer still to the border. To go there, you must get permission from Karabagh's Ministry of Defense, in Stepanakert. Karabagh's northernmost region of Shahumian has been overrun by enemy forces and is now occupied by Azerbaijan. It is not accessible.

Hotel and Place to Stay

The **Jraberd Hotel** in Jraberd (Martakert) offers 19 dark and spartan rooms. There's only cold water, and it's only in a shared bath on the first floor. Each room has a balcony, but there aren't any views. Regular rooms 1,000 dram (about $2); Deluxe rooms 1,500 dram (about $3). Located on Azatamartikner Street, which is also known as Lenin Prospekt. Getting a room here is only marginally better than sleeping in the street.

Dadi Vank is a stunning monastery that just might be the oldest in all of Karabagh. The buildings that have survived to this day were all built early in the twelfth and thirteenth centuries. The complex is unequaled in its mystery and majesty among the churches of Karabagh. According to legend, the monastery was originally established in the first century AD, but was destroyed and then rebuilt roughly 800 years ago. Scholars are undecided, but if the legend is true, then Dadi Vank would gain distinction as the oldest monastery in Karabagh.

Historians believe that Dadi Vank, with more than 20 buildings of both an ecclesiastical and residential nature, was the grandest monastery in all of medieval Armenia.

The complex today consists of a three-story bell tower that dates back to 1334, and several other buildings, some of them with elaborate engravings and inscriptions on their walls. The largest of the buildings is the church of St. Dadi, which was completed in 1214. Its main altar is used daily by the local villagers, and it frequently displays an assortment of gifts and messages that they have left behind.

Dadi Vank Monastary

On the outside of the southwestern wall, there's a bas-relief of a model of the church being offered to God. Below it there is an inscription, written in Armenian. It says, "I, Arzu Khatun, obedient servant of Christ…wife of King Vakhtang, ruler of Artik and all Upper Khachen, with great hopes have built this holy cathedral on the place where my husband and sons are laid to rest. Done in 663 [AD 1214] of the Armenian calendar." Inside, frescoes adorn the larger walls.

Extensive renovations were begun in 2003, much of it of questionable quality and workmanship. We saw evidence of carelessly spilled-mortar that had been allowed to conceal and fill-in the engravings and etchings on the exterior walls. New roofing was being installed, as well.

To get there, drive west nine km (20 minutes), past Martakert and to the village of Kusapat. Continue westward past the large village of Getavan, which is 53 km (three hours drive) from Martakert. Just after Getavan there is a military checkpoint, and the monastery is just a bit farther. We have usually been able to purchase gasoline at Getavan. The roads leading to Getavan are in poor condition and are mostly unpaved. Expect muddy and impassible conditions in early spring.

Travel time from Stepanakert to Dadi Vank (124 km) is about four hours.

The road to Dadi Vank winds past the **Sarsang Reservoir** and along the **Tartar Canyon**. The Tartar River's swift but shallow waters helped carve out this canyon. Don't be surprised to see the occasional remnants of destroyed tanks and other military hardware along the sides of the road. Even this remote area didn't escape the war. Sarsang is the largest body of water in Karabagh, and this is a great place to stop to rest when driving to Dadi Vank. This area is remote and forested, with sheer rock cliffs that cling to the sides of the roads, occasionally sending rocks crashing down. The unlikely appearance of the ancient monastery adds to Dadi Vank's mysterious charm. The best time to visit is in the summer, when you can go and still get back to Stepanakert before dark.

West of Dadi Vank monastery, in the town of Tsar, another ancient religious site fared less well. **The Monastery of Tsar**, built in 1301, was deliberately destroyed by the Azerbaijan authorities during the Soviet era. The monastery was blown up, two thirteenth century chapels were razed to the ground, and the pride of Tsar, the Church of the Holy Virgin, was dismantled. The elaborately engraved stones of the church were used to build storehouses, and they are today visible in the foundations of barns built by the Azeris. The author Boris Baratov documented the destruction, both in words and photographs, in the book A Journey to Karabagh: Paradise Laid Waste.

RETURNING TO ARMENIA

There are two primary routes out of Karabagh and back to Armenia. The easier of the two is the same way that you would have arrived if you were following the advice in this guidebook—through the Kashatagh Region and west to Goris. You'll be returning on the same road that brought you to Karabagh, and the journey will be simpler and faster.

Sarsang Reservoir, northern Karabagh

Karvachar (Kelbajar)

The alternate route to Armenia takes you past Dadi Vank on a much longer and more adventurous route. If you wish to travel on this road you will need permission from the Karabagh Foreign Ministry, which is located at 28 Azatamartikner Street in Stepanakert.

Traveling west of Dadi Vank, you will enter the region of **Karvachar (Kelbajar)**, which is a military zone. The road from Karvachar to the southern region of Lake Sevan in Armenia is poor even by local standards, and the journey can take at least five hours in a four-wheel drive vehicle. Military commanders may not allow you to pass, and even if they do the journey might not be safe because of risk that there may still be land mines in the area.

There's a military checkpoint 10 km west of Dadi Vank, and within the region of Karvachar. There's a fork in the road at the checkpoint. The southwest road goes to the town of Karvachar (Kelbajar), which is a distance of about 20 km. The northwest road goes to Sevan. We've traveled on both roads, but we were able to travel only as far south as the town of Karvachar because of a military roadblock. The scenery is beautiful, but historic sites were not accessible.

The alternate road, from Dadi Vank to Vardenis, near Lake Sevan, was mostly a rough trail when we traveled it in 2003, but it was open all the way to Armenia. If you decide to make this journey, we recommend that you bring along an Armenian-speaking guide and that you carry your passport with a current Karabagh visa and appropriate. There are no services on this trail, so you will need to be certain that you have a full tank of gasoline in your car before entering the region. You should also carry bottled water and some food.

APPENDIX 1

The authors of this guide have traveled extensively throughout Eastern Anatolia—historic lands of Western Armenia. Their travels and research have allowed them to create a large stock of photography of the ancient Armenian sites that survive there, as well as a manuscript documenting conditions and describing the region. Limited resources made it impossible to include these materials in this guidebook, but the authors hope to be able to publish their research and photography in a future comprehensive guide to Armenia, Karabagh, and Historic Lands of Armenia. Excerpts of some of their writings on the region are presented below.

PRESERVATION OF HISTORIC LANDS

Eastern Anatolia (Western Armenia)

Although the modern Republic of Armenia is quite small, the historic homeland of the Armenian nation encompasses much of Anatolia, in a vast region that is known geologically as the Armenian Plateau. At times this homeland has reached as far west as the Mediterranean coast and as far east as the Caucasus. Eastern Anatolia—a region that includes Lake Van and the Biblical Mt. Ararat—is at the heart of this historic homeland. Their recorded history here dates back more than 3,000 years, and the Armenians had lived here throughout all those centuries—until 1915.

In 1914 there were about 2 million Armenians living in Eastern Anatolia (Western Armenia) under the sovereignty of the Ottoman Empire. Today there are none and the area is populated mostly by Kurds. The entire Armenian population was either killed or expelled first by the Ottoman and later by the Kemalist Turkish authorities. The massacres began in the 1890s and culminated with the Genocide of 1915 to 1923. Most of the physical evidence of their three-millennial existence is gone, too.

A handful of the priceless and irreplaceable architectural monuments of the Armenian nation have survived, however. Some of the most dramatic surviving examples of this architecture, and hence of Armenian history, are found in Van and in Ani, and these are two areas that draw tourists despite their remote locations. The publicity that these monuments have received as a result of tourism has helped deter the authorities from razing them. It has not deterred them from neglecting them, however, and they are today in ruins and some are at risk of being lost forever.

Van

The historic Armenian capital city of Van lies on the southeastern shore of Lake Van, in the region of Vaspurakan. This had been a thriving cultural center with a population of 80,000 until the genocide of 1915, at which time it was obliterated. Today, visitors can walk where the city once was situated, and struggle to see the remnants of foundation walls for the roughly 5,000 buildings that were once churches and homes.

For most travelers, Van's biggest attraction is the Church of the Holy Cross at Aghtamar Island. This church, which is all that remains of an ancient monastery,

Photograph: A shepherd in northern Karabagh

Appendix

Ruins of the ancient Armenian Capital city of Van

is also called simply "Aghtamar." It is one of the holiest sites of the Armenian Church. It is also architecturally unique, and a masterpiece of tenth century Armenian architecture. The church owes its survival at least in part to its secluded location on the island.

Art historians say that the architect of Aghtamar made the stones speak for themselves. "As a testament to his fugitive existence," writes the architectural historian Herman Vahramian, "man brings life to stone." The carvings on the exterior of the church tell the story of Genesis. Bas-reliefs depict Adam and Eve, as well as a serpent. On the west façade, the image of King Gagik, the patron of the church, is carved in the act of donating the church. Biblical icons such as David, Goliath, and Jonah also adorn the walls. The worn and damaged frescoes on the interior walls tell the story of the Annunciation and the Nativity, the massacre of the innocents, the Baptism, and shows Jesus during the bathing of the feet.

The church is today in great peril. Tragically, vandals are destroying the priceless and irreplaceable Christian artifacts. During several visits beginning in 1997 and as recently as 2003, we have tracked deliberate defacement of the engravings on the building. The faces of the religious figures have been smashed, and as one walks around the church one notices that every carved relief that is within arms length of the ground has been damaged.

Yedi Kilesi

The name given to the village of Yedi Kilesi, which is located just 16 km outside the town of Van, is a bit of a misnomer today. This Turkish name means "Seven Churches" but there has been so much destruction of the seven ancient Armenian churches for which the village was named, that there are no longer seven of them, and it's difficult to even tell from the exterior of the structures that they are churches at all.

This site was once the Armenian monastery of Varagavank, and this was the seat of the archbishop of Van, beginning sometime between 1003 and 1022. Varagavank was destroyed by the Turkish army on April 30, 1915, during their siege of Van. The nearby and adjacent homes of the Armenians were occupied by Kurds, and the vicinity of Varagavank is today an impoverished Kurdish village.

Ani

Ani is the capital of an ancient Armenian kingdom that flourished about 1,000 years ago and the region is home to the oldest human settlements of Anatolia. During its heyday, Ani boasted a population of about 100,000, 30,000 of whom lived in an underground city just outside the city walls, and it was said to be the city of a thousand and one churches. Its location on the ancient Silk Road brought many travelers—including Marco Polo—and helped it to thrive. Today Ani is uninhabited and its cultural relics appear to have been abandoned to the elements. Of those thousand-and-one churches, only a scattering of them have survived.

The first recorded reference to Ani dates to the fifth century AD, although historians believe that there was a settlement there much earlier. Ani became a very important center of Armenian culture beginning in the ninth century and within 100 years (by AD 971) it had become a capital of an Armenian kingdom ruled by the Bagratid dynasty. Ani became an important crossroads for merchant caravans in the Near East, and this helped to ensure the vitality of the settlement.

The remarkable proto-Gothic churches of Ani exhibit architectural elements which predate their appearance in Europe by more than one hundred years, making them significant architecturally, as well as historically.

Most of the structures were built of stone. The core of each stone block was a combination of stone rubble and concrete, with surface layers of neatly cut stone. Many of

The 10th century Church of St. Gregory stands in ruins at the Armenian capital of Ani

the smaller churches have a similar floor plan with an open central space surrounded by four, six, or eight apses. The interiors of a few of the churches are still covered by frescos depicting stories from the lives of Christ and the church's patron saint.

Seismic activity is one of the greatest threats to the site. Several churches have collapsed during earthquakes, and wind and sand erosion are further weakening the structures. Relic hunters have robbed the site of valuable artifacts and have damaged the buildings through erratic digging.

Historic photographs and further information on the architecture and history of Ani is available online at www.virtualani.freeserve.co.uk.

Kars

Kars is important to tourists today primarily as a launching point from which to visit Ani, one of Armenia's ancient capitals. This is because visitors to Ani must purchase tickets not at Ani, but from the tourist office in Kars, which is located 40 kilometers away. Kars was quite a bit more important at one time, having been the seat of an independent Armenian kingdom during the ninth and tenth centuries. The town was founded by Armenians, and then overrun by Seljuk Turk invaders in the eleventh century. There was nearly one century of Russian rule beginning in 1828, and a brief period of peace. This period of Russian rule also gave Kars its wide avenues and grid layout of streets. Armenian poet Yeghishe Charents was born here during this era, in 1897. Although he is now ignored in Kars, he is honored with a museum in Yerevan [see Chapter 4, Yerevan].

Kars was bounced back and forth by Turkey and Russia, who were each looking for a forward garrison. Turkey seized Kars in April 1918. Armenia recovered Kars

Church of the Holy Apostles, built more than 1,000 years ago, features relief carvings of the Twelve Apostles

shortly thereafter, and it was restored to Armenia as a part of the first Armenian Republic of 1918. But then Turkey invaded the fledgling Armenian Republic in 1920, and took Kars, Ani, and Gyumri. Turkey withdrew from Gyumri, but it still occupies Kars and Ani.

Today the population of 145,000 in Kars is roughly 80 percent Azeri and 20 percent Kurdish. There are more Azeri Turks living in Kars than anywhere else in Turkey, and they are mostly the descendants of immigrants who arrived during the era of Russian sovereignty over the area, from 1878 until 1920.

In the old quarter of town one sees many stone buildings from the era of Russian sovereignty. This quarter of town is also the location of the Armenian Church of the Holy Apostles. A bas-relief of the Twelve Apostles adorns the drum of the church, just below the conical roof. The church had been converted to a mosque, although this isn't apparent at a glance because it has no minarets. A new large mosque has been built adjacent to the church, as well.

Vandalism at the Church of theHoly Cross, Aghtamar

UNESCO WORLD HERITAGE SITES

The ancient Armenian churches at Ani and on Aghtamar Island are priceless cultural treasures that deserve to be protected for all posterity. The World Heritage Convention is a UN-sponsored treaty that encourages the protection of cultural and natural properties of "outstanding universal value." There's no doubt that Ani and Aghtamar are cultural properties of outstanding universal value. Still, the treaty cannot do anything to save them from destruction.

There are 754 sites on the World Heritage List, which is managed by the United Nations Educational, Scientific and Cultural Organization (UNESCO). Turkey is a party to the World Heritage Convention and it may therefore designate or recommend properties for the World Heritage List. Once a site has World Heritage status, the home nation is obligated to protect the designated location. Nominations must come from the government on whose territory the property is located, however. Therefore, sites cannot be included without the host government's involvement. Consequently, Armenian sites in Turkey, and elsewhere outside of Armenia's borders, have not been inscribed on the World Heritage List.

Frescoes are still visible on the interior walls of this ruined Armenian church at Yedi Kilesi, near Lake Van.

Armenian sites in Turkey are not merely ignored and neglected by the authorities. They have been actively defaced and destroyed. UNESCO has reported that only 913 Armenian Churches and monasteries were left in Turkey after 1915. By 1974, 464 had been completely destroyed, 252 were in ruins, and 197 require extensive restoration. At Ani, ancient Armenian inscriptions and frescoes have been defaced and covered with plaster. Stone monuments and *khatchkars* have been smashed.

Various international organizations have reported on the destruction of Armenian sites in Turkey. For example, the Global Heritage Fund (www.globalheritage-fund.org), whose mission is to preserve mankind's most important cultural sites, lists Ani as an endangered site. Ani is also listed as an endangered site by the Yerevan-based Research on Armenian Architecture (www.antares.am/raa). More information about UNESCO World Heritage Sites is available on their website (www.whc.unesco.org).

APPENDIX 2
VOLUNTEER ACTIVITIES

Unskilled Volunteer Programs

The program of the shortest duration for organized volunteer work in Armenia is available through the US-based Land and Culture Organization. Volunteers serve for four weeks during the summer, working on the rehabilitation of ancient monuments in Armenia and Karabagh. Service can be reduced to three weeks in exceptional circumstances but is more often extended than reduced. Skilled labor is not required. Contact: Land and Culture Organization; PO Box 1386; Hoboken, NJ 07030 (Tel. 212-689-7811; Toll-free 1-888-526-1555) (E-mail: lcousa@aol.com) (Internet: www.landandculture.org). In Yerevan contact: Land and Culture Organization; 5 Vardanants Street (Tel. 52-91-71) (E-mail: info@landandculture.org).

Professional Volunteer Programs

Medical students can participate in volunteer programs for short periods by making independent arrangements through the Armenian American Medical Students and Housestaff Association. Contact: Maral Mardiros or Gayane Ambartsumyan (E-mail: aamsha@aamsha.org) (Internet: www.aamsha.org).

Public Health programs can be arranged on an ad hoc basis through the American University of Armenia, which has an office in Oakland, California. Contact: AUA; 300 Lakeside Drive; Fourth Floor; Oakland, California (Tel. 510-987-9452) (E-mail: info@aua.am) (Internet: www.aua.am).

Lawyers and law students may be able to arrange projects of varying lengths with Arlex, an international law NGO based in Armenia, which operates out of the same office as the Armenian Volunteer Corps. There is no office in the US. In Yerevan contact: Tom Samuelian, Director (Tel. 58-42-91) (Internet: www.armenianvolunteer.org).

The Law Department of the American University of Armenia occasionally has lecturing opportunities for experienced lawyers. In Yerevan contact: Matthew Karanian, Associate Dean (Tel. 51-27-55) (E-mail: mkaranian@aua.am) (Internet: www.aua.am). In the US contact: Stephen Barnett, Dean (E-mail: barnetts@law.berkeley.edu).

The Armenian Youth Federation (AYF) Summer Intern Program invites college students to spend two months in Armenia during their summer break as volunteers with government agencies, private companies and other organizations. The program allows students to gain experience in their chosen professions while helping Armenia (Internet: ayf.org).

The Armenian Assembly of America also helps to place volunteers with government offices in Armenia. These volunteers have typically been college students who are alumni of the organization's summer internship program in Washington, DC, however (Internet: www.aaainc.org).

Social Programs

For work with children, the Armenian Church Youth Organization of America (ACYOA) sponsors the Armenian Service Program. Typically 12-18 volunteers, aged 18 to 28, spend two weeks as counselors at a children's camp. The campers are children who have lost family members. Contact: Karen Khatchadourian (Tel. 201-281-6149) (E-mail: asp@acyoa.org) (Internet: www.acyoa.org).

Appendix

The Canadian Youth Mission to Armenia (CYMA) also sponsors children's camp counselor programs and many other projects that last from three weeks to one month (Internet: www.armenianchurch.ca/cyma).

Opportunities to help disadvantaged children In Yerevan are sometimes available through the Orran Center. The Center provides children with guidance, helps them with their studies, and feeds them a hot meal every weekday. Call them in Yerevan at 53-55-90. In Tsaghkadzor, which is about 30 minutes from Yerevan, there's a children's camp that accepts volunteers in the summer (Tel. 0-23-52-70; 0-23-53-70).

World Vision Armenia is a religious-based charity that sponsors child sponsorship programs for disadvantaged children in Armenia's earthquake-zone city of Gyumri. Contact: World Vision; 34834 Weyerhauser Way South, Federal Way, Washington 98001 (Tel. 253-815-1000; Fax: 253-815-3140) (E-mail: wv@arminco.com) (Internet: www.wvarmenia.am).

Semi-skilled laborers are welcome at Habitat for Humanity, which organizes volunteer opportunities in partnership with Habitat Armenia in their Global Village program. The program builds houses for families in need. Contact: Habitat Armenia; 27 Aygestan-Ninth Street, Yerevan (Tel. 57-24-35) (E-mail: armenianhabitat@netsys.am). In the US (Tel. 1-800-422-4828 ext. 2549) (Internet: www.habitat.org/GV)(www.hfharmenia.org).

Environmental Programs

The Armenian Tree Project accepts volunteers in its quest to reforest Armenia. They have an office in the US, as well as in Armenia. Contact: Armenian Tree Project; 65 Main Street, Watertown, Massachusetts 02472 (Tel. 617-926-8733) (E-mail: info@armeniatree.org) (Internet: www.armeniatree.org). In Yerevan (Tel. 56-99-10; 55-30-69) (E-mail: atp@ultranet.com).

The Birds of Armenia Project accepts proposals from volunteers to perform ornithological research both in the field and in the lab. Contact: Levon Janoian, Project Manager; Birds of Armenia Project; American University of Armenia; 40 Marshall Baghramian Avenue; Yerevan (Tel. 51-28-16) (E-mail: boa@aua.am).

Long-Term Organized Programs

The Armenian Volunteer Corps, in partnership with Birthright Armenia, arranges both short-term and long-term volunteer programs in a wide array of government offices, law and medical offices, in education, public health and social work, and much more. The programs are as short as two weeks and as long as one year. If you're not sure where you fit, this is a good organization to talk to first. Apply by March for programs that begin in June. Contact: Nouneh Sukiassian, Fund for Armenian Relief; 630 Second Avenue; New York, NY 10016 (Tel. 212-889-5150) (Internet: www.armenianvolunteer.org). In Yerevan (Tel. 58-42-91) (E-mail: info@avc.am).

Pyunic is an association for the disabled that will accept volunteer workers. Contact: Pyunic USA; 6606 Cantaloupe Avenue; Van Nuys, California 91405 (Tel. 818-785-3468). In Yerevan (Tel. 56-07-07) (E-mail: pyunic@arminco.com).

Welcome to the Armenia Marriott Hotel,

easily the most **rewarding** way to stay in Armenia

By choosing **Armenia Marriott Hotel**, you will not only stay

in the very heart of Yerevan's Center and

in the most spacious standard deluxe rooms in the city,

but also will join the **Marriott Rewards** premier frequent traveler program,

that rewards members with 10 points or 3 miles

toward dream vacations, ski or golf trips,

cruises and more for each dollar spent at

any **Marriott Hotel and Resort** worldwide.

thinking of you

Marriott.
ARMENIA YEREVAN

Republic Square, Yerevan, 375010
Republic of Armenia
Tel: 374 1 599 000
Fax: 374 1 599 001
Reservations: 374 1 599 002
marriott.com/evnmc

APPENDIX 3
INTERNET SITES

Environment

www.armenianforests.am
prevention of deforestation, Armenia

www.armeniatree.org
reforesting, tree farms, Armenia

www.ecotourismarmenia.com
advocates of green tourism, Armenia

www.eatsc.com/arm/cultural_heritage.html
eco-agro-tourism, South Caucasus

www.worldlakes.org
data on Lake Sevan, Armenia

Government

www.artsakh.org; nkr.am,
Ministry of Foreign Affairs, Karabagh

www.armeniaemb.org
Armenian Embassy, US

www.armeniaforeignministry.com
Foreign Ministry, Armenia

www.artsakhworld.com
historic sites, Karabagh

www.gov.am
Government (Parliament), Armenia

www.mnpiac.am
Ministry of Nature Protection, Armenia

www.nkrusa.org
Karabagh's Office, US

www.president.am
information about Armenia's President
Robert Kocharian

www.usa.am
US Embassy in Armenia

News and Information

www.armeniadiaspora.com
news for diaspora Armenians

www.armeniainfo.am
tourism development agency in Yerevan

www.armenianow.com
news from Armenia

www.eurasianews.com
analysis and news about Armenia and Eurasia

www.groong.com
news service

History and Culture

www.cilicia.com
comprehensive information about historic
sites in Armenia

www.armeniaguide.com
travel information, lots of links

www.armenianhighland.com
history, culture

Non-profit Organizations

www.armeniafund.org
humanitarian organization, Karabagh highway project

www.armenianvolunteer.org
volunteering clearinghouse

www.himnadram.org
Hayastan All Armenian Fund, Karabagh
highway project

www.lcousa.org
Land and Culture, restoration of ancient
sites, Armenia and Karabagh

www.localhands.org
public health in Karabagh

www.pyunic.am
advocates for the disabled

Commercial Sites

armenianphotography.com
specializes in Armenian photography

kurkjianimages.com
stock photos from around the world

stonegardenproductions.com
photography and book publishing

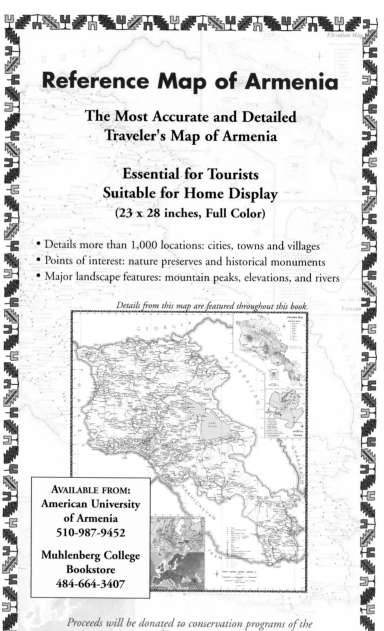

APPENDIX 4
Ecology Organizations
Armenia

Armenian Botanical Society
Eleonora Gabrielian (President)
Tel. 52-77-68
Preservation of Armenia's botanical cover

Armenian Forests
Jeffrey Tufenkian (President)
38 Moskovian Street #10
Tel. 54-15-29
info@armenianforests.am
www.armenianforests.am
Advocacy to protect forestland

Armenian Society for the Protection of Birds
Mamikon Ghasabian (President)
Tel. 51-28-16
Vasil Ananyan (Tour Guide)
Vananian72@yahoo.com

Association of Nature Protection
Dorik Poghosyan (Chairman)
(Tel. 56-34-31; 25-40-68)
ecocentr@pnas.sci.am
Promote natural resources maintenance

Association for Sustainable Human Development
Karine Danielian (President)
Tel. 52 23 27
ashd@freenet.am
Sustainable development advocacy

Armenia Tree Project
Susan Klein (Director)
Tel. 55-30-69; US Tel. 617-926-8733
www.armeniatree.org
trees@arminco.com
Reforestation, community tree planting

Birds of Armenia Project
Levon Janoian (Project Manager)
Tel. 51-28-16
Ornithological research and conservation at the American University of Armenia

Byurakan
Melania Davtian (President)
Tel. 52-44-84; 57-22-46; 56-37-19
bee@arminco.com
Ecology education

Center of Bird Lovers
Martin Adamyan (Contact)
Tel. 28-11-82
adamians@freenet.am
Birding, promotion of biodiversity

Eco-team of Armenia
Artashes Sarkissian (Chairman)
Tel. 52-92-77
ecoteam@arminco.com;
Renewable sources of energy

Ecological Assembly of the Women of Armenia
Rita Aivasova (President)
Tel. 26-80-04; 58-02-54
ecocentr@pnas.sci.am
Ecological research

Eco-tourism Association of Armenia
Zhanna Galyan
Tel. 39-75-52; 27-87-28
www.ecotourismarmenia.com
zhanna@freenet.am
Association of ecology organizations

Ecology Fund of Armenia
Boris Mehrabian (President)
Tel. 23-69-00; 22-30-58
nih1@pnas.sci.am
Scientific evaluation of Armenia's ecology

Environmental Survival Organization
Boris Gabrielian (President)
Tel. 27-92-68; 56-80-27
rhovan@sci.am
Support research on biodiversity

Environmental Public Advocacy Center
Aida Iskoyan (President)
Tel. 53-06-69; Fax 53-92-55
epac@arminco.com
Environmental advocacy organization

Flora
Sveta Mkrtchian (Chairman)
Gyumri (Tel. 69 + 3-35-86)
Advocacy center

Forestry Association
Karen Ter Ghazarian (President)
Tel. 58-36-55; 58-06-72
frec@mail.freenet.am
Education regarding tree maintenance

Greens Union of Armenia
Hakob Sanasarian (President)
Tel. 28-14-11; 25-76-34
armgreen@ipia.sci.am
Environmental advocacy

International Academy of Ecology
Gevorg Pirumian (Chairman)
Tel. 55-86-35
Training courses in ecology, research

Khazer Ecological and Cultural Organization
Amalia Hambartsumyan (Chairman)
Tel. 53-44-72; 53-81-87
khazer@nature.am
Preservation of cultural inheritance

Nature Protectors
Eduard Javruian (Chairman)
8, Charenc Street, Biology Faculty of the Yerevan State University
Tel. 63-31-89; 55-67-78
Advocates against poaching

Protect our Forests Coalition
protectourforests@yahoo.com
Coalition of environmental organizations in Armenia

Sustainable Development
Victoria Ter-Nikoghosian (President)
Tel. 24-73-91; 22-50-63
Education on environmental legal issues

Tapan Eco-Club
Hrant Sarkissian
Tel. 73-33-22
grant@tapan.infocom.amilink.net;
tapan@acc.am
Protects natural environment, preserve and reconstructs cultural-historical monuments

Yerevan Environmental Association
Sona Ayvazian (Contact)
Tel. 58-55-78; 52-69-14
sona@transparency.am

Youth Ecological Group - YEG
Sergey Arevshatian (President)
Tel. 56-22-45
ecocentr@pnas.sci.am
Increases the awareness of ecology

Government

Ministry of Agriculture
Tel. 52-46-41
www.minagro.am
Environmental matters related to agriculture

Ministry of Health
Tel. 58-24-13
www.armhealth.am
Responsible for environmental health matters

Ministry of Nature Protection
Tel. 53-31-81 Fax: 53-49-02
www.mnpiac.am
Environmental protection and monitoring.

Georgia

Caucasus Environmental NGO Network
Nana Janashia, President
Tel. 99532+ 92-39-46; Fax: 92-39-47
info@cenn.org
www.cenn.org
Public awareness, conservation projects

Georgian Center for the Conservation of Wildlife
Ramaz Gokh
Tel. 99532 + 32-64-96; Fax 53-74-78
office@gccw.org
www.gccw.org

Noah's Ark Center for the Recovery of Endangered Species (NACRES)
Levan Butkhuzi (Contact)
Tel. / Fax 99532 + 53-71-25
info@nacres.org
www.nacres.org

Russia

Center for Russian Nature Conservation
PO Box 57277
Washington, DC 20037
Tel. 202-778-9573
www.wild-russia.org

International Organizations

Bat Conservation International
P.O. Box 162603
Austin, TX 78716
Tel. 512-327-9721
Internet: www.batcon.org

Conservation International
1919 M Street, NW Suite 600
Washington, DC 20036
Tel. 202-912-1000
Internet: www.conservation.org

Earth Share
7735 Old Georgetown Road
Betheseda, MD 20814
Tel. 800-875-3863
Internet: www.earthshare.org

National Audubon Society
700 Broadway
New York, NY 10003
Tel. 212-979-3000
Internet: www.audubon.org

Nature Conservancy
4245 North Fairfax Drive, Suite 100
Arlington, Virginia 22203
Tel. 703-841-5300
Internet: www.nature.org

Wildlife Conservation
2300 Southern Boulevard
Bronx, New York 10460
Tel. 718-220-5100
Internet: www.wcs.org

World Resources Institute
10 G Street, NE, Suite 800
Washington, DC 20002
Tel. 202-729-7600
Internet: www.wri.org

World Wildlife Federation
1250 Twenty-Fourth Street, NW
PO Box 97180
Washington, DC 20090
Tel. 1-800-CALL-WWF
Internet: www.wwf.org

GLOSSARY

Sightseeing

aygee	park
bert	fortress
bulur	hill
despanadoon	embassy
dzor	gorge
djanapar	road
gavit	church hall
gyoogh	village
Hayastan	Armenia
hyooranots	hotel
jahm	church
kaghak	town
kar	stone
khatchkar	stone cross
leech	lake
poghots	street
sar	mountain
shuka	market
tangaran	museum
vank	monastery
yekeghetsee	church

Food

agh	salt
beebar	pepper
breendz	rice
paneer	cheese
tsiran	apricot
dzook	fish
kaht	milk
hav	chicken
hahts	bread
djoor	water
lavash	flat bread
loleek	tomato
mees	meat
matsun	yogurt
soordj	coffee
shakaravaz	sugar
varoong	cucumber

Greetings

Hello	barev
Hello (polite)	barev dzez
How are you? (fam.)	vonts es
How are you? (polite)	vonts ek
Fine, thank you	lav em, shnorhakalootyoon
OK	voch eench
Very good	shat lahv
Very bad	shat vaht
Getting by (slang)	kah-mahts, kah-mahts
What's up? (slang)	Eench kah
Nothing much	Voch me bahn
I'm tired	hoknats em
I'm sick	heevand em
I'm happy	oorahkh em
Goodbye	tstesootyoon
What's your name?	Anoonut eench eh
please	khundrem
goodnight	baree geesher
Have a good trip	baree djanapar

People

Father	Hayr
Mother	Mayr
Brother	Yeghbayr
Sister	Kooyrik
Friend	unker
Grandmother	Tatik, metz Mayr
Grandfather	Papik, metz Hayr

Getting by

yes	ayo
no	voch, cheh (colloquial)
I	yes
you (polite, plural)	dook
you (fam., sing.)	du
who	ov
what	eench
where	vortegh, oor
when	yerp
why	eenchoo
how	eenchpes
I want	oozoom em
I don't want	chem oozoom
I know	eemanoom em
I don't know	chem eemanoom

Traveling

hotel	hyooranots
room	senyak
bathroom (toilet)	zoogaran
elevator	verelak (leeft)

taxi	(taxi)
bus	avtoboos
bus station	avtoboosakayan
airplane	otanav
airport	otanavakayan
subway	metro
street, road	poghots, djanaparh
highway	mayrooghee
I'm hungry	sovats em
I'm thirsty	tzarav em
restaurant	djasharan
café	srdjaran
postage stamp	namakaneesh
letter	namak
Post Office	post
telephone	herakhos
telephone number	herakhosee hamar
movie	(kino)
luggage	djahmbrook
laundry	lvatskatoon

Shopping

store	khanoot
market	shuka
open	bats
closed	pak
cheap (inexpensive)	ezhan
expensive	tahng
money	pogh

Weather

hot (weather)	shoke
cold (weather)	tsoort

Directions

left	dzakh
right	ach
straight	oogheegh
stop	kangne
up	verev
down	nerkev
here	aystegh
there	ayntegh

Time

What time is it?	zhamuh kaneesn eh?
today	aysor
tomorrow	vaghuh
yesterday	yerek

Food

barbecue	khorovatz
apricot	tsiran
bread	hahts
cheese	paneer
cucumber	varoong
food	kerakoor
green vegetables	kanachee
rice	breendz
sugar	shakaravaz
tomato	loleek (pomeedor)
yogurt	matsun
beef	tavar
chicken	hav
egg	dzoo
fish	dzook
Lamb	vochkhar
meat	mees
warm	tak
cold	pagh
spicy	ktzoo
sweet	kaghtstr
salt	agh
pepper	beebar

Beverages

coffee	soordj
tea	tey (chai)
water	djoor
cold water	saruh djoor
milk	kaht
yogurt beverage	tahn
beer	garedjoor, (peeva)
wine	geenee
vodka	oghee

Colors

red	karmir
orange	narndjagooyn
yellow	degheen

green	kanach	house	toon
blue	kapoyt	monastery	vank
brown	srjagooyn	mountain	sar
black	sev	museum	tangaran
white	spitak	road	djanapar
dark	mook	stone	kar
light	bahts	stone cross	khatchkar
		town	kaghak
		village	gyoogh

Numbers

one	mek	camera	loosankarchakan, (aparat)
two	yerkoo	film	(plyonka)
three	yerek		
four	chorse		

Commands

five	heeng	stop	kanghnee
six	vets	sit	nustee
seven	yot	come	aree
eeight	oot	look	nahyee
nine	eenuh	let's go	gnatseenk
ten	tas	go	gnah
twenty	kuhsahn		
thirty	yeresoon		

Questions

forty	karasoon	How do I go to Yerevan?	Vonts em gnoom Yerevan?
fifty	heesoon		
sixty	vahtsoon		
seventy	yotanasoon	Where are you going?	Oor ek gnoom?
eighty	oohtanahsoon	Do you know?	Geetek
ninety	eenneesoon	Where is?	Oor eh?
one hundred	haryoor	What is?	Eench eh?
thousand	hazar	How much does this cost?	Sa eench arzhee?

many (a lot)	shaht
few	keech

Weekdays

Monday	Yerkooshahptee
Tuesday	Yerekshahptee
Wednesday	Chorekshahptee
Thursday	Heenghshahptee
Friday	Oorpaht
Saturday	Shahpaht
Sunday	Keerahkee
Every day	ahmen or

Sightseeing

Building	shenk
Church	yekeghetsee, zham
Embassy	despanatoon
Fortress	bert
Hill	bulur

Photography from
around the world.

REFERENCES

In addition to their original field research, the authors used the following sources for the historical, environmental, statistical and other background information.

Architecture

Architectural Ensembles of Armenia, O. Khalpakhchian (1980)

Documents of Armenian Architecture (Levon Azarian, Armen Manoukian, editors) Haghpat (Vol. 1) 1969; Khatchkar (Vol. 2) 1977; Sanahin (Vol. 3) 1970; Amberd (Vol. 5) 1978; Goshavank (Vol. 7) 1982; Aght'amar (Vo. 8) 1974; Ketcharis (Vol. 11) 1982; Ani (Vol. 12) 1984; Haghardzin (Vol. 13) 1984

Armenian Genocide

A Problem from Hell: America and the Age of Genocide, Samantha Power (Basic Books, 2002)

The Burning Tigris: The Armenian Genocide and America's Response, Peter Balakian (HarperCollins, 2003)

History of the Armenian Genocide: Ethnic Conflict from the Balkans to Anatolia to the Caucasus, Vahakn N. Dadrian (Berghahn Books, 1995)

Ecology and Conservation

Assessment of Capacity Building Needs for Biodiversity of Armenia (UNDP, 2002)

Biodiversity of Armenia, First National Report (Armenian Ministry of Nature Protection, 1999)

Changes in the Waterbird Community of the Lake Sevan-Lake Gilli Area, Balian et al (2002)

Important Bird Areas in Europe: Priority Sites for Conservation (BirdLife International, 2000)

Isotopic Evidence of the Persistent Dominance of Blood Lead Concentrations by Previous Gasoline Lead Emissions in Yerevan, Armenia, Robert Kurkjian and A.Russell Flegal (Environmental Research, 2003)

Lake Sevan Action Program, Main Report (Armenian Ministry of Nature Protection, 1999)

Lead Isotope Tracking of Atmospheric Response to Post-Industrial Conditions in Yerevan, Armenia, Robert Kurkjian et al (Atmospheric Environment, 2002)

Long-Range Downstream Effects of Urban Runoff and Acid Mine Drainage in the Debed River, Armenia, Robert Kurkjian et al (Applied Geochemistry, 2004)

Metal Contamination in the Republic of Armenia, Robert Kurkjian (Environmental Management, 2000)

National Environmental Action Program, Main Report (Armenian Ministry of Nature Protection, 1999)

National Report on the State of the Environment in Armenia in 2002 (Armenian Ministry of Nature Protection, 2003)

Strategy on Developing Specially Protected Areas and National Action Plan (Armenian Ministry of Nature Protection, 2003)

History and Culture

Armenia: A Historical Atlas, Robert Hewsen (University of Chicago Press, 2001)

Armenia: Portraits of Survival and Hope, Donald E. Miller (University of California, 2003)

Armenian Van / Vaspurakan, Richard Hovannisian (Mazda Publishers, 2000)

Armenian Folk Arts, Culture and Identity, Levon Abrahamian, Nancy Sweezy, editors (Indiana University Press, 2001)

The Armenian People, from Ancient to Modern Times, Richard G. Hovannisian, ed. (St. Martin's Press, 1997)

Looking Toward Ararat: Armenia in Modern History, Ronald Grigor Suny (Indiana University Press, 1993)

Pride of Small Nations, Suzanne Goldenberg (Zed Books, 1994)

Karabagh

Black Garden: Armenia and Azerbaijan Through Peace and War, Thomas De Waal (New York University Press, 2003)

The Caucasian Knot: The History and Geopolitics of Nagorno-Karabagh, Levon Chorbajian, Patrick Donabedian, and Claude Mutafian (Zed Books, 1994)

Literature

A Captive of the Caucasus, Andrei Bitov (Weidenfeld and Nicholson, 1993)

The Crossing Place, Philip Marsden (Harper Collins, 1993)

The Human Comedy, William Saroyan (1943)

Reference Guides

A Field Guide to Birds of Armenia, Martin S. Adamian and Daniel Klem, Jr. (American University of Armenia, 1997)

Armenian Info Text, George Mouradian (Bookshelf Publishers, 1995)

Handbook of the Birds of Armenia, Martin S. Adamian and Daniel Klem, Jr. (American University of Armenia, 1999)

Rediscovering Armenia, Brady Kiesling, author; Raffi Kojian, editor (2001)

INDEX

Yerevan Yerevan Yerevan Yerevan Yerevan Yerevan
Yerevan Yerevan Yerevan Yerevan Yerevan Yerevan
Yerevan Yerevan Yerevan Yerevan Yerevan Yerevan
Yerevan Yerevan Yerevan Yerevan Yerevan Yerevan
Yerevan Yerevan Yerevan Yerevan Yerevan Yerevan
Yerevan Yerevan Yerevan Yerevan Yerevan Yerevan
Yerevan Yerevan Yerevan Yerevan Yerevan Yerevan
Yerevan Yerevan Yerevan Yerevan Yerevan Yerevan
Yerevan Yerevan Yerevan Yerevan Yerevan Yerevan
Yerevan Yerevan Yerevan Yerevan Yerevan Yerevan
Yerevan Yerevan Yerevan Yerevan Yerevan Yerevan
Yerevan Yerevan Yerevan Yerevan Yerevan Yerevan
Yerevan Yerevan Yerevan Yerevan Yerevan Yerevan

Fly non-stop to Yerevan three times a week from London Heathrow

With a flight every Wednesday, Friday and Sunday, our non-stop service to Yerevan is ideal for business or leisure travel to Armenia. And with our Club World service, there's extra comfort and convenience available too. To book, visit www.britishairways.com, call us on 0870 850 9 850 (UK), 1-800-AIRWAYS (North America) or (1) 521 383/528 200 (Armenia) or see your travel agent.

Services operated by the independent carrier British Mediterranean Airways Ltd

BRITISH AIRWAYS

oneworld

Regions of Armenia and Karabagh

Legend for Armenia Reference Map
Pages 147, 150, 154, 170, 172, 188, 202, 204, 220, 222

●	Village	✈	AIRPORT
⚲	Site of former village or place	✝	CATHEDRAL, MONASTERY, OR CHURCH
○	Town	■	FORTRESS OR MONUMENT
★	Administrative center	♠	Grove, forest, or arboretum
═══	Category 1 road	Xfmr.	Transformer station
───	Category 2 road	✕✕✕	Descriptive name identifies type of location
-----	Category 3 road	R.	River
▲	Mountain	RM	River mouth
⠿	Gorge	FP	Fish ponds
)(	Pass	Res.	Reservoir
)(	Bridge	⌒	Marsh
▢	RAILWAY STATION		

Courtesy of the Birds of Armenia Project, American University of Armenia, Oakland, CA, 1999

Driving Distances in Kilometers
(kilometers x 0.6 = miles)

Administrative center ★	Yeghegnadzor ★	Vanadzor ★	Tashir	Talin	Stepanavan	Sevan	Noyemberian	Meghri	Khosrov Preserve	Kapan ★	Ijevan ★	Hrazdan ★	Gyumri ★	Goris	Gilli area	Gavar ★	Dilijan	Byurakan	Berd	Ashtarak ★	Artashat ★	Arpi Lake	Armaveer ★	Armash FP
Yerevan (capital)	123	121	158	70	140	62	173	371	66	300	136	45	125	240	160	97	100	40	167	24	31	166	43	60
Armash FP	62	181	218	130	200	122	233	313	40	242	196	105	185	182	220	157	160	100	227	84	31	226	87	
Armaveer ★	149	130	173	42	155	105	216	397	92	326	179	88	100	266	203	140	143	58	210	40	57	141		
Arpi Lake	289	101	146	96	132	228	151	537	232	466	167	211	41	406	326	263	138	140	333	142	197			
Artashat ★	92	152	189	101	171	93	204	340	35	269	167	76	156	209	191	128	131	71	198	55				
Ashtarak ★	147	97	134	46	116	86	197	395	90	324	160	69	101	264	184	121	124	18	191					
Berd	290	123	172	237	154	106	99	538	233	467	50	120	183	407	129	161	86	207						
Byurakan	163	115	150	50	132	102	213	411	106	340	176	85	105	280	200	137	140							
Dilijan	223	37	80	170	62	40	85	471	166	400	36	57	97	340	124	75								
Gavar ★	220	113	162	167	144	36	160	468	163	397	111	53	172	337	68									
Gilli area	283	161	210	230	192	98	209	531	226	460	160	115	227	400										
Goris	117	357	398	310	380	302	413	131	202	202	376	285	365											
Gyumri ★	248	60	101	55	83	137	152	496	191	425	133	170												
Hrazdan ★	168	94	137	115	119	17	129	416	111	345	93													
Ijevan ★	259	73	122	206	104	76	49	507	202	436														
Kapan ★	177	421	458	370	440	362	473	71	274															
Khosrov Preserve	107	187	224	136	206	128	239	355																
Meghri	248	492	529	441	511	433	544																	
Noyemberian	296	96	145	243	127	125																		
Sevan	185	71	120	132	102																			
Stepanavan	263	31	18	138																				
Talin	193	115	156																					
Tashir	281	49																						
Vanadzor ★	244																							

Courtesy of the Birds of Armenia Project, American University of Armenia, Oakland, CA, 1999

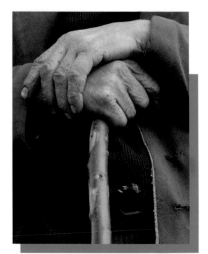

The best resource for Armenian photography
armenianphotography.com
888-266-7331